PAGAN
SPIRITUALITY

About the Authors

Joyce and River Higginbotham have taught Paganism classes throughout the past decade. They have planned and organized local and national Pagan gatherings, written articles for Pagan publications, appeared on radio and television broadcasts, spoken at Christian and Unitarian Universalist churches, and attended interfaith councils. They also helped found the Council for Alternative Spiritual Traditions, which hosted public Pagan and alternative events in the Midwest.

To Write to the Authors

If you wish to contact the authors or would like more information about this book, please write to the authors in care of Llewellyn Worldwide and we will forward your request. Both the authors and publisher appreciate hearing from you and learning of your enjoyment of this book and how it has helped you. Llewellyn Worldwide cannot guarantee that every letter written to the authors can be answered, but all will be forwarded. Please write to:

Joyce and River Higginbotham
℅ Llewellyn Worldwide
2143 Wooddale Drive
Woodbury, MN 55125-2989
Please enclose a self-addressed stamped envelope for reply,
or $1.00 to cover costs. If outside U.S.A., enclose
international postal reply coupon.

Many of Llewellyn's authors have websites with additional information and resources. For more information, please visit our website at:

http://www.llewellyn.com

PAGAN SPIRITUALITY

A GUIDE TO PERSONAL TRANSFORMATION

Joyce & River Higginbotham

Llewellyn Publications
Woodbury, Minnesota

First Edition
Fourth Printing, 2011

Book design and layout by Joanna Willis
Cover image © 2005 by Comstock
Cover design by Gavin Dayton Duffy
Interior illustrations by Llewellyn art department

Excerpt from "Magic of the Ordinary: Recovering the Shamanic in Judaism" by Gershon Winkler, published by North Atlantic Books, copyright © 2003 by Gershon Winkler. Reprinted by permission of publisher.

The authors wish to thank and acknowledge Shambhala Publications for permission to incorporate and paraphrase material by Ken Wilber, Blackwell Publishers, Inc., for permission to paraphrase the eight colors of the spiral from Don Edward Beck and Christopher C. Cowan's *Spiral Dynamics: Mastering Values, Leadership, and Change,* © 1996, and Roman & Littlefield Publishers, Inc., for permission to reprint the figure "Societal Types by Degree of Sex Stratification" from *Sex and Advantage: A Comparative, Macro-Structural Theory of Sex Stratification* by Janet Saltzman Chafetz, page 115, © 1984.

Llewellyn is a registered trademark of Llewellyn Worldwide Ltd.

Library of Congress Cataloging-in-Publication Data
Higginbotham, Joyce, 1961–
    Pagan spirituality : a guide to personal transformation / Joyce & River Higginbotham.
      p.   cm.
    Includes bibliographical references and index.
    ISBN-13: 978-0-7387-0574-3
    ISBN-10: 0-7387-0574-8
    1. Neopaganism. I. Higginbotham, River, 1959– II. Title.
BF1571.H53 2005
299'.94—dc22

                2005045145

Llewellyn Worldwide does not participate in, endorse, or have any authority or responsibility concerning private business transactions between our authors and the public.
    All mail addressed to the author is forwarded but the publisher cannot, unless specifically instructed by the author, give out an address or phone number.
    Any Internet references contained in this work are current at publication time, but the publisher cannot guarantee that a specific location will continue to be maintained. Please refer to the publisher's website for links to authors' websites and other sources.

Llewellyn Publications
A Division of Llewellyn Worldwide Ltd.
2143 Wooddale Drive
Woodbury, MN 55125-2989
www.llewellyn.com

Printed in the United States of America

This book is dedicated to Ken Wilber
For having thrown down the Gauntlet
and
To all those who courageously pick it up
And accept the challenge it offers to their spiritual growth

CONTENTS

EXERCISES

FIGURES

INTRODUCTION

For more than a decade we have introduced people to the ideas and principles of the modern Pagan movement, teaching classes at churches, bookstores, homes, conferences, and festivals. Many of you reading this are already familiar with our introductory book, *Paganism: An Introduction to Earth-Centered Religions*, in which we set out a number of concepts central to modern Paganism.

As noted in our introductory book, there is debate among Pagans as to what name should be used to describe the modern movement so as to distinguish it from historical Paganism. The noted author and Druid, Isaac Bonewits, has developed what some consider a classic definition of the types of Paganism. Bonewits uses the word "paleopaganism" to describe "the original tribal faiths of Europe, Africa, Asia, the Americas, Oceania and Australia." A few of these tribal faiths, such as Hinduism, Taoism, and Shintoism, whose adherents number in the millions, have survived to the present. He then uses the word "mesopaganism" to describe re-creations of paleopagan systems which are usually interwoven with influences from Judeo-Christianity. Some of the examples he gives are Freemasonry, Rosicrucianism, Theosophy, Voudoun, Santeria, and Sikhism. His third category is "neo-paganism," which he defines as religions created since the 1960s which "have attempted to blend what their founders perceived as the best aspects of different types of paleopaganism with modern 'Aquarian Age' ideals."[1]

For the sake of simplicity, we use the word Pagan throughout this book to refer to the modern neo-Pagan movement. If the focus of a section is on ancient peoples and cultures, then we will reference them explicitly.

When we began teaching classes about Paganism over a decade ago we immediately discovered that our students really yearned to connect spiritually, to find that point where they intersect with the universe, and to have an experience of being seen and heard by whatever has ultimate meaning for them. Their desire to develop active and creative spiritual relationships was strong, and was frequently what brought them to Paganism. As teachers and facilitators of the learning process, we began searching for ways to help our students connect. We created experiences we hoped would enable them to open to spiritual energies and take part in the constant and creative exchange of the universe. We introduced them to energy workings, manifesting, and divination skills. We offered them opportunities to listen to their inner selves, the natural world, and consciousness at large, and to commune with their concept of spirit and the Divine.

As time passed, we noticed that certain approaches were more successful for some students than others. Students brought with them various sets of needs and we had to adapt the material, exercises, and our teaching methods in order to meet them. We began to recognize patterns in the types of needs the students expressed, and we noticed that what fed one set of needs did not necessarily feed another.

In order to understand what we were observing, we began to study human growth and development. We discovered that growth—including spiritual growth—involves an expansion of capacities, and that capacities unfold in a recognizable pattern as skills build one upon the other. We realized that what modern Pagans think magick is, how they think it works, and what they view as ethical is based on a combination of their beliefs (conscious and unconscious) and developmental capacity. Our study of development helped us begin to make sense of what we were experiencing with our students so we could respond more effectively. At the same time, we learned a lot about our own growth and what did and didn't feed us spiritually. Learning about development in others brought to mind developmental spaces we have traveled through, transitions we made with more or less success, and issues with which we continue to struggle. It is no exaggeration to say that we grew as much as or more than our students as we explored the contours of human development.

Even so, it did not occur to us to share with you what we learned about development, as we used this knowledge behind the scenes with our students. We applied what we discovered to make classes better, but did not teach development per se. What changed our minds was a comment made by Ken Wilber in his book, *Integral*

Psychology. Ken Wilber is a modern philosopher who writes on many topics including history, psychology, and spirituality. His theory of developmental spaces is one of several we examine in the first two chapters. As we were reading along in *Integral Psychology*, we came upon a section in which Wilber offers a fairly piercing criticism of new paradigm spiritualities, or those focused on Gaia, web-of-life theories, ecology, matriarchal religions, and the new physics.

About these new spiritualities Wilber says:

> . . . simply learning systems theory, or the new physics, or learning about Gaia, or thinking holistically, will not necessarily do anything to transform your interior consciousness, because none of those address the interior stages of growth and development. Open any book on systems theory, the new paradigm, the new physics, and so on, and you will learn about how all things are part of a great interconnected Web of Life, and that by accepting this belief, the world can be healed. But rarely will you find a discussion of the many *interior stages of the growth of consciousness* that alone can lead to an actual embrace of global consciousness . . . no hints about how these interior transformations occur, and what you can do to foster them in your own case—thus truly contributing to a worldcentric, global, spiritual consciousness in yourself and others. . . .[2]

He notes that while these new spiritualities encourage a more unified life, they do not appear to be effective paths to one, as they do not offer sustained spiritual practices that support higher levels of development. He concludes that "sadly, in claiming to offer a completely 'holistic' view of the world, they often prevent or discourage people from taking up a genuine path of interior growth and development, and thus they hamper the evolution of just that global consciousness that they otherwise so nobly espouse."[3]

Well. His comments so aroused us that we immediately named this section of his book "The Gauntlet" and engaged in many spirited debates about it, alternating between the conclusion that Wilber's head is full of rocks and that he might be making some very good points.

The Gauntlet wouldn't go away. It irritated us and goaded us. Although Wilber does not identify Paganism by name, it seemed to us that his comments include some aspects of it. If his criticisms are applicable to modern Paganism, are they well founded? Hasn't he *read* any books written for Pagans by Pagans, we wondered? And then we realized that there really aren't many, if any, books in Pagan literature that address developmental issues directly. Or even indirectly for that matter. The modern Pagan movement is new enough that it is still in the process of defining itself. Many Pagan books currently in print are devoted to describing one or another tradition, or this or that practice, as a means of articulating what modern Paganism is. This is normal to our way of thinking, and we would be surprised if Pagan literature were not addressing these issues at this point. To a large extent, Paganism is still trying to find its feet, and to expect the movement to be focusing on developmental issues already may be premature.

And yet, the modern Pagan movement isn't starting completely from scratch. We believe that Paganism is arising in a postindustrial world and is a postmodern movement. As such, it has the advantage of arising from a worldview that is capable of holding multiple perspectives at once, of testing all beliefs in the light of reason and direct experience, and allowing the different realms of human experience (Wilber's four quadrants discussed in later chapters) to enjoy their independent expressions without being subjugated one to another. However, this postmodern perspective raises the bar for Paganism. The Pagan movement is taking shape in a culture that on the whole has progressed quite a distance from the worldviews in which most mainstream religions were formed, and thus has larger skills and capacities available to it if it is willing to make use of them. Whether or not the Pagan movement is able to take advantage of its unique position will depend in large part on the developmental capacities of individual Pagans. For even though Paganism arises in a postmodern paradigm, each person who identifies as a Pagan is born at the most basic level of human capacity and must grow through each space in sequence. Not everyone makes every transition, naturally, but the more that Pagans can expand to greater capacities, then the greater will be the capacities of the movement as a whole.

This has profound implications for Pagans, indeed for everyone, as it emphasizes the importance of continued growth and expansion. It is this fact more than anything that convinced us to share with you what we learned about spiritual development and its application to Paganism. We hope the information presented in this book helps you come to a greater understanding of the process of growth in general, and to see your own developmental experiences more clearly.

The book begins by exploring two models of personal development, the first based on Ken Wilber's developmental spaces and the second on James Fowler's stages of faith. We offer our view on how these models apply to modern Paganism, and then in chapter 2 look at development within cultures. The cultural models offered here include Spiral Dynamics, developed by Don Beck and Christopher Cowan, and a variety of other theories from several authors, including Ken Wilber, Karen Armstrong, Riane Eisler, Janet Chafetz, and Gerhard Lenski. In chapter 3 we turn the developmental focus onto magick, which we believe comprises the bulk of modern Pagan spiritual practice. We review the basic principles of magick as we have interpreted them, and in the remaining chapters examine each of the four types of magick individually (that is, communing, energy work, divination, and conscious creation), provide exercises to help you develop your magickal skills, and help you move forward in your growth. We also explore how each of the types of magick is likely to be experienced by Pagans depending on their developmental capacities.

Our general assumption is that most of the readers of this book are Pagan, or if not Pagan, at least interested enough in modern Paganism to pursue their study to this level. However, it's certainly not a requirement that you be a Pagan to read this book. If you are reading this book in order to understand a friend or family member who is a Pagan, please begin with our introductory book as it will give you a thorough overview of the movement as a whole. As with the introductory book we continue to offer examples here that bridge from Christianity to Paganism, showing both commonalities and differences. We hope this bridging will help those with a Christian background who are new to Paganism, or Christians and others who are not Pagan but are curious about the movement, to gain a greater understanding of modern Pagan ideas and principles.

Because this book more or less picks up where the introductory one leaves off, we have kept the same format. This means that we have included discussion questions, journaling, visualizations, and other exercises, and we are again writing jointly. This book can be studied individually or with a group, and works well in a class setting. We suggest that you acquire a notebook to use as a journal in which you can write your thoughts and experiences, answer discussion questions, and keep track of projects, magickal pages, and your magickal plan for the year.

Finally, we wish to note that both our introductory book and this one are essentially overviews. Unfortunately, there is not time or space in which to present every theory of development that may be relevant, or every perspective of magick that can be explored. If you have an interest in a particular Pagan tradition, group, or magickal practice, please consult with your bookseller or search the Internet for related information. There are many resources available that may give you the detail you are looking for in specific areas. Concerning spiritual development and Paganism, we know we have only scratched the surface of a topic that has profound implications for the future of Paganism. We hope this book is only the first of many yet to come on this topic by a variety of authors. We also hope our discussion of these subjects opens doors for you, and helps you gain clarity and understanding regarding your own spiritual path. May our efforts here encourage you to open to your own unfolding, and to embrace the many joys and challenges that await you along your journey.

1

Growth and the Individual

LIFE IS THE EXPERIENCE of growth, change, and transformation. To be alive is to evolve. To evolve is to connect with the world in new and deeper ways. Sometimes change happens almost without effort while at other times it feels strained and difficult. Sometimes transformation is exciting and welcome, and at other times threatening and overwhelming. But there is no avoiding growth and change. It is embedded in you.

Each of you have experienced numerous transformations during your life. From the moment you took your first step you began a lifelong movement toward the new and unknown. You expanded the limits of your world. You pushed your boundaries larger, and then larger still. And not only physically, but cognitively, emotionally, morally, socially, and spiritually as well. Concerning your spiritual growth, the concepts of God that you had at age five may not be adequate for you at age twenty, and the concepts of God you had at age twenty may not be adequate again when you reach your forties and later, your elder years. Across the span of your life you may travel through a variety of views about who and what ultimate authority is or isn't, what the purpose of life is, what your values and taboos are, and the importance (or not) of ritual, myth, and symbols.

The focus of this book is spiritual growth and development as experienced by Pagans. We believe this issue is very important, especially since many new Pagans have no real idea of where they are headed spiritually or why, and because most books on Paganism do not discuss development directly or in connection with what Pagans might experience at various points in their growth. If you have ever wondered where you are going spiritually as a Pagan, then learning about development, how it applies to Paganism in general, and to you in particular, will be time well spent.

Not only is this topic of interest to you individually, but it is important to the entire Pagan movement, as Paganism will only be as powerful and effective as the people who practice it. If you desire Paganism to be a serious and influential spiritual philosophy in this culture, then you must strive for the highest level of development you are capable of reaching. Paganism cannot point the way to any level of spiritual enlightenment that its members are not experiencing.

It is our hope that the developmental models we explore in the chapters ahead will help you understand and advance in your spiritual growth. Such models can help you see patterns in yourself and the culture where now you see only disorder. They can be very helpful, but remember that models are only road maps. They are a way of describing reality but are not the reality they are describing. Models cannot predict your life experience or the path your growth will take. They can, however, point out the contours and shapes of human experience and hopefully provide you with greater knowledge and confidence.

In this chapter we examine two personal developmental models, one from modern psychology and the other from faith development. In chapter 2 we continue our exploration by including a model of cultural development. We relate each of the developmental perspectives to Paganism in general as we go, and in chapter 3, to magick specifically. Chapters 4 through 7 explore each of the four types of magick we identify individually, apply the developmental models to them, and offer activities to help you move forward in your spiritual growth and exploration.

Growth as Expansion

Volumes have been written on the nature of human growth and development. It is beyond the scope of this book to explore all the definitions and models of development from so many theorists. And yet, we need a basic understanding of what growth is in order to explore it in relationship to Paganism.

It seems intuitively clear to us that growth is a process of expansion. Think for a moment about your own growth—beginning as an infant, becoming a youth, going through school, entering adulthood. If you have siblings, children, nieces, or nephews, you have observed the same growth patterns in them as you experienced yourself. As development unfolds, an individual can do more and grasp more. Earlier skills are not lost but incorporated into new capacities. The wiggling of arms and legs becomes learning to sit up and roll over, then becomes crawling, and finally becomes standing and walking. The walking could not happen without the earlier skills, and so each experience of growth embraces what came before and adds something more to it. Crawling is a skill that is whole and complete in itself and perfectly adequate for the infant at a certain stage. But while complete at one level, the skill of crawling becomes only a part of greater skills once the infant begins to walk. While the skill of crawling is adequate, the skill of walking can be viewed as more adequate. The infant has embraced a greater capacity.

Growth as an expansion of capacity is not limited to childhood development but seems to be found wherever there is life. In the realm of biology, there are subatomic particles, then atoms, then molecules, then cells, then organs, then entire organisms. Each of these levels contains those that came before it and adds a greater capacity to it. Even in the sociocultural, or "man-made" arenas, such as the spoken and printed word, there is the expanding pattern of images, then symbols, then letters, then words, then sentences, then paragraphs, then chapters, then books.[1]

The order in which expansion occurs seems to be important since it is not possible to have a sentence if one does not first have words, and one cannot have words without the letters or phonetics that form them. There would be no human bodies if there were no cells, and no cells if there were no molecules. It is possible, for example, for an infant to learn to sit up but because of injury or disease, never be able to crawl or walk. However, no infant can walk who cannot even sit up, and no organ can function if it is not comprised of cells.

The picture of growth we are suggesting is one of expansion in which *wholes* expand to become *parts* of greater wholes, whose capacities exceed those of the prior whole. Psychologist Arthur Koestler coined the term "holon" to describe these wholes.[2] Ken Wilber, philosopher and psychologist, whose work we examine below, visualizes Koestler's holons as capacities which are nested one within the other, like layers of an onion. The capabilities of earlier development are still present in the expanded capacity, which is dependent upon the earlier skill or ability. Wilber refers to this nested phenomenon as the Great Chain of Being, or the Great Nest of Being.[3] This Great Chain or Nest embraces increasing orders of wholeness and capacity, beginning with the most basic unit of matter, then expanding to include organisms, mind, soul, and spirit.

The concept of growth as expansion into greater orders of capacity requires the ranking of capacities at some point. Which capacities must come first in order to support those which come later? Answering this question places development in an ordered sequence. To say that written words are composed of letters, and one needs to understand letters before one can write words, is a ranking of order. It implies a hierarchy of structure (or as Koestler would say, a "holarchy"[4]) and a progression from one capacity to another. It does not imply a judgment of worth or importance. Indeed, letters are indispensible to written words and are not of "lesser" or diminished importance. Koestler believes that the holarchy of development is open-ended in both directions; its inner and outer reaches have not been discovered, and may never be. He suggests we abandon the view of the individual as a "monolithic structure" and replace it with "the concept of the individual as an open hierarchy whose apex is forever receding, striving towards a state of complete integration which is never achieved."[5]

If the idea of ordering developmental sequences is uncomfortable for you, keep in mind that you and most other people act intuitively from assumptions of ranking everyday. Most people will agree there is a greater reach and capacity in being able to walk to places than to crawl to them, and much more can be conveyed through the paragraphs of this book than a study of the letter "B." For reasons we will examine in chapter 2 in the section on Spiral Dynamics, the idea of ranking or hierarchy is currently out of favor and frequently associated with repressive systems of one type or another. But as Riane Eisler, author of *The Chalice and the Blade*, reminds us, there is a big difference between actualization hierarchies and domination hierarchies.

As Eisler explains it, a domination hierarchy is a system of ranking "based on force or the threat of force. These *domination hierarchies* are very different from a second type of hierarchy, which I propose be called *actualization hierarchies*. These are the familiar hierarchies of systems within systems, for example, of molecules, cells, and organs of the body: a progression toward a higher, more evolved, and more complex level of function. By contrast, as we may see all around us, domination hierarchies characteristically inhibit the actualization of higher functions, not only in the overall social system, but also in the individual human."[6]

We propose that the holonic view of development is an actualization hierarchy. As Wilber puts it: "This is a ranking, to be sure, but a ranking of increasing inclusiveness and embrace, with each senior level including more and more of the world and its inhabitants, so that the upper or spiritual reaches of the spectrum of consciousness are absolutely all-inclusive and all-embracing—as we said, a type of radical universal pluralism."[7]

my journal

Take the following categories one by one and identify all the ways in which you are comfortable in that area of your life: (1) finances, (2) emotions, (3) career, (4) spirituality, (5) your mind, and (6) your body.

Next identify all the ways in which you are unsatisfied or uncomfortable in each of these same areas.

Study these two lists. Do you see any patterns or connections between them?

Focus for a moment on your list of spiritual discomforts. Why are those items on your list? What is going on spiritually that is not working for you? What has happened to bring you to this point? Are other people or situations factors in your discomfort, and if so, how? What can you do to resolve these discomforts?

Hang on to your journaling from this exercise as you will need to refer to it in this and later chapters.

The Growth Process

As the self expands to embrace wider capacities, it does so first by identifying with the new level or capacity, and then by integrating it into its structure. Eventually, the self begins to separate its sense of identity from the prior level and prepares itself to move to the next, unless something occurs to arrest it or hold it there. Wilber notes that complete mastery of a given level of development is not required for growth to continue, only basic competency, with the self gaining an essential grasp of the skills and capacities offered by a given developmental space.[8] We discuss Wilber's developmental spaces in detail below.

As discussed earlier, *wholes* expand to become *parts* of greater wholes, whose capacities exceed those of the prior whole. So it is that new skills emerge from earlier ones. For this reason, if a problem occurs at one level it can continue as a distortion into later levels. Wilber compares this to a skyscraper. Each floor of the building rests on the floor below, and a tilt in the first floor will cause a tilt in the second, and so on up the structure.[9] Imbalances can be corrected by an individual once he or she gains capacities large enough to see the problem and decides to work to correct it. We look at specific problems, or pathologies, that can arise at different points in the developmental process in the next several sections.

Although we are using the word "self" as though it describes a unitary structure, the self is really a composite of many separate capacities. Wilber calls these various capacities "developmental streams," which include morals, ethics, emotions, cognition, social skills, creativity, altruism, sexuality, spirituality, and self-identity, to name but a few.[10] Each of these streams develops at its own rate, with some expanding faster than others, although Wilber notes that all of them follow the same developmental sequence, beginning with what he terms the archaic and moving toward the nondual, discussed in detail below. This means, for example, that a person can be well developed in say, artistic or charitable activities, but poorly developed in social skills or self-esteem. However, even with the different streams operating at different levels within the same individual, the self tends to identify with only one level of development at a time.

Wilber states that each time the self changes to a new level, it "sees a different world."[11] It has new problems, new perspectives, new needs, and new values. It has a different sense of time, identity, morals, acceptable motivations, social structures, technology, and religious experience. It is as though there is a level of "food" that satisfies the relational needs of the self at each level, from physical food, to emotional food, to mental food, to spiritual food. As Wilber notes, another way of describing growth is the process of "learning to digest subtler and subtler levels of food."[12]

The self can temporarily experience a level of consciousness outside of its usual level when it has a "peak experience." A peak experience occurs when the self briefly experiences a more expansive level than the one from which it operates on a daily basis. Renowned psychologist Abraham Maslow studied peak experiences and identified some of their characteristics. Maslow is the psychologist who defined a "hierarchy of human needs" that begins with hunger and thirst, and moves up through safety, belongingness, love, and esteem. The highest levels of the hierarchy he termed "self-actualization" and "transcendence," which are levels humans can aspire to when other needs are met. Maslow views peak experiences as temporary moments of self-actualization.

Some of the characteristics of peak experiences he identifies in his book *Religions, Values, and Peak-Experiences* include a perception that the entire universe is an integrated and unified whole; an experience of deeper than normal levels of concentration, listening, and feeling; an experience of timelessness and spacelessness; an acceptance of the world as it is, as being whole and beautiful in itself, with evil seen as having a proper place in the whole; a description of reality in terms of the highest spiritual values—for example, people not only exist but are sacred, the world not only exists but is sacred; the disappearance of fear and the resolving of the apparent polarities and dichotomies of life; a sense of being the creative center of one's actions and perceptions, feeling more self-determined and responsible than usual; and a tendency to become more loving, accepting, and selfless, combined with feelings of gratitude.[13]

Maslow notes that people having a peak experience "become larger, greater, stronger, bigger, taller people and tend to perceive accordingly."[14] Wilber points out that peak experiences can occasionally jolt an individual into the next level of growth, but if not, are translated at the level occupied by the person at the time.[15]

Developmental Space

As we noted earlier, one difficulty in discussing human development is in choosing from among the many models and systems we could present. We are indebted to Ken Wilber for making our task simpler. Wilber has engaged in extensive research into the writings of developmental psychologists and spiritual writers of both Eastern and Western traditions, and has done an unsurpassed job of cataloging and correlating various models. Those of you who wish to study developmentalism in more detail can begin with Wilber's *Integral Psychology*, referenced in the bibliography. His charts at the back of the book present an unparalleled comparative study of several dozen models of development.

From his studies Wilber designed a model of development based upon levels of human consciousness. He describes these dimensions of being as *developmental spaces* into which people grow.[16] Each developmental space contains a way of being and of seeing the world. As people grow into these spaces, they have the potential to expand into them and acquire the skills that are characteristic of that space.

Wilber identifies nine developmental spaces, the first five of which he considers to be *personal*—that is, centered in the individual and his or her sense of self—and four of which he characterizes as *transpersonal*—that is, taking the self beyond its boundaries and into realms outside of space and time. For the first five developmental spaces, Wilber accepts the names given to them by the noted psychologist, Jean Gebser, with some adaptations. These five spaces he calls the archaic, magical, mythic, rational, and vision-logic. The last four, or transpersonal spaces, he names the psychic, subtle, causal, and nondual.[17]

It is unfortunate that Wilber and other psychologists have chosen "magical" as the word to describe the second developmental space, since "magick" is a term of art for Pagans which describes a predominant mode of Pagan spiritual practice. The sense in which Pagans use the word "magickal" and the sense in which Wilber and other psychologists use "magical" cannot be reconciled. We feel that if we adopt "magical" as the name for the second level, it will lead to confusion and misunderstanding for both Pagans and non-Pagans. Since Wilber and others use a variety of words to describe the second developmental space including egocentric, narcissistic, naive, and self-centered, we feel it is just as accurate to refer to this stage as the *egocentric*. Other than this change, however, we adopt the Gebser/Wilber terminology for the nine developmental spaces.

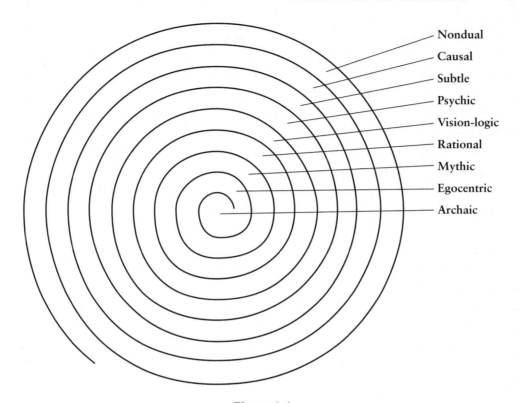

- Nondual
- Causal
- Subtle
- Psychic
- Vision-logic
- Rational
- Mythic
- Egocentric
- Archaic

Figure 1.1
Wilber's Nine Developmental Spaces

As we go through Wilber's nine spaces we will also include insights from other developmental psychologists, including Jim Marion, a Catholic and former monk, who applies Wilber's model to Christianity in his book *Putting on the Mind of Christ: The Inner Work of Christian Spirituality*. Marion's particular additions are the Dark Night of the Senses and the Dark Night of the Soul, which he adds between two of Wilber's levels. We believe that those of you who are Christian or have a strong background in Christianity will find Marion's insights useful and enlightening.

Although similar to his concept of growth as layers of an onion, we picture Wilber's nine developmental spaces on an expanding spiral (see Figure 1.1).

The Personal Spaces

ARCHAIC. The first experience of human consciousness Wilber discusses is the *archaic*, normally experienced during the first three years of life. In these early years, the sense of self is largely diffuse. At first, a baby cannot distinguish itself from its environment. The discovery that the toes it sees are its toes and part of itself, while its mother and rattle is not, is a major step in development.

The archaic self is governed by basic and primary bodily needs, such as hunger, thirst, and the desire for warmth. It is essentially concerned only with itself and has only a rudimentary awareness of others. Adults can occasionally be thrust back into the world of the archaic self in cases of severe accident and trauma, or through diseases such as Alzheimer's.

For the most part, the self at this level is helpless and dependent on others. Its means of defending itself are limited, but it uses what abilities it has available. These include sensation, perception, symbols, impulses, and instinct. Its means of coping include wish fulfillment, hallucination, and perceptual distortion. If something goes wrong in the development of the self at this point, psychological pathologies may develop which can express themselves throughout childhood and adulthood. These may include psychosis, hallucinations, and being overwhelmed by impulses. Treatment is difficult for these problems because the damage to the self occurs at such a basic, primal level that it is hard to access. Wilber notes that some success has been experienced with techniques such as Janov's primal scream and Grof's holotropic breathwork,[18] which are examples of deep level therapy techniques.

EGOCENTRIC. The second type of human consciousness generally begins to unfold between the ages of three and six. In this developmental space the self becomes aware that its emotions and the emotions of others are distinct and separate. The world of this self is narcissistic, and one in which the self cannot distinguish between its inner symbols and the outer world. Marion notes that children in this stage believe that the sun and moon follow them and obey their wishes.[19] They believe they can make it rain or snow if they wish it. If they hide their heads, for example, they think the rest of them cannot be seen, even though they are standing in full view. This is because they believe their perspective *is* reality and what they wish to be so is so. Their needs, pleasures, and wishes are all there is.

While the archaic self is content with only material food, such as warmth, shelter, nutrition, and water, the self at the egocentric level needs emotional food as well. Such emotional food includes power, safety, security, affection, and (for adults) sex.

The egocentric self tends to defend itself by projecting its feelings onto others, splitting the world into black and white, and emotionally fusing with others. Wilber notes that if something goes wrong at this level, or development is arrested here, resulting pathologies can include grandiose fantasies, persistent and extreme narcissism, and borderline personality disorder.[20] Treatment might involve a strengthening of the sense of self and the development of appropriate emotional boundaries.

MYTHIC. The third developmental space is the *mythic*, which begins around age six, and is the first of the "mental" levels. Concepts are forming and the self is able to use them to order the world. The self becomes aware, for example, that the concept of a dog is different from that of a cat; and also that the concept of mommy is different from that of daddy. The self, then, begins to sense the existence and importance not only of objects but also of roles, and may begin to explore them by playing at being a mommy, a doctor, or a fireman.

This level is called the mythic because the roles the self begins to adopt are seen by it to be larger than life. They are universal models or archetypes. The grandiose view of the self experienced in the prior level is transferred to the mythic "gods" of this level, and these gods become the self's source of authority. Marion states such gods will likely include the self's parents, teachers, nation, religious deities, and even Santa Claus.[21] Although the self now realizes it cannot command the world at its whim, it believes the gods of this level can do so.

The self learns that if it follows the rules of its authorities it is "good" and if it doesn't, it is "bad." The self wholeheartedly embraces the beliefs and conventions of its parents, peers, and culture. Religious symbols and ritual are interpreted in a concrete and literal way. Whatever its family says is right, is right. Whatever its religion says is right, is right. Whatever its nation does, is right. Tolerance for other beliefs and cultures is beyond the capabilities of the mythic self. The suggestion of tolerance, in fact, is seen as a betrayal of the authorities to which the self owes its loyalty and sense of worth. The self will, therefore, aggressively defend its point of view and attempt to convert others to its beliefs.

Beginning with this level, and continuing for the next two, the self shifts from being fed by emotional food, to being fed by mental food. This includes concepts, rules, theologies, discourse, introspection, and study.

A sense of belongingness and safety is important to the mythic self. It is in the process of integrating its feelings and impulses with its new concepts. If something goes awry at this point of development, pathologies that develop can include neurosis, anxiety, depression, feelings of guilt, scrupulosity, and obsessive compulsive disorder. Wilber states that the new conceptual self can be frightened and overwhelmed by feelings it receives from the body, such as anger and sex, and the self can react to them by forcibly repressing the feelings. Techniques aimed at treating this level (as well as the first two levels) are frequently called "uncovering techniques," because they attempt to uncover and reconnect the self to its alienated parts in order to befriend and integrate them. Wilber suggests therapeutic approaches such as psychoanalysis, Gestalt Therapy, and Eugene Gendlin's focusing,[22] which are a few examples of uncovering therapies.

RATIONAL. The fourth developmental space is the *rational*, which is typically reached in young adulthood. The self's worldview is still mythic at this point and continues to internalize the roles which surround it and to learn the cultural "scripts" it is expected to follow as an adult. This process will result, however, in the self beginning to move from being "me"-centered to an awareness of its place in the grand scheme of things, and hence to an awareness of the "we" of its society.

The rational self also begins to develop its logical skills, and to grapple with abstractions and universal concepts such as "freedom" and "equality," and "gravity" and "speed of light," and discovers these abstractions apply to all people, even those who do not hold its worldview. This discovery begins to shake the self loose from its dependence on a mythic worldview. This process frequently generates a lot of conflict and turmoil, both inner and outer, particularly if the self's parents, society, or religion insist it remain in a mythical, literal understanding of the world.

The development of reason will lead the rational self to examine and critique the rules and roles of its society. This is normal. The self will expend time and energy explaining and rationalizing the beliefs of its culture and religion to itself. It will reframe its myths so that they fit into a logical framework. Those that can't be explained rationally may be abandoned. Marion observes that people operating from the mythic level may look at those at the rational level and declare that they have "lost their faith."[23]

Pathological problems that occur at this level frequently relate to the adoption or inability to break free from unhealthy "scripts" learned from the self's family or culture. Problems can include isolation, reaction formation, repression, and projection of the self's repressed feelings onto others. Treatment generally focuses on identifying and uprooting unhealthy ideas and replacing them with more reliable scripts. Techniques can include role playing, unmasking, cognitive therapies, and creation and enacting of personal mythologies.

VISION-LOGIC. The fifth experience of human consciousness Wilber identifies is *vision-logic*. At this level the self is fully capable of abstract thought and is able to understand and integrate many different perspectives. The worldview of the self, which so far has shifted from "me" to "us of this group," now moves to "all people on this planet."[24] For the first time the self's perspective becomes truly global and moves beyond narrow definitions of race, national origin, gender, and religion. Instead, there is only humanity. The self becomes tolerant of other cultures and beliefs and appreciates many points of view. It sees that humanity lives in a global society, and wants to promote standards of education, technology, international law, and human rights that guarantee the most freedoms for the most people.

The vision-logic self tends to become more integrated and self-aware and is frequently able to work through buried traumas, repressions, and unhealthy beliefs and behaviors. This is a difficult time for the self, however, as it must decide who it is according to its own values and conscience. It may decide it is something quite different from what its parents, friends, scriptures, or faith community has said it must be. Sometimes this means that the self must construct new beliefs for itself, which can include an entirely new vision of the Divine. This can be a painful and disillusioning process.

If the self is not able to process the demands of this level, it can fall into hopelessness. Cynicism can creep in and the self can abandon its concern with ethics and act in bad faith. If it is blocked or unsupported in its redefinition of its values and beliefs, then its self-esteem might be dealt a severe blow. Therapies for this level might focus on building self-esteem, examining and building healthy and functional beliefs, and articulating a vision of the world, the self, and the Divine that will lead to a sense of meaning and purpose.

At this point the self is poised for a momentous leap. Until this moment the self has identified, although in wider and more expansive contexts, with itself only as it exists in this body. Stop and think for a moment of how you view yourself. Most likely, you think of yourself as "Mary" or "John," who lives in a certain place, has a certain job, certain interests and talents, and certain friends. There is nothing unusual about this, and for your everyday interactions it is usually sufficient. By the time you reach the sixth type of human consciousness, however, you will become aware of a "transpersonal" part of yourself. That is, one that extends beyond the personal *you* that you know, into deeper realms. The self at this level may become aware of an inner witness which resides in a realm outside of space-time. As the self becomes aware of this expanded part it may begin to develop the skills of this expanded self, such as clairvoyance, telepathy, and so forth.

The Transpersonal Spaces

PSYCHIC. Because such skills are now consciously available to the self for the first time, Wilber calls the sixth level *psychic*. Here the self does indeed begin to develop psychic skills, have out-of-body experiences, and become sensitive to energies. It may become proficient in dream interpretation, prophecy, divination, and energetic healings. The experiences at this level are frequently rich in sensory and emotional images and effects, and can feel very sharp, meaningful, and pleasurable.

Less reliance is placed by the psychic self on the opinions of others as it becomes more self-directed. Its moral concern shifts from "all of us humans" to "all earthly beings," whether human or not; its worldview expands, consequently, from one that is global to one that is shamanic.[25] It is able to embrace and encompass all that lives even as shamans are able to connect with all life forms spiritually and energetically through trance. The self embraces what Wilber refers to as Nature Mysticism, which can be an ecstatic, awe-inspiring experience of unity with nature and all things that exist on the planet. This sort of encounter is one of the most frequent we hear Pagans relate, either as a peak experience or as part of an overall awakening that shook them out of their prior worldview permanently. Beginning at this level and continuing into the next, the self moves from being fed by mental nourishment to being fed by "soul" nourishment, which includes psychic visions, contemplation, meditation, and union with the Divine.

Pathologies at this level can include getting lost in the experiences and sensations of the psychic realm, or developing a split between body and spirit. If the self has leftover issues from the narcissistic level, it can develop a grandiose ego, especially now that it perceives it has psychic powers at its disposal. Wilber recommends the "path of yogis" as a means of treatment, particularly the practices which properly open, balance, and align the chakras, or energy centers, of the body.[26]

As the self travels through the psychic level, Marion believes it will eventually experience one of two "dark nights," this first one being the Dark Night of the Senses. This term comes from St. John of the Cross, a Carmelite priest of the sixteenth century, who observed this Dark Night in himself and others under his guidance. The Dark Night comes on unexpectedly and can last from weeks to months. The enjoyment the self felt in discovering and using its new spiritual, psychic powers disappears. The pleasure the self felt in prayer, meditation, and ritual evaporates. Everything becomes difficult, dry, and stripped of meaning. All the rich sensory images and feelings disappear and the self finds no pleasure in spiritual experiences and exercises it used to enjoy. At the same time, the individual is tormented by repressed material which explodes into his or her consciousness, including anger against those in authority, discontent, sexual desires, temptations, and struggles with spiritual forces. This period eventually fades, according to St. John, and the individual generally emerges less self-centered and more truly compassionate of others. St. John identifies a second Dark Night which Marion places between Wilber's subtle and causal levels.

SUBTLE. The seventh developmental space Wilber identifies is the *subtle*. The multidimensional development of the self continues and expands to include union with the Divine and spiritual realms. The worldview of the subtle self expands from the shamanic to the archetypal, or forms of creative patterning. The self also shifts from Nature Mysticism to what Wilber calls Deity Mysticism, and moves from identifying with all earthly beings to all sentient beings, whether incarnate or not.[27] Marion believes that at the subtle level, the self has immediate access to angels, spiritual teachers, and guides.[28]

During spiritual experiences, the subtle self tends to experience ecstasy and bliss, as well as sounds, visions, and interior illuminations. The illuminations do not contain the rich sensory content of the psychic level, but tend to come nonverbally and intuitively. The self begins to experience brief moments of union with Spirit, during which all mental and emotional images fade away. The self still identifies with gender roles, and so the practice of tantra may be particularly fruitful at this level, a practice which Wilber describes as "archetypal gender union."[29]

Pathologies at this level are similar to those experienced by the psychic self. Marion notes that with the advent of visions and illuminations there is a danger of hallucinations, and if the self still has unprocessed issues and repressed emotions at work, the content of the hallucinations can be negative and frightening.[30] The self can also experience an agony of withdrawal between the moments of union that are beginning to happen to it. According to Marion, this agony eventually becomes St. John's second "dark night," the Dark Night of the Soul.[31] During this Dark Night the self feels abandoned by the Divine between its moments of union, which causes great spiritual (and sometimes even physical) pain, hopelessness, and fear. The self may feel as though it is left hanging, unable to move forward or back, and feels in terror of being abandoned by the Divine in this state forever. The self will not leave this Dark Night—perhaps for many years—until it grasps that it can never "leave" or "be left" by the Divine, as the Divine is everything and everywhere. When the self gains this realization, it begins to relax into the next level of development.

CAUSAL. The eighth developmental space Wilber identifies is the *causal*. At this stage the self experiences a sense of freedom and release. It leaves Deity Mysticism behind, usually because it perceives that the concept of Deity implies "otherness," and its experience in the Dark Night has taught it that Spirit is not "other," since there is nowhere Spirit is not. The self begins to transcend its old notions of God and move into union with Spirit itself. During spiritual moments, all images leave the self and it rests in an emptiness it perceives to be outside of time and space. This shift takes the self to what Wilber terms Formless Mysticism.[32]

According to Marion, the causal self is characterized by peacefulness and a certain emotional detachment. The self lives in the present moment and chooses whether to act or react in a given circumstance. He describes the prayer of the causal self as a sinking down into the Ground or Void, and notes that the self is content with silence and communes without thought. Marion also believes that the causal self engages in spiritual work as it sleeps.[33]

The pathologies of this level can include becoming overly detached. Since the self is beginning to see everything as Spirit, it may begin to feel careless, in a detrimental way, about the needs of people and the world. The self can shift from an overattachment to the physical world to an overattachment to silence and formlessness. Staying involved in the world and selfless service can help prevent this problem.

NONDUAL. The ninth and final level of consciousness Wilber identifies is the *nondual*. In this space the self comes to a direct awareness that there is nothing that is not Spirit. Since there is no place where Spirit is not, then searching for the Divine is a waste of effort. The self shifts from Formless Mysticism to a blending of form and the formless in what Wilber calls Nondual Mysticism, and moves from identifying with all sentient beings to all of manifest and unmanifest reality.[34]

The self begins to let go of even the archetypal forms it embraced at the causal level, and may drop all its earlier notions of the Divine. As Meister Eckhart, the thirteenth-century Christian mystic put it, "I pray God to rid me of God,"[35] a statement which continues to perplex conventional theologians and no doubt contributed to his teachings being condemned by the Catholic Church. The self instead sees itself as emerging directly from the sea of Spirit Consciousness, and realizes it has had access to all of Consciousness at every point in its development. That is, the archaic and narcissistic levels are as perfect an expression of this Consciousness as any other. The self realizes there is not more Spirit at one level than another. Wherever the self finds itself in terms of its development and life situation is perfectly adequate for accessing all of Consciousness. In its spiritual practice the nondual self relaxes and lets go of searching and striving for Spirit. As the self realizes that Spirit is all that is, it becomes content to rest quietly in this awareness.

questions to discuss

1. Is there any developmental space discussed that makes you uncomfortable? Why? Is there any level you wish you could skip, or believe you have skipped?

2. Which development space do you believe you are in now?

3. Can you think of examples of people whose developmental streams have developed noticeably unevenly, with highly advanced development in one area and significant underdevelopment in another? What do you think caused this situation and what might resolve it?

4. Can you give examples of people who seem to be more well rounded or evenly developed? Why do you think they've had more success in balanced development?

Stages of Faith

In this section we take a look at a model of faith development proposed by psychologist James Fowler who spent many years researching and mapping faith development in children and adults. He set out the results of his study in the book *Stages of Faith*. Fowler identifies seven "stages" of faith development, which he calls undifferentiated, intuitive-projective, mythic-literal, synthetic-conventional, individuative-reflective, conjunctive, and universalizing. We discuss each of them below.

Fowler acknowledges that most people define faith as a body of doctrine or belief. As you will see in the discussion of his model, there is a stage of development which defines faith in this manner, but faith according to Fowler is much broader than this. Fowler sees life as comprised primarily of relationships that form what he calls a "covenantal triad," which he describes as a triangle created with yourself on one point, other people on the second point, and some shared center of value and power at the third point.[36] This shared center of power can include family, country, church, school, and social clubs, to name a few.

Each self is a member of many such triads. From these relationships the self chooses values that bring order and meaning to its understanding of itself and the world. As the self grows and changes, so do the relationships it chooses to devote itself to, and the meanings it takes from them.

Fowler proposes that there is a difference between "movement through the seven stages" and "conversions." He defines a conversion as a change of content in beliefs, while a stage change involves moving from one stage to another. It is possible, then, to change the content of one's beliefs without changing stages, and to change stages without changing one's beliefs. They can also occur together, or one can trigger the other. In other words, it is not a necessity to exchange one set of beliefs for another in order to grow spiritually.

As we explore these seven stages, note their similarities to Wilber's nine developmental spaces.

STAGE 0—UNDIFFERENTIATED. The departure point for development is the pre-stage Fowler calls the undifferentiated, which occurs in infancy. In the undifferentiated state, the self begins the experience of faith as a trust relationship between itself and those who nurture it. The infant's faith structure centers around fears of rejection and deficiencies in its environment. The strength of this stage is the forming of a foundation of trust. The danger lies in the failure to build this foundation. The infant self will begin to transition to the next stage with the development of thought and language.

STAGE 1—INTUITIVE-PROJECTIVE. This stage generally occurs between ages three and seven. The self is now able to use speech to sort its experiences. It assumes that its perspective is the only perspective that exists, and in fact, is unable to take another's perspective. When it comes to spiritual matters, children combine pieces of stories to explain God. Even children from nonreligious homes do this. Fowler notes that religious symbols and language are so prevalent in this society that every child, regardless of upbringing, will have formed an image of God by the time he or she starts school.[37]

The self's imagination is uninhibited and will produce enduring impressions which it will have to translate rationally in later years. It can be permanently influenced by the stories adults tell it. Imagination is the strength of this stage, and also its danger. Since fact and fantasy are indistinguishable to the self, frightening images can threaten to overwhelm it, especially when misused by adults to enforce conventional rules and beliefs.

Transition to Stage 2 is triggered by the onset of certain rational skills and the desire of the child to sort out what is real and what is not.

STAGE 2—MYTHIC-LITERAL. This stage generally begins around age seven and continues until adolescence. The child's reasoning skills blossom and he or she begins to demand empirical proof in order to separate fact from fantasy. The self begins to be able to take perspectives outside of itself and to engage in inductive reasoning. Fowler notes that probably the greatest gift of this stage is the ability to narrate one's experience.[38] At this stage the self gives meaning to its experiences through the medium of stories. A Stage 1 child appreciates stories and is deeply influenced by their images, but cannot create them until this stage. The self in Stage 2 is unable, however, to distance itself from the stories it creates. It is caught within the story, it *is* its story. The self defines who it is by the roles it plays in its stories.

Images of God become fully anthropomorphic (that is, endowed with human characteristics) at this stage and always take the forms promoted by the self's family, religion, or culture. It believes that there is an order to the world, that God created this order and is also constrained by it. It believes that if it follows this order it is "good" and will be rewarded by God. If it breaks with the order, it is "bad" and will be punished, a concept Fowler calls reciprocal fairness.[39] Beliefs and symbols are taken literally in this stage.

The strength of this stage is the use of story and myth-making to give meaning to what the self observes. The danger in this stage comes from the immersion of the self into the story and the taking literally of its themes and symbols. The self might acquire a lasting image of itself as "bad" and try to overcome it by becoming a perfectionist.

The transition to Stage 3 begins when the stories begin to conflict with the self's reasoning abilities.

STAGE 3—SYNTHETIC-CONVENTIONAL. The third stage can begin as soon as the self has the ability to reflect on its own thinking, which typically begins in adolescence. The self is now capable of forming and testing hypotheses and using them to discover solutions. It is also capable of distancing itself from the stories told in the prior stage and reflecting on them. The self realizes it can compose stories that project itself into the future, and so begins to form its own personal myth.

The self also develops deeper interpersonal relationships, such as with best friends, and later, in dating. God in the prior stage was rather impersonal—the keeper of order who rewards and punishes as it is due. But with growth into deeper interpersonal relationships, God becomes very personal and knows the self intimately. Fowler remarks that God at this stage resembles a "divine significant other."[40]

Authority is identified as being "outside," and the self depends on the expectations of others to define its faith relationships. The self is aware of having values but is generally unable to focus its reflective abilities on the value system itself. For this reason, a certain degree of mystery exists around the edges of its beliefs, surrounding those things it can't explain and doesn't particularly want to. There is an aversion to asking too many questions, especially if the self is being raised in a household still in this stage. But as Fowler observes, many adults never leave Stage 3.[41] Those raised in Stage 4 homes may have an easier time transitioning to Stage 4 themselves.

At this stage the symbols of the sacred are confused with the sacred. Any attempt to demythologize a symbol is seen as an attack on what is considered holy and sacred. The strength of this stage is the forming of the self's own story, or myth, regarding itself. The danger comes from locating the source of authority outside of the self and losing autonomy.

The transition to Stage 4 can be brought on when the person leaves home, finds him or herself at odds with authority, or observes conflict between authorities. Not everyone transitions to the next stage. Whether or not a person does so may depend on the structures in which he or she is immersed. Fowler notes that situations which can slow or prevent a transition include remaining at home, early marriage, joining a sorority or fraternity, or involvement in a conventional Stage 3 religious group.[42]

STAGE 4—INDIVIDUATIVE-REFLECTIVE. The fourth stage can emerge when two things happen: there is a disruption of reliance on outside authority, and the self is willing to take responsibility for its own choices.[43] The ideal age for the emergence of Stage 4 is during the twenties. Fowler states that if the transition is delayed until the thirties or forties, it usually takes longer and causes more disruption. The adult in transition to this stage will struggle with issues of individuality versus identification with a group, unexamined feelings versus critical reflection, self actualization versus being for others, and the relative versus the absolute.[44]

This stage is a time for questioning and critical reflection and the beginning of mentally detaching the symbols from what they represent. While demythologizing allows the symbols to be translated into concepts which can be shared and discussed with others, it can also bring a sense of sadness, confusion, and grief. The strength of this stage lies in the development of thoughtful deliberation. Its danger lies in that same self-reflection which may be unable to see beyond itself and so become self-absorbed, or absorbed in the concepts it creates.

Transition to Stage 5 begins when the mental constructs the self created begin to feel flat. An inner voice breaks through containing images and feelings from a deep part of the self. The self begins to wonder if reality is not more complex than the image of the rational world it has created.

STAGE 5—CONJUNCTIVE. In this fifth stage of faith development, the self is able to see multiple perspectives at the same time. It begins to see a pattern to things and suspects that everything is "organically related" to everything else. The self is able to let things speak in their own voice and begins to feel a sense of detachment. That is, it is able to assimilate its observations of reality regardless of the effect this has on the self's beliefs or worldview. It appreciates its own and others' symbols because it understands the greater wisdom which they reflect. The self believes that contradictory views are actually contradictory, however, and will attempt to combine the seeming differences. As a part of this process, however, it is willing to interact with ideas or groups which are frightening to its outlook. Its sense of fairness cuts across ethnic, national, and religious lines.

The Stage 5 self begins to sense there is more to itself than the clear boundaries and identity it created in the prior stage. Stage 4 generally identifies itself with its conscious awareness but Stage 5 incorporates the unconscious as well. As

Fowler notes, the self comes to accept that "truth is more multidimensional and organically interdependent than most theories or accounts of truth can grasp. Religiously it knows that the symbols, stories, doctrines, and liturgies offered by its own or other traditions are inevitably partial, limited to a particular people's experience of God, and incomplete."[45]

The strength of this stage is the ability to see the incompleteness of all beliefs, including one's own. The danger lies in this ability leading to cynicism, feelings of lack of purpose and meaning, or of being frozen by uncertainty.

STAGE 6—UNIVERSALIZING. The sixth and last faith stage identified by Fowler is Universalizing. The self at this stage makes its experience of the Divine real in its person, and does so without regard to its own protection. Such a self is often seen by some elements in the society as subversive. Examples of people Fowler believes have reached the sixth stage include Gandhi, Martin Luther King, Jr., Mother Teresa, and Thomas Merton, among others.[46]

The community of this self includes everyone and everything. It is comfortable with people at any developmental space and from any religion. However, this self is not perfect and can exhibit poor judgment and habits in some areas of life. Even so, it tends to create what Fowler calls a "zone of liberation" around itself which attracts others to its vision, freedom, and generosity.[47]

Stage Demographics

Fowler firmly believes people are born genetically equipped to develop in faith. He believes that spiritual development is a natural and expected process and should be met with encouragement. His views are in agreement with Wilber and others that while each stage of development is adequate, each additional stage is more adequate.[48]

He thinks it essential that faith communities create a "climate of developmental expectation" to assist people in navigating whatever stage they are in, and then move to the next when they are ready.[49] To do this he suggests that groups provide rites of passage, activities, and service opportunities that are faith stage appropriate.

% in each Stage

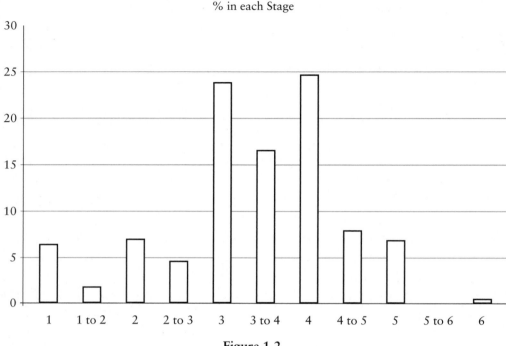

Figure 1.2
Stage Demographics

The results of Fowler's faith development study are worth noting. Researchers tested the stage development of 359 people. Although Fowler observes that the sample may not be satisfactorily random, the results are interesting nonetheless.[50] In the 0–6 age group, 88% were in Stage 1 and 12% were transitioning to Stage 2. In the 7–12 age group, the largest number (72.4%) were in Stage 2 and the next largest (17.2%) were transitioning to Stage 3. In the 13–20 age group, the largest number (50%) were in Stage 3 and the next largest (28.6%) were transitioning to Stage 4.

Combining the results for the twenties, thirties and forties, the largest number (39%) were in Stage 4 and the next largest (21.5%) were in Stage 3. A sizeable percentage (13.8% and 14.6%) were transitioning from Stage 3 to 4, or from Stage 4 to 5, respectively. Beginning at age 50 development was distributed fairly evenly across Stages 3, 4, and 5. In the over 60 age group, the largest number

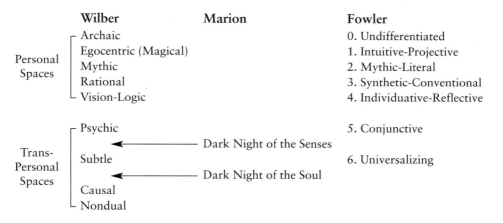

Figure 1.3
Correlation of Developmental Spaces, Dark Nights, and Stages of Faith

were in Stage 3 (24.2%) and the next largest in Stage 4 (27.4%). Only one person in the entire study was measured at Stage 6, and was in the over 60 age group.

Looking at the study as a whole, the percentages of people in each stage are shown in Figure 1.2.

If we add the percentages for the transition levels to the lower stage level (that is, count a person transitioning from Stage 2 to 3 as still being in Stage 2), then by far the largest percentage of the study population as a whole is in Stage 3, with the next largest in Stage 4. If we extrapolate this to the U.S. population as a whole, we could expect the majority of U.S. citizens to have a mythic-literal (Wilber's mythic) worldview, with the next largest percentage holding a synthetic-conventional (Wilber's rational) worldview.

Integrating the Models

While working with this material we found it helpful to combine the models in order to study their interrelationships. Figure 1.3 is a table of the models showing Wilber's nine developmental spaces, Marion's Dark Nights, and Fowler's six Stages of Faith in relation to each other.

questions to discuss

1. Do you recognize any of the stages of faith as places you have been in your life? Where do you believe you are now?

2. Do you recognize any of the stages of faith at work in people you know? What are they and how do you recognize them?

3. Is there a stage you would like to be in now? Is there a stage you wish you could avoid?

4. Has any situation in your life become clearer after learning about developmental spaces, and stages of faith? If so, how and for what situation?

5. How has the content of your faith changed since you became a Pagan? How important is that content to you? Do you think you could change the content of what you believe and still be a Pagan?

6. Do you think you changed faith levels when you became a Pagan? If so, from what to what? Could you have changed levels without becoming a Pagan? If so, what might your beliefs and lifestyle be like now?

 **exercise**

Making a Personal Timeline

Take a fresh sheet of paper, or turn to a new page in your journal, and draw a personal timeline. Begin with your birth and write your birth date at the beginning of the line. Then mark important events that happened to you, or that happened to others but which had a significant impact on you. Include events that you remember and those that others have told you about. Continue until you reach the present.

Be sure to mark the happiest events in your life, your proudest moments, your most embarrassing moments, physical traumas, and emotional traumas. Note watershed moments, when your world or beliefs shifted suddenly and dramatically. Are these moments attached to specific events or do they seem to have happened independently? Note changes in your spirituality, striking changes in belief, and peak experiences. Also note the developmental spaces and stages of faith you believe you have occupied. Have you gone through any "dark nights" or periods of spiritual dryness or grieving during any of these stages?

Choose an event from your timeline that is significant to you and write about it as a story. Keep this timeline with your other journaling as we will be referring to it in later chapters.

 **exercise**

Knotworking

Cut strands of yarn, heavy string, twine, or leather cords between ten and twenty-four inches in length. We do not suggest sewing thread as it is too fine and will probably be too difficult to work. Sit quietly for a moment with the materials in front of you. Breathe deeply and slowly, and let yourself relax. Let go of the stress of your day and any tension that you feel. As you breathe in and out, imagine that the cords in front of you represent the strands of your life, the strands of your self. Remember a few of the events of your life you identified in your timeline, and see how those events and your reactions to them helped shape who you are. This self that is you is complex and rich, composed of many facets, woven in and through your experiences, expectations, and beliefs. What aspects of yourself do these experiences reflect—such as your outward personality, social nature, sexuality, interest in art and beauty, mental abilities, motor skills, health, emotions, and religious and moral feelings, among others? Take several moments and acknowledge these different aspects of yourself.

Now pick two or three aspects that you feel the most drawn to at this time. These could be aspects you feel you express a lot or which you would like to develop more. Choose a strand of the yarn or cord for each aspect. Do not choose more strands than is possible to tie together in a knot. As you pick each strand, identify what part of you it represents.

When you are finished, gather all the strands together in your hand and sit with them quietly for a moment. Do these aspects of yourself have anything to say to you right now? Why are you drawn to them over other aspects you could have chosen? How do they represent who you are now, or possibly, who you wish to become? Notice that as you begin doing the knotworking, all these aspects of who you are become bound together in a way that makes the whole stronger and more durable.

Holding all the strands together in one hand, tie a knot near the end. The sort of knot you tie is up to you, though a simple loop is fine. As you tie this knot acknowledge the vast ground of potential from which you arise, and say the following or similar words: "I honor the potential that is me and out of which my self emerges. I embrace my connection to this potential within my spirit and honor my spiritual feelings and desires. I honor the unlimited creativity that expresses itself as the sea of possibilities in which I live, and I honor the Ground on which this potential arises and on which I rest."

After a few moments, move about a third of the way down the length of the cord and tie a second knot, saying the following or similar words: "I honor my body for the gift that it is, from my individual atoms and cells to myself as a whole organism. I acknowledge and bless even the parts of my body that I don't like, or that are injured or diseased. I honor all that I am in the self that is my body. I am grateful for all that my body has been for me in my past and open myself to a deeper relationship with it in the future." Spend a few moments sending joy and acceptance to all parts of your physical being.

An inch or so further down the cord, tie a third knot and say the following or similar words: "I honor my mind and all its abilities. I am grateful for my reason, my thoughts, and the communication and exchange I have with both inner reality and the outer world. I open myself to the power of thought and intention, and accept responsibility for how I use them in my life. I am grateful for all that my mind has made possible for me in the past, and open myself to a deeper relationship with it in the future." Spend a moment sending warmth and acceptance to your mental being.

After a few moments move another inch or so down the cord, tie another knot, and say the following or similar words: "I honor my emotions, my feelings, my gut instincts, and my intuitions. I honor the power of internal and external images and the feelings they arouse in me. I recognize and embrace the power that my emotions represent, and accept responsibility for using this power in ways that are beneficial to myself and others. I am grateful for all that my emotions have made possible for me in my past, and open myself to a deeper relationship with them in the future." Spend a moment sending love and acceptance to your emotional being.

Finally, move to a point near the end of the strands opposite from where you began, and tie one last knot. As you do, say the following words, or similar thoughts in your own words:

"I embrace where I am in my growth at this time, and I acknowledge all the places I have traveled in order to arrive where I am now. I acknowledge all the aspects of myself that come together to help make this growth possible, and I especially embrace the gifts that are my body, my mind, and my emotions. I accept responsibility for my spiritual growth, my beliefs, and the actions that flow from them. I open myself to further growth and the development of new capacities and perspectives. I step courageously into the unknown that lies before me, because I trust myself, the universe, and my concept of the divine to support me in my journey."

For the next several weeks carry your strand of knots with you if you like. You may tie the ends together to make a bracelet or necklace, hang it on your rearview mirror, keep it at work, or tie it to a drum, prayer feather, or dream catcher. We also suggest that you have it available to put on your altar for the blessing rituals set out in the last four chapters.

Paganism and Personal Development

In this section we share some of our reflections on the relationship between Paganism and personal development as discussed in this chapter. We agree that growth occurs for everyone, Pagans included, and that developmental models can be good means of identifying patterns of human growth. We do not think that Pagans are exempt from developmental patterns, and have observed that capacities seem to open for Pagans in the same order as for others.

We also agree with Koestler's vision of growth as a series of embedded wholes, where each whole is adequate in itself, each new level adds yet more capacities, and so becomes even more adequate. The self continues to expand and never loses the skills it gained earlier. We agree with Riane Eisler that such a view is consistent with the worldview adopted by many modern earth religions that any system of ordering should be one which helps individuals or societies reach their fullest potential, and should not be used for repression or control. We also find the view of wholes embedded within wholes to be in harmony with our view of the structure of the living universe and magick, as we explore in later chapters of this book.

Concerning peak experiences, we have had them and know that many Pagans have, too. It is also clear to us from experience that Pagans suffer from arrested growth and pathologies as much as the general population. Indeed, Paganism's magickal aspects can provide a fertile opportunity for people to exhibit pathologies, particularly narcissistic ones, frequently under the guise of psychic or magickal "powers." This can be a troublesome area for teachers, group leaders, and advisors, and we address some of these issues in the last four chapters.

Finding a faith community which operates on a literal, mythic, Stage 3 level is not difficult in the United States. This is due to a couple of factors, one of which is that a sizeable number of the population in all age groups is likely in Stage 3, as suggested by Fowler's study. Therefore, a significant percentage of churchgoers are interpreting their beliefs and religious experience in mythic or mythic-rational terms. This situation is reinforced by the fact that the major religions of the world arose in cultures where the majority of the population was in Fowler's Stage 2 or Stage 3. This means that Stage 2 and 3 images, beliefs, and worldviews dominate much of mainstream religions' scriptures, doctrines, and teachings. It can be difficult to be anything but mythic-literal or mythic-rational in a faith where one is surrounded by beliefs created from such a worldview, and which demands its followers stay at that level in order to be true believers.

This may be one of several reasons people are turning to alternative spiritualities. Their urge to grow is propelling them and they are not getting adequate support from their faith communities. Their communities frequently do not provide the "climate of developmental expectation" that Fowler recommends. His study also tells us there is a significant percentage of older adults that are in Stage 4, and if they stay in their faith communities, are likely pressing for change so that their needs can be met. Indeed, some mainstream religious groups are advancing to keep pace with their Stage 4 members, but it is our observation that these groups are not yet in the majority.

Overall, it's our observation that faith communities offering a postconventional (Stage 4 or greater) spirituality are still rare, though becoming somewhat more common. River was raised a Presbyterian, and while growing up observed the struggle between those who wanted to remain at a Stage 2 to 3, mythic-literal Calvinist view of Presbyterianism, such as the Evangelical Presbyterians, and those who wanted to move toward a more rationalized approach, as in the Presbyterian Church USA. We both continue to observe similar phenomena in a variety of Christian denominations.

Some postconventional faiths have swung so wholeheartedly into the rational camp that the rational is all that is allowed. In some cases there is no Divine, spiritual, or Ultimate component to be found at all. Sometimes these faith communities can be every bit as restrictive, prejudicial, and repressive as mythic ones. They can also neglect developmental streams beyond the mental. The development of mental faculties is only one stream within human beings, there being also the physical, emotional, altruistic, creative, social, and so on. How do strictly rational faiths deal with the body and emotions, the experience of visions, trance states, ecstasies, or even meditation? Some rationally-based faiths do address these areas, but many are neglectful or even hostile.

Against this background of religion in the United States, we believe Paganism is in a unique position to encourage growth across all developmental spaces and streams. We believe that Paganism is truly a postmodern religion, and is being formed within a worldview that is comfortable holding a variety of perspectives. Paganism as a whole does not require its adherents to adopt one belief system or dogma, or to be primarily at one stage of faith or another. This results in a great deal of freedom for Pagans to explore a variety of belief systems, and to combine elements of belief and practice from a variety of traditions—ancient and modern—in a way that would not be permitted in most mainstream religions.

A second reason we believe Paganism is in a unique position in regard to developmental issues is that Pagans are not shy about using all the skills and methods they have acquired in a developmental space, even after leaving that space as their primary expression. And use them they do, in movement, role-playing, sex, drumming, individual and group energy raising, dreamwork, shamanic journeys, projections, fantasy, wish fulfillment, vision quests, spellwork, storytelling, myth-making and enacting, guided and individual meditations, regressions, herbology, energy cleansing, theological debates and discussions, silent retreats, reading and study groups, and in social action and political activism. There generally is no censure in Pagan culture for combining practices or skills from several developmental spaces; indeed there seems to be a genuine appreciation of all levels, including the most basic ones. The archaic, egocentric, and mythic levels in particular do not seem to be used, as may happen in some faiths, to control members through fear, to enforce conventional taboos, or to arouse the self-preservation instincts of the faith community.

There are dangers for Paganism, of course, in the integration of practices from a multitude of developmental levels and streams. These can include confusion and a sense of loss of direction for individuals, particularly if teachers and advisors do not have training in spiritual development and are unable to point the way to the next capacity. Other dangers include the tendency of one developmental space to "take over" and force itself on others because it is "better," more politically correct, or happens to be the space occupied by the high priest or priestess at the time. A person or group that gets unhealthily "stuck" in one of the first levels, such as the egocentric, may project its egocentric pathologies onto others and cause disruption in the community. Pagans who are not well informed about spiritual development, or not well balanced themselves, can also create negative impressions of Pagans in the greater culture by not presenting themselves or the movement accurately and positively.

Teachers and counselors within Paganism need to be ready to spot these problem areas and encourage healthier responses. This can be difficult if those in teaching and advisory positions lack training in developmental issues. Admittedly, such training is scarce in Paganism at the moment. There is a definite need here which we hope to begin to fill with this book, as well as to encourage those in leadership positions to educate themselves and others on these issues.

We have also struggled with the question of whether Pagans experience the Dark Nights of the Senses and Soul, as discussed by Jim Marion. There is no doubt that Pagans go through difficult moments in life, as does everyone; moments which strain belief, faith, and trust. But the Dark Nights described by St. John of the Cross refer to spiritual dryness and spiritual abandonment brought on by God and suffered by the soul until God chooses to stop the experience.

Such a concept makes sense in a framework where God is a transcendent, anthropomorphic being, capable of withdrawing Its presence from the soul as It wishes. The Pagan view of the Divine is generally more immanent than this, if not entirely immanent, as discussed in some depth in our introductory book. Combine the view of a more immanent Divine with one of an interconnected universe—that is, where the universe might be composed of embedded or enfolded layers of consciousness that may flow unceasingly from and through a Divine Ground—and you have in Paganism a spirituality that is disposed to view separation from the Divine as essentially impossible. Given this theological disposition, we suggest that Paganism may tend to view Dark Nights less as something the Divine is doing and more as a crisis within an individual. Such a crisis could be brought on for several reasons.

One possibility is the general grieving process that occurs every time a person shifts permanently to a new level of development and abandons an old one. Neither Wilber, Marion, nor Fowler discuss this grieving in much detail, but we have experienced it ourselves and observed it in others. It seems to us to be a perfectly natural part of the separation phase Wilber describes. Especially for adults, moving to a new dimension of consciousness often involves big, upsetting shifts in worldviews, values, goals, moral embrace, friends, and associates. Letting go of who one was before is just not easy and often occurs before the person fully knows who he or she is going to become next. Sometimes after a transition, people wish they could go back to the way they were before, even though they know they wouldn't fit there anymore. The process of growth and separation and the emotions it raises can lead to a sense of loss and grieving which could be described as a Dark Night.

Somewhat ironically, we have also observed a certain euphoria that briefly occurs when a person transitions to a new developmental level. This euphoria exhibits as a large influx of energy that sustains the person for a while, sometimes a long while, but when it begins to fade the person can get discouraged, disillusioned, and depressed. They can lose their interest in spiritual practices that excited them before, and working with their new "powers" or capacities becomes hard work. We have noticed this phenomenon to one extent or another at every level. As the person becomes fully integrated in the skills and worldview of a level, the excitement, thrill, and newness wears off and a period of dryness seems to be unavoidable. This pattern does seem to become more intense with each stage of expansion, as though the bigger space the self occupies lets in much larger amounts of energy—in the same way that larger lung capacity lets in more air—and so the resulting "let down" from the integration of this energy becomes correspondingly more intense. This loss of euphoria following integration of a capacity may be described as a Dark Night by some.

As Wilber points out, when people move into new developmental spaces they shift in the type of "food" they need to feed them. The things that inspired, nourished, thrilled, challenged, and sustained them before now feel dry, empty, and meaningless. What happens if a person experiences a shift in "food" needs in a faith community where no one else has shifted or will likely shift, where the institution is not going to support a shift, and the person knows he or she can expect to be fed the same dry food over and over for the rest of their lives? We don't know about you, but this depresses us just thinking about it! Such a situation is particularly agonizing in a religious community, such as a monastery or other close group, where the lifestyle and theological perspective is not going to change to fit the changed person. To live in a faith community where few people—possibly no one—are at the new level of growth must be extremely painful and could certainly bring on a Dark Night. If the individual is deeply depressed by their situation, the Dark Night could go on for years. In fact, St. John notes that some monks and nuns report being in a Dark Night for the remainder of their lives. We have wondered if such a Dark Night would have continued if these monks and nuns had been able to move to an environment that better fed their new selves.

As Marion points out, a great deal of repressed material comes exploding up into consciousness during Dark Nights—particularly sexual fantasies, resentment against superiors and church authorities, and visions of torment by Satan. Let's look at each of these problem areas from the Pagan perspective. Concerning sexual issues, Paganism does not require celibacy, chastity, or even monogamy, and is generally sex-affirming. Communication about sexual issues and desires, honesty about one's needs and tastes, and the forming of responsible relationships (even those considered "alternative" or taboo in mainstream culture), are frequently accepted. While a Pagan could certainly be sexually repressed, Pagan culture does not enforce the type of sexual restrictions that Christians may experience.

Regarding resentment against superiors and religious authority, Pagans generally do not vow obedience to a religious leader, are not limited in their beliefs to approved dogma, and are fully responsible for the formation of their conscience. While a Pagan could resent someone in authority, Pagan culture does not give the sort of power to church leaders that many Christians experience. Concerning satanic torments, Pagans don't share Christian beliefs about Satan since most Pagans do not adopt Christian mythology. Many Pagans view Christian mythology from the same perspective as they would any other belief system, such as say, Egyptian mythology. Nor do Pagans tend to see the world as engaged in a pitched battle between the forces of good and evil, as do many Christians, and so would not usually envision themselves as the recipient of an attack by Satan.

These observations lead us to wonder whether certain aspects of Dark Nights are not in some instances brought on by Christian beliefs and culture, while other aspects—such as loss of euphoria or grief—may simply be inherent in the process of growth regardless of one's belief system. If both of our suppositions are correct, then we shall see over time how the Pagan experience of Dark Nights, if Pagans do experience them, resembles or differs from those recorded by Christian observers.

As noted above, Paganism has not adopted one single, official dogma, but studies centuries of mythology. Most Pagans are open to a variety of views and perspectives concerning the Divine. Because of this approach to religious belief

Paganism is a very appealing spirituality to those who are transitioning from the rational to the vision-logic level (Stage 3 to 4). And since many Pagans are strongly oriented toward nature and the earth, and are beginning to have Nature Mysticism experiences, it is also a very appealing spirituality to those who are transitioning from vision-logic to the psychic level (Stage 4 to 5).

While Wilber, among others, has criticized the Pagan and "New Age" movement for its emphasis on Gaia, "web-of-life theories," and experiences of interconnectedness, as discussed in the Introduction,[51] we believe that such an emphasis is stage-appropriate at the vision-logic and psychic levels (Stages 4 to 5). In our opinion, such experiences need to occur and be integrated before further development can happen. Web-of-life theories are perfectly adequate for their developmental space. At more expanded levels they may not be, and the developing self may likely go on to embrace more inclusive views of interconnectedness if growth continues.

Whether Paganism is able to support its members all the way to Wilber's nondual space will be seen in time. The fact that we haven't seen much of it yet either in Pagan practice or literature is, in our opinion, likely due to the youth of modern Paganism. Compared to any of the mainstream religions, modern Paganism is a brand new arrival. It has had only fifty or sixty years to establish itself, which is just the blink of an eye. The two of us became familiar with the movement before the word Pagan had even been widely adopted. There has certainly been little time to map spiritual and mystical experience from the Pagan perspective, or even to grow Pagans with the maturity to be able to map such experiences. St. Teresa of Avila and St. John of the Cross, some of the first to map spiritual development for Christians, came along 1600 years after Christianity had begun. Is Paganism, which has barely had time even to name itself, already supposed to be operating at these levels? We think those who criticize the movement on this basis should be a bit more patient.

Regardless of pressures from governments or religions, some individuals have always managed to grow to the most expansive levels of spiritual development. Pagans need to remember that it is not the content of belief that "makes" you grow or "keeps" you from growing, though we understand that beliefs can create roadblocks. The permission to grow ultimately comes from within, and no religion or culture is powerful enough to stop every individual all the time.

Does Paganism have the spiritual depth to take its adherents all the way to Fowler's Stage 6 or Wilber's nondual space? The most honest answer is that time will tell. Paganism has several things going for it, including the fact that its modern incarnation did not begin in a predominantly egocentric or mythic culture, and so has not had to battle its way forward against the cultural inertia experienced by most world religions. We examine these cultural developments and where culture is at present in the next chapter, but one can argue that modern Paganism is coming along at a good time developmentally. The emergence of Paganism now, in a postmodern world, offers a golden opportunity for spiritual exploration and creativity, an opportunity which will hopefully be enhanced by Paganism's honoring of multiple perspectives and beliefs, and balancing of the responsibilities of the individual with planetary and communal concerns.

 questions to discuss

1. What do you think Paganism's goals should be in regard to fostering the personal and spiritual development of Pagans? Do you think Paganism adequately encourages development? What kinds of discussions have you heard Pagans having about spiritual growth, if any? Is the environment of Paganism conducive to development? Explain.

2. Do you think that growth is a natural process or one that a person must make happen? How and when did you form this belief? What experiences is it based on?

3. Did your family or religion of origin ever discuss spiritual development? What did they believe about it? Do you agree or disagree with them now? What would their opinion be of the material presented in this chapter?

4. What does Paganism offer you in terms of your faith development right now? Is it meeting your needs? In what ways is it meeting them or not? What would it take to change those aspects that are not meeting your needs?

2

Growth and the Culture

NO INDIVIDUAL DEVELOPS IN isolation. While some aspects of development are personal, such as those involving brain maturation, general motor skills, or physical trauma, many others are intimately connected to the society or culture in which the individual lives. Even brain maturation can be slowed or arrested by a culture that is isolated, regressive, or in a recurring state of crisis that threatens its members' survival. To understand individual development, then, means that one must also understand cultural development.

Koestler's concept of the holon can be extended into the realm of culture, since a culture is in essence a holon made up of individuals. The shared inner meanings of cultural symbols, as well as external cultural structures such as laws, politics, arts, sciences, educational systems, churches, and institutions, are created by individuals each operating from a personal point of development. Although individuals are *wholes* in and of themselves, when they band together they create a larger or more expansive structure in which the individual becomes a *part* of a larger *whole*.

Within this new whole called culture, we would expect that the level of development representing the majority of its members with political power will receive the largest share of resources. Those resources are then used to build institutions and other social structures that mirror the level of development of those members of the culture. As the average level of individual growth changes within that society, so we would expect to see cultural beliefs, expectations, and structures shift to keep pace. In this chapter we take a look at cultural formation and how it impacts the development of individuals and the belief systems in which they operate.

Culture in Developmental Space

The first developmental model we examine in regard to culture is an extension of Wilber's developmental spaces and is based on types of social structures and technologies. Social structures begin with the tribe and progress through the village, empire, and nation-state. Technologies begin with foraging and hunter-gatherer, and progress through horticultural, agrarian, industrial, and informational. Wilber correlates each cultural structure and technology to his developmental spaces up to vision-logic. Keep in mind that when Wilber identifies a cultural type, he is referring to the general or overall level of development experienced by a given society at a given time. Obviously not every individual in a society is at the same level, but the weight of cultural expression and use of its resources will tend to settle around one level at a time. We have developed Figure 2.1 to show the correlation between the levels of personal development and cultural type, according to Wilber. Each triangle represents a layer of growth, with the bottom of the triangle stating the level of individual development and the sides stating the corresponding aspect of cultural development.

Beginning with the first level, the archaic, Wilber notes that this term applies to all structures which existed before the appearance of hominids on the planet. Early human beings formed a foraging, hunter-gatherer technology and lived in groups of families or tribes.[1] A tribe was bound together by kinship and lineage. It drew its boundaries in relation to others according to the identity of common ancestors. A tribe did not have a worldview which enabled it to unify groups except through blood relationships. As issues over scarcity of land, food, and other resources arose, this worldview became inadequate as a means of interacting with other groups, and so it expanded into Wilber's magical (our egocentric) level, and the village became the primary social structure.

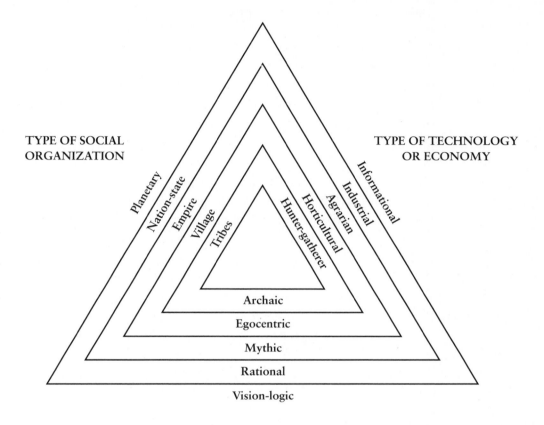

TYPE OF SOCIAL
ORGANIZATION

TYPE OF TECHNOLOGY
OR ECONOMY

Planetary
Nation-state
Empire
Village
Tribes

Informational
Industrial
Agrarian
Horticultural
Hunter-gatherer

Archaic

Egocentric

Mythic

Rational

Vision-logic

DEVELOPMENTAL SPACES

Figure 2.1
Culture in Developmental Space

This more expansive worldview allowed tribes and families to broaden their embrace and organize within a larger context composed of individuals from many lineages. By combining forces in this fashion, humans were able to solve the problems which arose at the earlier level, and technology advanced to the horticultural.

Wilber notes that the type of societies in which women historically held the most power were horticultural. In these societies, women shared power equally with men and often produced as much as 80% of the food.[2] Tools for food production were simple, such as hoes and digging sticks. Cultivated areas were small and near the homesite, and therefore easy for women to access even when pregnant or nursing. However, with the later development of the plow and agrarian culture, and the shift to a fully mythological society, the majority of food production and the balance of power shifted to men.[3] Images of the Divine changed as well, from the predominantly feminine to the masculine, from the Great Mother to the Great Father. As Wilber puts it, " . . . where women work the fields with a hoe, God is a Woman; where men work the fields with a plow, God is a Man."[4]

Feminist sociologist Janet Chafetz points out that this shift was not so much a function of male oppression as it was genetic necessity. Women who plowed had much higher rates of miscarriage. In agrarian cultures, fields were larger and much further from the homesite, and pregnant and nursing women had limited mobility.[5] What began in biological necessity, however, eventually became a difference in status. The value of an individual in a mythological society is based on the type of role he or she plays, and those roles which help to maintain or improve the power of the society are viewed as more valuable. Therefore, more status is given to roles in the public sector or those related to economic production.

As Chafetz notes, a biological constant for women is that they carry babies in their bodies and so are less mobile. Women experience increased miscarriage and child mortality if they engage in heavy labor, the predominant form of economic production in agrarian cultures, and so their participation is limited in order to protect their own and the group's survival. With women less physically mobile, it is more efficient for them to take care of the young, which means that they remain close to home. Since they remain close to home it is also more efficient for them to manage domestic matters. Chafetz concludes that "since many societies have had a large share of their productive activities moved away from the homesite, these fetters on female mobility restrict women's opportunity to specialize in productive roles."[6] As societal development continues into the present, however, biological needs and limitations drive fewer and fewer of the lifestyle choices for men and women, gradually freeing both sexes from biological constraints.

This freedom would not develop quite yet, as the next worldview to arise would be the mythic. At this level, the economy is agrarian and the societal structure is the empire. As Wilber noted above, the shift from horticultural to agrarian is usually marked by the development of the plow and other heavy farming equipment; and as Chafetz notes, women are historically most disadvantaged and experience the highest levels of sexual stratification in agrarian-mythic cultures.[7] As a means of ordering society, however, empires have a wider embrace than the earlier village structure and can provide stability over more territory. Members of empires are usually bound together by a common mythology under rulers who are legitimized by it. As the empire expands, conquered peoples are frequently required to adopt the prevailing mythology or be killed or exiled. Since a mythological culture can get rid of unbelievers, it is usually very unified. As Wilber drily puts it, "nothing so wonderfully concentrates a community as the prospect of being burned at the stake for disagreeing with its worldview."[8]

According to both Wilber and cultural historian Karen Armstrong, empires reach their limitations when they run into each other. Empires have not yet attained the worldview that allows them to formally recognize the existence of other nations, and instead see them as competitors. The might of the empire is wielded in an attempt to bring all peoples of the world under the power of its mythology. Other empires and their mythologies are incompatible with this mindset and so must be destroyed. Encountering other empires eventually begins to raise questions and doubts. The first response to this discomfort is to prop up the myths with rational reasons, an in-between stage Wilber calls mythic-rational. Reason will continue to grow, however, and eventually will replace the mythic worldview.

The rise of reason had unprecedented effects on all aspects of human understanding, including the social, religious, scientific, and artistic. To understand just how unprecedented these effects are, Wilber sets out his concept of the four "quadrants" of human experience in what he calls the "integral approach." These quadrants are (1) the *Inner I*—which is your private, personal, subjective experience, (2) the outside of *Outer It*—which is what can be observed about yourself and the world externally, (3) the *Inner We*—which includes shared meanings and experiences, such as the fact that you understand the meanings of the language we are using in this book, and (4) the *Outer Its*—which is the observable structures and institutions of a society.[9]

All four quadrants of human activity exist all the time, but their interrelationships are affected by developmental progression. The earlier the level of development, the more merged the four quadrants are, and the less able individuals and societies are to separate them.

So, for example, if the world of *Outer It* is confused with the inner subjective experience of the *Inner I*, as might occur in an egocentric or mythological society,

Upper Left—I	**Upper Right—It**
Internal Individual	External Individual
• subjective	• objective
• internal processes	• mechanistic
• thought, emotion, intuition	• science, observable phenomenon
• how I experience my Self	• how I experience the external World
Lower Left—We	**Lower Right—Its**
Internal Collective	External Collective
• subjective	• objective
• shared cultural meanings	• structures, organizations
• language, mores, etc.	• governments, laws
• how my Self and your Self experience each other	• how we express our culture in physical form

Figure 2.2
Wilber's Four Quadrants

then one would not be surprised by a statement such as the one offered to refute Galileo, that since the body has seven orifices in the head, and there are seven types of metal, then obviously there can only be seven planets.[10] The four quadrants cannot be properly separated until development reaches a certain point, most typically the rise of rational faculties beyond the role of justifying the position of the ruling mythology. When the four quadrants are freed from each other, scientists are free to make discoveries that disagree with church or civil authorities, artists can paint themes that are unsanctioned or even sacrilegious, and individuals can explore interests that go beyond what survival or the society dictate. Concepts of fairness, rightness, and justice that are independent of the prevailing mythic worldview begin to develop.

In the earliest eras, what is right is what has to be done to secure the survival of one's self, children, and tribe. Later, what is right is what the ruler and mythology says is right and can be backed up by force. With the rise of reason, what is right is what is universal, fair, and just. Neither biological nor mythological constraints pass muster in a rational society. The old social relations based on power or biological necessity are intolerable to reason. And so we observe the rise of liberation movements, of all types, wherever rationality takes center stage. In Wilber's words: " . . . this inescapably means that the widespread emergence of the women's movement was not primarily the *undoing* of a nasty state of affairs that easily could have been different, but rather it marked the *emergence* of an altogether *new* state of affairs that was in significant ways *unprecedented*."[11]

According to cultural historian Karen Armstrong, the shift in Western culture from the mythological stage to the rational took approximately three hundred years and reached fruition around the year 1600. She notes that in the beginning of the shift most scientists, explorers, and even theologians believed they were simply discovering new ways to be religious, uncovering more aspects of God.[12] By the year 1600, innovations were occurring at a rapid pace and Europeans were able to meet their material needs more easily. Since they didn't need to spend all their waking energies on keeping warm and avoiding starvation, they had more resources available, both in time and money, to invest in new advances. This marked the beginnings of capitalism and an industrial culture.

The new inventions needed people to build, operate, and repair them. People who for generations had been illiterate subsistence farmers now needed greater skills, and were trained to work a trade or otherwise support the new technologies. This work was more complex than subsistence farming and the training for it required that workers become more educated and literate. Armstrong notes that as more workers became literate they began to demand a say in their workplace and towns, and so began to exert pressure towards more democratic forms of government.[13] The new technologies, then, propelled a large strata of people into the rational level of development by pulling them out of their previously isolated, illiterate circumstances, and requiring them to become more cognitively mature.

As increasing numbers of individuals grew into the rational level of consciousness, universal reasonableness began to replace divisive mythology. Empires gave way to modern states who were able to recognize each other and make room for each other politically. When the modern state uncoupled itself from mythology, it accomplished the separation of church and state, although these concepts would take some time to mature. In 1605, Francis Bacon stated in his *Advancement of Learning* that science must be separated from myth. John Locke, who lived from

1632 to 1704, wrote in his *Letter Concerning Toleration* that church and state must not interfere with each other, that a government must tolerate all religious beliefs and concern itself only with administering governmental affairs. The separation, or differentiation, of Wilber's four quadrants was beginning in earnest.

Locke considered himself a Deist; that is, he believed there was a Divine Being and that the natural world gave evidence of the Divine's existence, the truth of which reason would demonstrate to each person. His religious and secular views were radically new, but in time his position on the role and form of government became the standard for the modern secular state.

Interestingly, the leaders of the American Revolution, particularly Washington, John and Samuel Adams, Jefferson, and Franklin were Lockeian Deists. The Declaration of Independence mentions the "God of Nature," not the Christian God, and the Constitution does not mention God at all. The Pledge of Allegiance, written in 1892, also did not mention God. The words "under God" were added in 1954 by an act of Congress during the McCarthy era to distinguish Americans from the "godless Communists." Despite the growing trend toward a rational worldview, however, many Americans at the time of the Revolution were mythic-level Christians who were unable to relate to the rational secular ideals of the Founding Fathers. Deism was considered a Satanic belief system by most Christians of the revolutionary era.[14]

Over the next one hundred years, however, rationalism had a tremendous impact on religion. Although evangelical Christianity was the dominant faith in the United States, by the mid-1800s it was based on a literal reading of the Bible, a personal conversion in Christ, and a rejection of all forms of mediation between the individual and God and the individual's interpretation of scripture.[15] It was very devoted to the reform of society and promoted the liberation of a wide variety of oppressed groups, including abolition, prohibition, feminism, women's suffrage, and penal and education reform. As Armstrong points out, what we have come to know as "fundamentalism" within Christianity in the United States is a very modern and rationalist development. These movements are not regressive, since the rational, literal way in which their members read the Bible was unheard of in earlier centuries. To the fundamentalist, doctrines are "facts" in the same way that data are "facts" to a scientist. Armstrong notes that modern fundamentalism "is a way of being religious in an age that values the *logos* of science above all else."[16] They are also embattled forms of religion, in that they see the rise of rationality as a competing faith that is conspiring to take over the culture and destroy religion, and strongly resist the separation of Wilber's four quadrants, particularly as expressed in the separation of church and state.

The rise of rationality obviously coexists with other levels of development which remain influential, while it continues to search for global solutions and a worldview that is pluralistic and noncoercive. As you watch world events unfold in the near future you may begin to recognize various developmental spaces we have discussed here, some of which precede the rational, showing themselves in the behaviors and ideals of groups and cultures. Meanwhile, the rational worldview strives to expand toward Wilber's vision-logic space, a space which is able to hold many perspectives at once and to unify opposites.

The unfolding of a vision-logic worldview is still in its infancy and is by no means assured. Although we are presenting these societal types as though one level flows automatically into the next, that is not the case. There is always the possibility that due to war or other crisis a particular society will step back to an earlier mode of being in order to meet basic needs and bring stability to the group. Even without the eruption of a crisis, each level of growth solves certain problems of the prior stage, but adds its own new problems. Wilber notes that "each new and more complex level necessarily faces problems not present in its predecessors."[17] Societies can face these new problems by expanding to meet them, applying old solutions that probably won't meet them satisfactorily, or retreating to a prior level completely. In the latter case the new problems also go away since the earlier worldview does not have the capacity to see them. As Wilber reminds us, evolution means that not only are there new wonders and abilities that unfold at each stage, but also new horrors. Any balanced account of history must acknowledge both.

If our culture is able to develop into vision-logic, then the form of cultural organization will be increasingly global and the economy will be information-based. Examples of the emergence of both are not hard to find. Global issues are already with us, as in the past one hundred years human society experienced its first World Wars and gained the capacity for mass destruction. A global perspective literally and concretely arrived in the 1960s when space travel and satellite pictures showed Earth from the viewpoint of space for the first time. Radio and television began bringing world events and cultural differences into our living rooms by the mid-twentieth century. Problems of a global nature have developed as societies deal with issues such as terrorism, health care, violations of human rights, interdependency of economies and monetary systems, and environmental concerns.

An information-based economy began in earnest with the invention of computers, and the Internet has made instantaneous global communication widely available, a situation which has never before existed. Cell phones and fax machines are everywhere and allow millions of people to interact nearly instantly. The impact of such rapid and accessible means of communication on the development of culture is still not fully understood, but it will undoubtedly have global consequences on many fronts, including the social, political, and economic. These developments may lead the culture to Wilber's vision-logic space and an embracing of emergent capabilities that are as yet unknown.

 questions to discuss

1. How would you describe the culture in which you live right now? What are the gifts and the problems it experiences? Do you think Paganism adds anything to its gifts? Does it have anything to offer in solving its problems?

2. Do you think Paganism glorifies the past? If so, how and why? If so, do you think it should and what do Pagans gain from such beliefs?

3. Do you agree or disagree that the sexes enjoy more cultural freedom now than in the past? Give a few examples.

4. Give examples from your personal experience of instances where the four quadrants have been confused or one quadrant has controlled the others. What beliefs brought about this situation? What happened and how did you and others respond?

If you could live during a different era in history than this one, which would it be? Why? What would your daily experience be like? How would your experiences differ from what they are now? How would you be different from who you are now, in terms of how you think, behave, and see the world? What aspects of living in this other time would be difficult? As a man? As a woman? What aspects would be rewarding? What things would you miss from the present? Are there any issues, personal or cultural, in this other time that you believe you would be drawn to create or resolve?

Write a brief story or personal myth about yourself in this other time, and describe your experiences, challenges, and triumphs. Be imaginative and creative! Are there any parts of your story, or aspects of this other self, you'd like to bring forward into your life today? Write or act out a dialogue between this other self and yourself today. What do they have to say to each other?

Spiral Dynamics

Spiral Dynamics is a developmental model that focuses on the values around which people organize their behavior. This model was developed by Don Beck and Christopher Cowan and is based on the work of their mentor, sociologist Clare Graves.

Beck and Cowan propose that just as "genes" organize biological information around which the body forms and functions, so do "memes" act as organizing structures that produce certain worldviews.[18] They propose that *value* memes emerge and evolve into levels of increasing complexity, a process they compare to a spiral vortex. Change from one level to the next occurs as a wave, with pressures building up within an existing worldview until a new system suddenly emerges. Each turn of the spiral marks the awakening of greater capacities, which they note are characterized by an expansion of psychological space, an expansion of conceptual space, an expansion in available choices, and increased behavioral freedom.[19]

Interestingly, Beck and Cowan also describe development of both individuals and cultures in terms of holons; that is, older value clusters remain inside the individual after they are integrated. They propose that people and cultures travel up and down the spiral in response to events and life conditions. This means that within the same society different people experiencing different circumstances will be at various places on the spiral. Even so, as with Wilber, they believe a culture generally centers around one overall level of the spiral at a time and so can be identified as being predominantly at one space or another. They also note that the levels of the spiral tend to alternate between those which focus on the individual and those which focus on group interests.

Beck and Cowan identify the turns of the spiral by color and divide them into two groups of development which they call First Tier and Second Tier. They identify First Tier thinking as "Subsistence" levels, as these have to do with the development of the human organism, basic survival skills, and the development of essential cognitive and social frameworks. Every level of the First Tier is marked by a belief that its way of thinking is the only or best way, and individuals at any First Tier level tend to resist or condemn the other levels. Beck and Cowan identify Second Tier thinking as "Being" levels, since subsistence needs are consistently met and the individual can expand into wider frameworks of values. They note that a radical shift of thinking occurs between the First and Second Tiers, as we will examine in more detail below. Generally, the individual at Second Tier thinking is able to see all the levels of the spiral simultaneously, travel them at will, and work for their healthy expression without being attached to any of them. We picture the spiral as illustrated in Figure 2.3.

The First Tier

BEIGE. The first value meme of the spiral is the Beige. At this level, as with Wilber's archaic and Fowler's undifferentiated levels, the sense of self is barely awake. Beige uses habits and instincts to survive and is driven by physiological needs. At one time, which Beck and Cowan place at one hundred thousand years ago, this level represented cutting edge thinking that distinguished humans from animals.[20] Today this level is found mostly with infants and the elderly, though a person can be arrested here from poor nutrition, disease, accident, or lack of stimulation. People can also regress to this level during mass disasters if basic needs are not met.

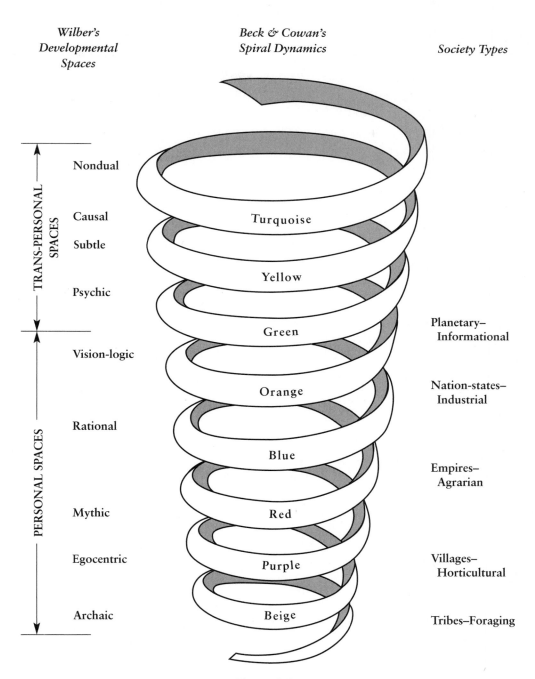

Wilber's Developmental Spaces

TRANS-PERSONAL SPACES
- Nondual
- Causal
- Subtle
- Psychic

PERSONAL SPACES
- Vision-logic
- Rational
- Mythic
- Egocentric
- Archaic

Beck & Cowan's Spiral Dynamics
- Turquoise
- Yellow
- Green
- Orange
- Blue
- Red
- Purple
- Beige

Society Types
- Planetary–Informational
- Nation-states–Industrial
- Empires–Agrarian
- Villages–Horticultural
- Tribes–Foraging

Figure 2.3
Correlation of Developmental Models

51

Beige is the beginning of the development of memory and a sense of time. Emotions bring on attachments to people and objects. As the sense of self develops, so also does a recognition of danger from a mysterious and uncontrollable environment. Beige discovers there is strength in numbers and once it reaches this realization begins to transition to the next level. Beck and Cowan put the current number of the world population at the Beige level at .1% and the percentage of power it exercises at zero.[21]

PURPLE. The second value meme on the spiral is Purple. Family and kin are most important to Purple, as the collective is better able to survive than is the individual alone. According to Beck and Cowan, this level was the cutting edge in human thinking about fifty thousand years ago.[22] As the understanding of cause and effect develop, supernatural reasons are given to explain events. Myths and legends abound and the culture is rich in folk stories, songs, and art. Social events are ritualized and customs are deeply valued, as is the preservation of sacred objects. Mystical signs are everywhere and one must obey the desires of spirit beings.

Purple is still very much with us today wherever there are sacred objects, rituals, and ceremony. It is a very powerful emotional value system. Purple is family heirlooms and mementos, the American flag, secret handshakes, and private clubs. Learning to bond in an intimate group is an essential aspect of development. An individual whose bonding needs are not met or who gets arrested at this level may turn to closely knit groups in order to find fulfillment. This might include the military, athletic teams, gangs, cults, or other "tribal" communities or religions.

As Purple's security needs are met it can begin the transition to the next level. It will begin to see its beliefs as superstitious and will want less tradition and ceremony. The transition increases as the self gains a greater sense of itself as an individual. Beck and Cowan put the current number of the world population at the Purple level at 10% and the amount of power Purple groups exercise in the world at 1%.[23]

RED. The third value meme is Red. In its healthy form, it is where ego and self-confidence develop, but it can be wild, raw, and impulsive. Beck and Cowan place its cutting edge emergence in the culture at ten thousand years ago.[24] As with Wilber's mythic-empire stage, Red eras are characterized by empires, warlords, imperialism, and the exploration of frontiers. The consensus decision-making style of the tribe gives way to strong individuals who take control. A Red leader uses both charisma and intimidation to maintain control and will exploit Purple superstitions to his advantage.

Reds live for the moment, do not plan well for the future, and aren't able to restrain themselves well. Today Red behavior is found in children between ages three and five and again in puberty. A healthy individual must learn to deal with limits and how to manage his or her personal power. Beck and Cowan note that most television shows and video games are built around Red themes.[25] Purple social needs must be met before Red can exhibit healthily. If life conditions are brutal, such as found in impoverished and war-torn countries and in poor urban areas, then the individual can be arrested at Red and may live out the theme of warrior. The positive aspects of Red include creativity, love of adventure and fun, imagination, and lustiness. Healthy Red expression includes organized activities, summer camps, and the martial arts. Beck and Cowan put the current number of the world population at the Red level at 20% and the amount of power Red groups exercise worldwide at 5%.[26]

The transition to the next level on the spiral begins when guilt and doubts concerning unbridled behavior creep into the Red mindset. The next level, which is Blue, is the level of law and authority. Cultures sometimes shift from Red to Blue when religion, backed by military force, imposes law and order. The gods during such transitions are often vengeful and wrathful, swift to punish those who don't fall in with the Red/Blue program. Beck and Cowan note, for example, that Moses' delivery of the Ten Commandments and his slaying of those opposed to them, marked the arrival of Blue for the ancient Hebrews.[27] The driving force during the Red/Blue transition is the elimination of impure thoughts and actions, and the conversion of those who think "wrongly."

BLUE. The fourth value meme is Blue. According to Beck and Cowan, this level's cutting edge occurred about five thousand years ago.[28] As with Wilber's "mythic" level and Fowler's "mythic-literal," Blue offers eternal absolute principles, order, and gives life meaning and purpose through a prevailing belief system. This level expresses itself in young people as they experiment with concepts of right and wrong and fairness, and solve problems with the help of authority figures. When this level is expressed healthily, we find some of the happiest and most comfortable people and societies. Everyone has a place and stays in it. The society is orderly, punctual, and hierarchical. Scouting and patriotism are examples of healthy Blue. Words and books are very important to Blue. Beck and Cowan note that when a Red society attacks a Blue one, it almost always burns its libraries first.[29]

Blue's sense of self, however, comes from a source outside itself. It is taught that things are black and white, with no room for gray. Understanding and tolerance are minimal. People and situations are not judged compassionately. Blues can also tend to isolate themselves by choosing to associate only with other Blues.

Once the Blue worldview has stabilized its culture, it begins to transition to the next level. Doubts creep in as to whether authority is all it's been painted to be. Different versions of "the Truth" arise and factions appear. People begin to rely on their own opinions, though cautiously at first. Beck and Cowan put the current number of the world population at the Blue level at 40% and the amount of power Blue groups exercise at 30%.[30]

ORANGE. The fifth value meme is the Orange. Orange is entrepreneurial, achievement-oriented, and competitive. Beck and Cowan place the cutting edge emergence of Orange at one thousand years ago, and its flowering in the West just after the Middle Ages.[31] Orange is frequently set into motion by a market economy and the creation of a middle class. It is marked by the rise of nation-states, industrialization, and the separation of science from superstition—Wilber's separation of the four quadrants. People begin to read and hunger for information. Orange wants opportunities to excel and express itself. On the positive side, Oranges are masterful, self-reliant, progressive, optimistic, and comfortable with risk. They think in terms of limitless possibilities.

On the negative side, Oranges do not think about long-term consequences and can act without conscience. The combination of these two factors in their worst manifestation leads to the exploitation of other cultures and the environment. Oranges are good with new ideas but not so good with interpersonal relationships. Because of their competitiveness, Oranges only superficially care about others, and then only those who are useful and only for as long as they are useful. Orange wants to appear successful, and is concerned about fashion and status symbols.

People arrested at this level seem driven, self-absorbed and hard, and ridicule emotions as weak.

The transition to the next level begins when Orange becomes aware of the needs of others and finds constant competition to be lonely. Orange discovers that what others think and want really is important. Beck and Cowan put the current number of the world population at the Orange level at 30% and the amount of power Orange groups exercise in the world at 50%.[32]

GREEN. The sixth value meme is Green. It is community-oriented, concerned with feelings and revitalizing spirituality. Beck and Cowan place the cutting edge emergence of Green at 150 years ago.[33] Greens are concerned with fairness, the spreading of resources and their wise use. Ecological concerns become important. Greens value sensitivity, consensus decision-making, and cultural awareness. In the workplace, "team building" and empowerment are important. Greens enjoy cooperative ventures, which resolves the loneliness of Orange. Greens tolerate a wide range of beliefs in religion, and are interested in spirituality. The spirituality which Greens adopt tends to be nondenominational. Dogmatism on all fronts is at a low. Gender roles are loosened, and social and racial distinctions are diminished.

A downside of Green is the pressure it exerts to do as the group does—watch out if you are not "politically correct." Greens can also get caught up in guilt over past behavior, on behalf of a group, country, or religion, and will expend a great deal of energy and resources in making reparations. Greens also frown upon drawing distinctions of any sort, even where it might be beneficial, which leads to a refusal to define values and form judgments. This can result in a confusing relativism and a tendency to flatten everyone to the same level, limiting opportunities to excel or stand out from the crowd.

Green begins a shift to the next turn on the spiral when it begins to question the value of all this togetherness. The cost of Green caring, especially in the form of "entitlements" of one sort or another begins to take a toll, and it becomes clear that the society cannot continue to provide for everyone as it has. The system may approach collapse under the expense. In addition, global problems worsen and may be pressing urgently for a response, but consensus decision-making is too time-consuming for Green society to mobilize in a timely way. The existing collective process cannot adequately respond to the complexity of emerging global issues, and so transitioning Greens begin looking for other solutions.

Beck and Cowan put the current number of the world population at Green at 10% and the amount of power Greens hold at 15%.[34] They believe that U.S. culture is only just now transitioning fully from Orange to Green.

The Second Tier

While the emergence of each turn of the spiral is a major step in development, Beck and Cowan note that the shift from First to Second Tier is a momentous leap and marks an extraordinary shift in thinking. More than just another step in development, they describe Second Tier thinking as a new starting point, like a "musical theme repeated but in a different key."[35] The Second Tier introduces complexity in thinking that surpasses even the best of the First Tier. As Beck and Cowan describe it, the conceptual space available is "greater than the sum of all the previous levels combined."[36] Ideas become multidimensional, all the value memes of the First Tier can be seen simultaneously, and viewed as legitimate. This is in contrast to First Tier thinking where each level believes itself to be the only legitimate one and often resists, or is in conflict with, the others.

YELLOW. Beck and Cowan place the cutting edge emergence of Yellow at fifty years ago.[37] As people transition to Yellow, they begin to see the entire spiral in perspective. They can handle more diversity and complexity, and balance contradictions. One of the most significant characteristics of a person transitioning to Yellow is the dropping away of fear. The need for safety, success and acceptance fades. Yellows care about group concerns but no longer need to belong. Given their greater perspective they often approach issues in ways no one else has considered.

As with Wilber's vision-logic space, Yellows are at ease with paradox and contradiction. Yellow can move freely among the first six levels of the spiral at will and interact effectively with persons at each level. Yellows are inner-directed, with strong ethics they have developed through their own reasoning, usually created from many sources. Whatever is appropriate to get a task done will be used, whether it is considered politically correct or not. They have no need for status or displays of power and they favor minimal consumption. In organizations they tend to keep a low profile and only bring attention to themselves because they are so skilled at solving problems. Beck and Cowan put the current number of the world population at the Yellow level at 1% and the amount of power Yellows hold at 5%.[38]

Yellows begin to transition to Turquoise as they become attuned to the global nature of issues and realize that no individual alone can address the problems facing all of humanity. A sense of community re-emerges as well as a respect for holistic wisdom.

TURQUOISE. The next meme on the spiral is Turquoise. Its emergence in the world is very new and still occurring, and Beck and Cowan describe it as being in an embryonic stage. They identify the number of people worldwide at this stage at .1% and the amount of power Turquoise holds in the world at 1%.[39]

Turquoise learns to value intuition and instinct as much as observation and experience, and is able to utilize conscious and subconscious aspects of the self as needed. This opens up more possibilities for ideas, solutions, and behaviors. Turquoise is able to move fluidly through all the levels of the spiral, even more so than Yellow. It senses an underlying order to things and sees the world as an organism where everything is connected to everything else. As with Wilber's psychic space, Turquoise defines community not only as embracing all humans, but including all life on the planet, whether human or not. They see issues as global in nature, tend to view situations from the "macro" level, and discover interactions not detected before.

Turquoise believes that reality can be experienced but not known, and that one can never know and understand all things. The sense of ego that tends to drive the lower levels of the spiral dissipates here. Since Turquoise is very new and is still in the process of emerging, both the gifts and the downsides of this value meme have not yet been fully experienced and so cannot be fully mapped.

CORAL. Although Beck and Cowan identify a further turn on the spiral, they confess that this level is unknown to them and has yet to emerge. One of the guiding principles of Spiral Dynamics they identify is the ability of human beings to create new levels on the spiral, and so they leave the Coral level open for whatever the next development will be. They have no doubt that as human history unfolds, so will new ways of being that center around new clusters of values.

my journal

The color I resonate with most on the spiral is:

The reasons why are:

The color on the spiral that makes me the most uncomfortable is:

The reasons why are:

Take out your personal timeline created in chapter 1 and spend a few minutes looking it over. Beginning with Beige, make a note of which times in your life you believe correspond to each color of the spiral. For example, with Beige you might identify infancy, periods of severe illness, or trauma. Notice whether the watershed moments and peak experiences you identified correspond with color changes or other developmental shifts. As best you can remember, make a few notes about the beliefs and worldview you held for each color.

Take a look at the period of your life that corresponds to the color you identified which makes you the most uncomfortable. Did something happen during this period in your life that contributes to your feelings of discomfort? Is there anything that you did or that you observed others doing that affected your feelings? Is there anything you wish you could change? How did you behave while you were in this period of your life? What were your values? Would you say you feel a lack of respect for people who exhibit the values of this color? Why or why not? If so, give a least five reasons.

visualization

Sitting in the Spiral

Get in a comfortable position. If you are sitting, put your feet flat on the floor. If you are lying down, put your arms down beside you and your legs out straight. Close your eyes . . . slow your breathing . . . breathe in . . .

breathe out . . . relax your muscles . . . breathe in . . . breathe out . . . feel the tension leave your neck and back . . . breathe in . . . breathe out . . . relax all the little muscles around your eyes . . . relax your spine . . . your legs . . . your feet . . . your hands and arms . . . keep breathing slowly. [*longer pause*]

Feel yourself becoming lighter and lighter . . . you are so light you are able to float right over to the window of this room [*adjust for your setting*] . . . open the window and look outside . . . waiting for you just outside the window is a large carpet that can take you anywhere . . . see yourself floating right out of the window and onto the carpet. . . .

You settle yourself onto the carpet and it begins to fly away . . . it takes you to a large spiral that sits on the ground and twists up and up into the sky. . . . This spiral changes colors as it goes around. . . . From where you are you can see it is beige where it rests on the bottom, and above that it becomes purple, red, and blue, among others. . . . You can see people traveling up the spiral from color to color. . . . Some of them are riding up a conveyor belt that slowly goes around the twists of the spiral. . . . Other people walk across the middle of the spiral on walkways that cross from side to side . . . some of these walkways are straight across, others go up and down from one color to the next. . . .

Look now for the color on the spiral that you identify as the one which makes you the most uncomfortable. . . . Your magic carpet flies you to this color and stops. . . . You step off the carpet and it stays docked against the side of the spiral. . . . In the side of the spiral you see a doorway. . . . You open this door and step into a room . . . this room is one level of the spiral . . . everything in this room—the walls, floor and ceiling—is the color of this level of the spiral. . . . If at any time you feel uncomfortable and want to leave, you can go back out the door you came in and wait on your magic carpet. . . .

On one of the walls in the room you notice a large picture window that looks out into a large gathering area. . . . In this area are assembled all the people living on the earth who resonate with the values of this color of the spiral right now. . . . There are many, many people in this area. . . . You can see them through the picture window, but they cannot see you. . . . Some of these people you might recognize. . . . Most of them you don't. . . .

You see a chair in the room . . . turn it so it is facing the picture window and then sit down on it. . . . Sit for a moment and look at all the people living at this level of the spiral. . . . As you sit quietly, become aware of a nurturing feeling or energy coming from the spiral. . . . It is radiating from all the levels of the spiral, the ones above you and below, as well as the one you are sitting in. . . . You can feel the spiral vibrate and hum with life, growth, love, and acceptance. [*longer pause*] This love is unconditional. . . . It nurtures every living thing. . . . Feel this unconditional love surround you. [*long pause, perhaps a full minute*]

Now turn your attention to the people you see through the picture window. . . .These people are currently living the value system that makes you the most uncomfortable right now. . . . Find that current of unconditional love you just experienced and direct this love to the people at this level of the spiral. [*longer pause*] There are no conditions on the love and acceptance you and the universe send to them. . . . Send this unconditional nurturing to everyone on this level now . . . those who have traveled it in the past, including yourself . . . and those who will travel it in the future. . . . With each inbreath, fill yourself with this unconditional love. . . . As you breathe out, see it blowing out from you to the people on the other side of the window. . . . Breathe it in . . . breathe it out. . . . [*repeat several times, matching rhythm to a breathing rhythm, watch the group*]

Now relax. . . . Take a few more breaths of unconditional love and support for yourself . . . keep what you need and release the rest. . . .

The spiral has a message to give you about this part of itself and the values it contains, this color that makes you uncomfortable. What is that message? [*long pause, one to two minutes, watch group for restlessness*] Now thank the spiral, bid farewell to it and the people on the other side of your window . . . stand up and head back to the door . . . go out the door and step onto your magic carpet. . . . The carpet carries you back toward the city where you began your journey [*adjust for your setting*] . . . you see the buildings ahead of you, the houses around where you sit, and finally this building. . . . The carpet brings you to the window where you started . . . you step off of it and float back in the window, across the room, and to yourself where you are now sitting or lying. . . . Feel yourself come back into your body and take a deep breath . . . move your fingers and toes and stretch a bit . . . take another deep breath . . . and when you are ready, open your eyes.

 questions to discuss

1. What message did the spiral leave with you? Do you feel more or less comfortable with the color of the spiral you visited now than before? In what ways?

2. Give two or three examples of people you know in the color that initially made you uncomfortable. What about their beliefs and behaviors are troublesome to you? Do you feel differently about them after studying development and seeing them as part of a continuum of growth?

3. What color of the spiral do you aspire to most? What attracts you to it? What can you do to help yourself reach it?

4. Of the Pagans you know, what color or colors of the spiral do you think they most represent? Why? How does this compare to most non-Pagans that you know?

5. Have you ever experienced a worldview clash with someone? Do you believe they were operating from a different set of beliefs than you? Which set of beliefs on the spiral were they operating from, and which were you? What happened in this encounter? How did it end? Would you do anything differently if you were to have the encounter now?

Paganism and Cultural Development

In this section we offer our opinions on cultural development as it relates to Paganism. As we discussed in the Introduction and first chapter, the modern Pagan movement is new to the religious scene. Modern Paganism emerged into public view in Britain and the United States approximately fifty years ago, and has since grown into a sizeable movement. Most of the major religions of the world, by way of contrast, were established in late horticultural to agrarian periods. This puts their origins solidly in Warrior Red and Mythic Blue societies, at the historic height of male dominance and female disadvantage. The scriptures of the world's religions were also written during these periods and reflect the Red and Blue male-dominated worldview in which they were formed. By the time of the Middle Ages, however, an Orange glow was discernible on the horizon of this Red-Blue landscape in the West. This Orange glow hinted at personal achievement and autonomy and the rise of reason. As the industrial age began to dawn, Orange drove a number of changes, including the Reformation. The Reformation added a more rational, modern tone to Christianity and helped open the door to a "personal relationship" with Deity and individual interpretation of scripture.

The Orange glow grew, and as it did so Red began to fade and the landscape became increasingly Blue-Orange. As Blue and Orange combined culture saw the development of nation-states and rule by law, individual autonomy, knowledge and inventions, and the beginnings of industrialization. So it continued for several hundred years, until Green would appear faintly on the horizon. With the emergence of Green came a growing sense of community, interdependency, and relativism. Emergent Green saw the validity of many perspectives, unthinkable before, and so it seemed to Green that all absolutes were lost. Green became concerned with the search for meaning in a world without absolutes, a world that endured World Wars and developed terrible weapons. With Green the "postmodern" era began in earnest.

The Green glow on the horizon grew brighter through the 1900s and finally set off a flash of change among America's youth in the 1960s. As with the Reformation centuries earlier, the 1960s marked a permanent shift in cultural thinking. With these changes, Blue began to fade and the landscape began to look increasingly Orange, a shift still in progress today.

Onto this background of cultural development would appear the modern Pagan movement, cautiously at first but gathering steam through the 1970s and continuing to grow ever since. It is our opinion that modern Paganism is unquestionably a postmodern religious movement. Unlike the major religions of the world, it originated in an industrial society after the rise of reason and the development of secular nation-states, at a time when interdependent, relativistic Green was on the cutting edge and rugged-individualist Orange was beginning to head into its full strength.

We believe that much of Pagan philosophy is a mixture of Orange and Green. This is not to say that Pagan practice doesn't incorporate elements from every level of the spiral, as it does, but we believe that the movement overall is based on postmodern Orange and Green principles. Orange is evident in that there is a great deal of emphasis on personal responsibility. The individual, not a mythology, determines beliefs, ethics, god images, and spiritual practices. Pagans are often fiercely independent and self-motivated. They do not want to be told what to believe or how to act on those beliefs, and are convinced their reasoning faculties are capable of discerning what is good and true. Many Pagans do not belong to formal groups, do not care to get caught up in group dynamics, and so practice their spirituality by themselves. Pagans demonstrate the very rational side of Orange in that they are frequently amateur scholars of religion, culture, and psychology. They understand that religion is a choice, mythology is not a given, and beliefs are constructed.

Paganism is also strongly Green and becoming Greener. Pagans are beginning to lose their sense of isolation and want to experience deeper community. Concern for members' input and feelings typically leads to consensus decision-making; the ability to cooperate and work together as a team is improving. Paganism's nondogmatic emphasis easily lends itself to Green's relativism and Pagans are comfortable with holding many perspectives, even contradictory ones. Green Pagans seem equally comfortable with intuition as with reason, are concerned with feelings, motivations, the subconscious, and the development of psychic and magickal abilities. Most Pagans we know are extremely concerned with issues of justice and fairness toward all creatures, not just humans. They are often highly environmentally conscious and try to shop and work at places that support their ethics. Many are involved in causes and political activism.

Green's comfort with multiple perspectives allows them to spot abuses inflicted by earlier levels of the spiral. This ability may be a precursor to moving into the

Second Tier where all levels of the spiral are seen clearly for the first time in their strengths and weaknesses. It also leads to the Green desire to make reparation for past wrongs. Combine this tendency of Green with Paganism's interest in ancient religions, its view of the Divine as feminine as well as male (possibly having emerged in part out of Romanticism), and you have a mix that is ripe for a glorification of some aspects of the past, and a condemnation of others.

The Romantic movement of the 1800s was a reaction to the excesses of Orange rationality. An explosion of scientific achievement and invention, combined with the rise of industrialism and a mechanistic view of the universe, led to the Orange belief that science and rationality could solve every problem. Everything could be explained from an exterior, mechanical point of view—Wilber's upper right quadrant. This is the quadrant of observable, *Outer It*. Scientific Orange believed that human beings could be reduced to outer mechanisms and explained in this fashion, including thought, feeling, intuition, behavior, and consciousness itself. Mechanistic science tended to reduce humanity to a machine.

The Romantics were outraged and countered with the contention that science and industrialization are the source of all humanity's ills, and people should return to a more "natural" state of living. They believed this meant a return to nature and a more primitive lifestyle. They turned their focus to Wilber's upper left quadrant, the realm of the *Inner I*, of personal experience. They declared that "true" reality was based solely on a person's inner subjective experience—love, appreciation for beauty, and spiritual ecstasy, especially that experienced in untamed nature. The most "perfect" peoples were those pure souls who lived in primitive times, specifically in hunter-gatherer and horticultural societies. They glorified these cultures and ascribed virtues to them we will examine further below.

Those involved in modern earth religions who want to condemn modern culture and glorify ancient ones, and believe ancient cultures to be more pure, just, spiritual, and environmentally wise than modern society, can find support in the Romantic perspective. This is not to say that Pagans cannot learn many important things from ancient cultures, and that there isn't wisdom to bring from them into our own time. But Pagans need to be careful about romanticizing the past and believing it to be something it was not.

A few facts should help sort this out. We present them in relation to the cultural types identified earlier: hunter-gatherer, horticultural, agrarian and industrial. Since we are not social scientists ourselves, we are relying on studies done by those who are. Whether or not you agree with the findings presented, we hope you will find them thought-provoking.

Concerning the position of women in relation to men in culture, Chafetz' macro studies are very revealing. We discussed some of her findings earlier in the chapter. Chafetz concludes that at best women have historically been able to share power fifty-fifty with men. At other times men have held nearly 100% of the power, but never have women held more than half.[40] Her findings are supported by other feminist sociologists, including Riane Eisler, Rae Blumberg, and Joyce Nielsen. Historically, women shared power with men equally in foraging and horticultural societies. Men exercise nearly all the power in agrarian societies, but in industrial societies the balance of power is again shifting to bring more power to women. Chafetz' reasoning is based on the biological fact that women carry babies in their bodies and, until the advent of bottle feeding, also had to nurse infants. As long as physical work was relatively light and close to home, women participated equally with men in the production and distribution of food and other products. As cultivation became physically grueling and located further from home, women were at a disadvantage relative to men, and agrarian culture supported this disadvantage. Now that industry has again created opportunities for women to participate and produce equally with men, conditions are returning to a state of balance. Neither we nor Chafetz are saying that conditions and opportunities for women today are perfect, but they weren't "perfect" in foraging and horticultural societies either. There is no advantage women would gain by returning to foraging/horticultural times that they are not enjoying now in most First World countries.

Unfortunately, primitive cultures were less kind in other ways. According to the extensive findings reported by sociologist Gerhard Lenski,[41] the average life expectancy in hunter-gatherer societies was 22 years, a significant proportion of infants were thrown away for population control, 10% had slaves, and 58% engaged in frequent or intermittent warfare.[42] By the horticultural period 83% of societies had slaves, 30% practiced cannibalism, and 94% engaged in frequent or intermittent warfare,[43] despite the fact that one-third of these societies, according to Chafetz, were matrifocal and worshipped a Great Mother. The rate of slavery would drop to 54% in the highly patriarchal, agrarian societies which followed, and by the industrial age it would drop to zero.[44] As Wilber points out, in the one hundred year period from 1770 to 1870, slavery was eradicated from every industrialized nation on earth. This is quite a feat, and one of which modern society can be proud.

Nor did primitive cultures necessarily possess more environmental wisdom. Tribal peoples sometimes stayed in one location until they depleted the area and had to move on. Eisler states that "many peoples past and present living close to nature have all too often been blindly destructive of their environment."[45] Theodore Roszak, advocate of the wisdom of tribal cultures, notes that primitive societies have "in their ignorance, blighted portions of their habitat sufficiently to endanger their own survival. River valleys have been devastated, forests denuded, the topsoil worn away; but the damage was limited and temporary."[46] Other types of damage were not so temporary. Ethnobiologist Jared Diamond, author of *Guns, Germs, and Steel*, notes that many scientists attribute the extinction of a number of species to hunter-gatherer societies, such as the giant kangaroo, the marsupial leopard, the one-ton lizard, the giant python and the four-hundred-pound flightless birds in Australia and New Guinea, the ground sloth and mountain goat in the Grand Canyon region, the dodo of Mauritius, the moa of New Zealand, the giant lemurs of Madagascar, and the flightless geese of Hawaii.[47]

Pagans can appreciate ancient cultures and the wisdom they offer without resorting to romanticizing them. Pagans do not need to justify their respect for the earth and its creatures, and their desire to make wise choices concerning resources. Nor do they need to justify including intuition, emotion, and moral sentiments as they make choices that impact the earth and their relationship to it. Pagans do not need to choose sides between the scientific rationalists and the Romantics—or Wilber's upper left and right quadrants—as both are essential. The *Inner* and the *Outer*, in both the personal and the collective realms, are all equally important. All four of these quadrants need to be expressed in a healthy and balanced way. History shows the effect of one quadrant dominating the others. Pagans can, if they choose, leverage their nondogmatic and multicultural perspective into a real respect for and integration of all the quadrants.

Looking beyond the influence of the Romantic movement, perhaps Pagans resonate with hunter-gatherer and horticultural societies because they most nearly match our own in terms of degree of sexual stratification. The degree of sexual stratification, or female disadvantage in a society, as Chafetz tells us, influences

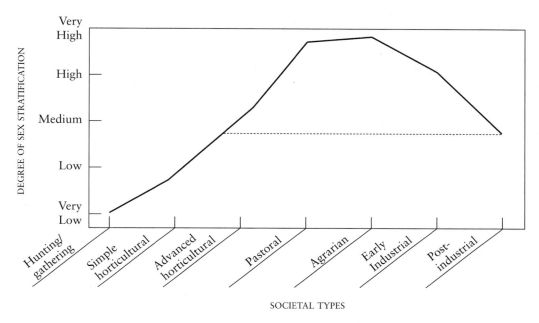

Figure 2.4
Degree of Sex Stratification by Societal Type

almost every aspect of a culture including mode of dress, division of work, size and nature of the economy, value given to various types of work, political power, religious roles and power, prejudice, types of marriage and divorce, abuse, size of families, and so on. Perhaps the values of the postmodern world, and therefore of postmodern religions, with their lower levels of female disadvantage, have more in common with early societies which also had lower levels, than with more recent societal structures that had high levels. Chafetz plots the degree of sexual stratification in the above graph (Figure 2.4).[48]

You will notice that Chafetz subdivides the horticultural, agrarian, and industrial periods into early and late (pastoral being the early form of agrarian), a distinction we have not made in this chapter for the sake of simplicity. The dark solid line represents her analysis of the degree of sexual stratification experienced in the different societies. You will see that the hunter-gatherer societies had very low levels and the horticultural had low to medium levels. By the pastoral/agrarian period the levels shoot to high and very high. Modern Middle Eastern cultures are examples of societies whose technologies and economies are still very much pastoral/agrarian, and their high levels of sexual stratification are well known.

By the early industrial period, female disadvantage begins to fall off again, and by the postindustrial period (Wilber's informational period)—which the United States currently occupies—the levels have fallen to medium, and according to Chafetz are continuing to fall. Her writings cited here are at least twenty years old. It would be interesting to see where she places sexual stratification in the United States currently. The dotted line is our addition. It begins at the postindustrial level and goes backward across time. Which period of history does it intersect? The horticultural. Because the level of sexual stratification found in the United States at the time of Chafetz' writing matches that of the horticultural period, perhaps this is one reason why Pagans are attracted to it and feel comfortable with the spirituality of that period. It is certainly food for thought.

Beck and Cowan note that each level of the spiral in the First Tier tends to believe that its perspective is the *only* right one. Blue Pagans may believe that their way to do ritual is the only right way and that their tradition is the only correct one. Green Pagans can pressure each other to conform to group norms—heaven help the Pagan who admits to having voted Republican! Or a Pagan may declare that anyone who doesn't recycle, doesn't shop at a certain store, buys fast food, isn't a vegetarian, works for a corporation, doesn't go to political demonstrations, and so on, isn't "really" a Pagan. No doubt this book's discussion of developmentalism will itself offend Pagans on several levels of the spiral. Mythic Blues won't find us mythic enough, rationalist Oranges won't find us rational enough, and Greens will be offended that we draw any distinctions and talk in terms of "levels" of growth.

Pagans need to be aware of their Green tendency to feel guilt for behavior they have not engaged in personally, that is, guilt on behalf of a country, race, gender, or other class of people. Our concern is not so much with the feelings per se but in how Pagans behave toward others in response. We have occasionally observed attempts by Pagans to feel better about past injustices, whether real or assumed, by engaging in blaming, demonization, and present acts of injustice. Taken too far, this behavior blurs healthy psychological boundaries by punishing individuals (through guilt, exclusion, or otherwise) for acts they haven't committed, and by projecting responsibility onto persons for issues that are not theirs. Group facilitators should keep an eye open for such behavior and help participants distinguish between the present and the past (whether personal or collective), distinguish between those who are actually responsible for the acts in question and those who are not, and never act unfairly in the present in response.

Although our experience leads us to believe that Paganism is philosophically at the Orange-Green level (Wilber's rational to vision-logic space), there are Pagans occupying every point of development. We have met a substantial number who are tribal Purple and mythic Blue, and equally sizeable numbers in rational Orange. The number of Green Pagans seems to us to be smaller but growing. We have met some Pagans who are clearly operating from Second Tier thinking—Yellow or beyond—extending into Wilber's vision-logic, psychic, and subtle spaces. However, in our experience these Pagans are few in number, again, we believe due to the youth of Paganism.

In addition to individual Pagans occupying every level of the spiral, Pagan belief and practice also incorporates elements from each level. Our experience indicates that this integration usually happens in a healthy fashion, though as with any group of people, things can occasionally get taken to an extreme. Purple elements within Paganism can be found in the reverence of sacred objects and mementos, use of robes, incense and rituals, ecstatic dance, drumming, and chanting, the sense of tribal connection, and in groups that maintain secret rites and membership. Red elements are found in some ecstatic and Dionysian paths, ceremonial magick, the study of weapons and metallurgy, vision quests, and other tests (even if symbolic) of skill and strength. The Guardian tradition, a sacred warrior path which serves as a security force at many Pagan festivals, is an excellent example of the healthy integration of Red-Blue in service to the community. Blue elements are found in Pagan scouting, pride in wearing of the pentacle, groups which promote exact ritual forms, codes of conduct followed at festivals (both implicit and explicit), and the creation of structured Pagan organizations. The strong Orange and Green elements of Paganism have already been discussed.

No matter where a culture, including Pagan culture, is located along the turns of the spiral, each person born into this world arrives at the archaic Beige level and must develop his or her capacities through each of the developmental spaces. No developmental space or turn of the spiral can be skipped or avoided without danger of arrest or pathology. It may be uncomfortable for Green parents to support their children, or members of a coven, as they grow into the wild Red stage or the conformist Blue stage, but grow into them they must. The key is to provide healthy expressions appropriate to each level (such as scouting instead of an urban gang), to help meet the needs of each level (such as physical security, emotional belonging, ego development, etc.), and then provide permission to keep moving forward.

As noted in the previous chapter, an individual is composed of many developmental streams, and spiritually can be at one level, socially at another, emotionally at another, and so on. Encouraging balanced growth among all aspects of the self is a worthy goal and one which Pagan leaders can foster. Many Pagan rituals, in fact, do focus on the self-development of the participants. Many encourage the participants to choose which facets of their development to work on within the ritual.

At some point, however, Paganism needs to look beyond the development of the self. No doubt the processing of personal issues will remain a large part of Pagan practice, as it is for many religions. In our opinion, if Paganism wishes to be in the forefront of the culture and point the way to deeper growth, then it must also be willing to look beyond the merely personal to the transpersonal. The embrace of Nature and Deity Mysticism, some shamanic practices, development of psychic abilities, and the openness to witness and participate in the cosmic flow Pagans call magick, are all steps in the right direction. But Paganism cannot stop there either. The challenge for Paganism as we see it is to identify transpersonal experience from its unique perspective and describe it in its own language. The transpersonal experiences recounted by the major world religions come wrapped in the language and beliefs (and cultural biases) of their respective theologies. How Paganism will interpret its own transpersonal experience and place it within a Pagan context is, in our opinion, one of the most exciting challenges facing the movement.

questions to discuss

1. Do you think religions help shape cultural development or not?
    Do you think they should? Give an example of a positive cultural
    development that you attribute to religion. Give an example of a
    development you believe is negative.

2. What do you think Paganism's goals should be in regard to encour-
    aging cultural development? Should Paganism get involved in such
    goals? Are you aware of any Pagans working on these goals now?

3. Do you think Paganism has an advantage over other religions in
    terms of fostering cultural development? If so, how and why? If
    not, why not, and is there anything Pagans can do to change it?

3

Growth and Magick

IN THE PREVIOUS CHAPTERS we explored developmental spaces, stages of faith, cultural organization, and the turns of the spiral. Now it's time to bring these new perspectives into the realm of magick and consider how Pagan spiritual practice fits into spiritual growth. This chapter will reacquaint you with our concepts of magick. Later chapters take each of the four types of magick we identify and examine them in more depth.

It has been our observation that when people start to focus on their spiritual development they can become anxious and feel they have to "work hard" to make any progress. Or they may compare themselves to others and become discouraged. If there is any advice we can offer as we begin this part of the book, it is to relax. Relax and enjoy the process. You did not worry when you were a child if your bones were growing; you did not fret over whether your organs were developing. If you enjoyed normal health you took these and many other things for granted. Your physical and cognitive development simply unfolded. Your body grew, your perspectives changed, probably without your being aware of it. Your growth was such a seamless experience that even now, looking back as an adult and searching for developmental shifts, it can be hard (or impossible) to say, "here is the point

I became aware that others existed," or "this is when I first became aware that people play roles."

It has been our observation that rather than being a process of hard work and sweat, development is often a matter of getting out of your own way. Sometimes spiritual effort has the effect of putting you into your own way, so let yourself relax. You don't have to prove anything to anybody, certainly not to us, and not to your friends or family either. In fact, continued growth for adults seems to consist in staying in a relaxed state of permission. Your mind, body, and spirit naturally want to change and evolve. Cells, attitudes, and insights all grow, die, and replace themselves. If you reach a point of stasis where you never change, then you are probably dead.

To live is to breathe and feel the rhythm of what comes in and what goes out. Like the rhythm of your breath, the universe folds in, the universe folds out. And as it does, everything changes.

So as you work with magick in the chapters ahead, give yourself permission. Give it in all the areas in which you most need to give it to yourself. Some areas you might want to consider especially are permission to listen and participate. Let yourself listen to your inner self, your subconscious, and your inner guidance. If you have a concept of the Divine, listen to what it has to say. And listen to what the universe is saying, not just the physical universe but the more abundant part of it that is beyond space and time. As the metaphysical writer Jane Roberts puts it in one of our favorite quotes, "the universe leans in your direction."[1] Trust the universe and listen to what it has to say. Turn your attention to the Ground from which your ideas of who "you" are and what "divinity" is arise. Listen to your multidimensional spirit, which holds more than what you identify as "you." Give yourself permission to listen and to open.

As for participation, give yourself permission to step into the universal flow we'll be talking about in the pages ahead. There's no need to stay on the side-lines—what fun is that? The adventure is all in the participating. Let yourself have fun with magickal pages, with feeling new things, doing new things, seeing things in a new way. When you listen to your inner self, the Divine as you conceive it, the multidimensional universe, and your multidimensional (or transpersonal) spirit, what does it inspire you to do? How do you want to *be* in the midst of things? There are ways in which you are willing to assist and be assisted in the universe and ways in which you are not. Discovering your beliefs, motivations and goals as they exist now is part of the process.

 questions to discuss

1. In what ways do you give yourself permission to expand? In what ways do you block or withhold permission? In what areas do you most need to give yourself permission?

2. What do you look forward to most about growing and changing in the years ahead? What about it worries you most?

3. What do you do now to listen to your inner self? To the universe? To your concept of the Divine? In what ways would you like to change how you listen and what you are able to hear?

4. Tell about a time when you felt that you were participating fully in the flow of the universe. What brought it about? How did it feel while you were having the experience? How do you feel about it now?

 visualization

Leaning Into the Universe

Get in a comfortable position. If you are sitting, put your feet flat on the floor. If you are lying down, put your arms down beside you and your legs out straight. Close your eyes. Slow your breathing down . . . breathe in . . . breathe out. . . . Relax your muscles . . . breathe in . . . breathe out . . . feel the tension leave your neck and back . . . breathe in . . . breathe out . . . relax all the little muscles around your eyes . . . relax your spine . . . your legs . . . your feet . . . your hands and arms . . . keep breathing slowly . . . breathe in . . . breathe out. [*longer pause*]

As you relax, you begin to feel very light . . . so light that you are able to float just above the floor. . . . Feel yourself becoming lighter . . . you are relaxed and floating in a cocoon of warm light . . . this cocoon is safe and surrounds you completely . . . you are able to float any-where you like within this cocoon. . . . Feel yourself float out of this room, around the corner, and down to the front door [*adjust for your setting*]. . . . The door of this building swings open before you . . . as you float closer to the door, you know that on the other side is a beau-tiful park. . . .

Float out the door and into the park . . . notice how beautiful it is, what a lovely warm and sunny day it is. . . . Lift your face to the sun . . . feel the wind on your face . . . take a deep breath and enjoy the beauty that surrounds you. [*longer pause, up to a half minute*] A short distance ahead you notice an oak tree. . . . It is a very ancient tree, with large and twisted branches. . . . You move toward it and feel its size and power. . . . Its leaves rustle above you and you stand in the shade it casts. . . . You approach the tree and lay your hand on its bark. . . . Its energy is very welcoming to you. . . . You have the feeling it has a lesson to share with you, and the tree invites you to come into itself to experience what it has to show you. [*longer pause*]

So you move closer to the tree and press yourself against it, from your feet to your head. . . . Your cheek is pressed against its bark. . . . Slowly you begin to feel yourself merge into the tree . . . not just your energy, but your entire body . . . like an effect in a movie, you feel your-self melt into the surface of the tree . . . cocoon and all . . . when you are ready later, you will be able to separate yourself . . . but for now you relax and allow yourself to be drawn completely into the tree. [*longer pause*]

You feel yourself being drawn up the trunk and out into one of the branches. . . . You see the branch spread out before you like fingers and the leaves wave in the breeze. . . . The oak tree pushes you out onto the branch, further, further, until you reach the very end. . . . At the end is a cluster of leaves, and there you see an acorn. . . . The oak tree urges you into the acorn, and so you go. . . . You wrap your cocoon tightly about you and squeeze smaller and smaller until all of you fits into the little acorn. [*longer pause*] For a moment nothing happens, and then a strong breeze comes along and begins to bend the branches of the tree . . . your little acorn dances around at the end of its branch, and suddenly it lets go and flies through the air . . . the wind whips you further away, and you fly away from the oak tree . . . down, down you fall, until you hit the ground, and you roll down a hill and come to a stop . . . a squirrel sees you rolling, runs toward you, scoops you up, digs a hole in the ground and drops you in it. . . .

You lie there in the dark, and the rains come and the warm sun shines on you . . . it seems that you lie there for quite a while . . . but then suddenly you feel your shell begin to burst open . . . your acorn cracks open and out comes the tiniest shoot of green. . . . Your shoot feels its way into the ground and begins to grow. . . . You can feel yourself stretch out from the small acorn and spread your roots like tiny threads through the soil. . . . You grow up through the soil into a small stem with just a couple of leaves. . . .

The winds and the rains come . . . the sun shines on you . . . the seasons pass in their turn . . . and through it all you continue to grow . . . you can feel your roots grow deeper and thicker in the soil . . . your branches grow taller and your trunk wider . . . and all of this happens without effort on your part. [*longer pause*] The sun shines on you and you accept its warmth . . . the rains fall and you accept the moisture and take it into yourself . . . your leaves grow and you absorb the sunlight as food . . . the winter comes and you accept the cold and the waiting, and your roots grow even as you sleep. . . . And all of this simply happens naturally. . . .You do not worry whether the sun will shine today or tomorrow . . . you do not fear the seasons. . . . You do not have to fret about how your roots get nourishment from the ground . . . or whether your branches are growing as they should . . . your leaves respond to the sunlight without any direction from you. [*longer pause*]

See yourself growing over many years, growing from a sapling to a large tree . . . stretch your legs out longer and longer and feel your roots grow deeper into the ground. . . . Feel yourself embrace the depths, the darkness, with faith that your roots will find their way . . . draw all the nourishment you need from the soil into yourself. . . . Stretch your hands above you within the tree, and let your arms move out into the branches as they become larger and longer. . . . Feel your strong and supple branches stretch out into the sky . . . embrace the sky. . . . Draw the power of the sun's nourishment into yourself. . . . You know you are growing larger and stronger . . . you are unfolding exactly as you should. . . . Let yourself expand even more . . . you are growing larger . . . larger even than the tree . . . let your spirit reach out from the tree and expand into the sky and the breeze . . . expand right out into space . . . expand yourself as far as you are able, embrace as much as you can . . . see that there is more to who you are than is contained within yourself. [*longer pause*]

Life supports you . . . and you give back to life . . . let yourself lean into the universe . . . rest yourself on it . . . know that it is trustworthy . . . you are a part of all things . . . you are connected into the Ground that supports everything. . . . Feel the multidimensional universe lean toward you . . . hear it sing with creative power. . . . Absorb it into your expanded self. . . . Absorb it into your roots, your leaves, your branches, your bark. . . . Be filled with the creative vitality of the universe itself. . . . With each breath in, pull in more and more of this energy until you cannot take in any more [*long pause, up to a minute*]

It is drawing close to the time to say goodbye . . . begin to pull yourself back into the limits of the tree . . . give thanks for sharing the universe's energy, and feeling its support of you . . . send a blessing to the sky, the earth, and the tree that you became . . . then begin to feel yourself shape shift from a tree to yourself again . . . your cocoon begins to separate itself . . . your bark turns to skin, your branches to arms, your roots to legs . . . you form back into yourself, within your cocoon. [*longer pause*] Your cocoon begins to float back through the park to where you entered . . . as you float toward the doorway you pass the ancient oak that invited you to join in this experience . . . thank this oak as you go past, and if it has a message or feeling to share with you, listen to what it has to say. [*longer pause, up to half a minute*] Continue to float through the park . . . ahead you see the door that leads back to this room . . . go to the door and float through it . . . shut the door behind you . . . now float back into this room, into your body . . . gradually let your cocoon dissolve back into your body . . . any excess energy flows easily away through your feet and down into the floor . . . take a moment and feel your body . . . take several deep breaths, [*longer pause*] stretch your arms and legs . . . when you are ready, open your eyes.

Be sure you are back and that you feel properly grounded. If you are leading a group, having the participants kneel with their hands on the floor to drain out excess energy, and giving them something to eat and drink will probably be sufficient. If anyone is cold, help them warm up with a hot drink, sweater, or blanket. Encourage everyone to share their experience during the meditation, and what feelings and images came to them during it.

Encourage everyone to do the walking meditation that follows as soon as is convenient or the weather permits.

Walking Meditation

As soon as you have the opportunity and weather permits, go for a walk outside and look for an acorn or a pinecone, or other seed of a tree. If the season is not right for finding these things, or if you live in an area where they are not available, then take an apple with you to eat. When you find the acorn or pinecone or other seed, find someplace comfortable and sit. Take a blanket or chair with you as needed. Sit and hold the acorn or pine cone in your hand, and put yourself into the meditative space of the earlier visualization. If you have an apple, slowly eat the apple and think of the apple tree from which it came, and then hold the seeds in your hand. Place yourself back in the visualization and imagine that you are the seed. Within you is the potential to sprout, root, and send out small branches. You can draw nourishment from the soil and the sun effortlessly, and feel them support you. Know that you are supported by a universe that is trustworthy. Know that the universe leans in your direction, and in return, feel yourself lean toward it. Let yourself expand and open to the power and vitality you sense in the vast multidimensional universe. Allow yourself to become bigger than you normally are and know that there is more to yourself than what lives as a physical being on this earth.

Stay in this space as long as you wish and then return to your surroundings. When you are finished, either plant the acorn, pinecone or apple seeds in the ground, or take them with you as a memento. Over the next several months, whenever you have the opportunity to be outside, even if you are just walking to work, occasionally turn your mind to the feelings you experienced here, and renew your sense of trust in a universe that supports you from its deepest levels.

A Review of Magick

Magick is the term used to describe Paganism's central spiritual practices. Magick is a term of art for Pagans and for that reason is spelled with a "k." It should not be confused with "magic," the popular term for stage tricks and sleight of hand. We divide magick into four areas based on the purpose and type of spiritual work done. These are *divination, conscious creation*,[2] *energy work*, and *communing*. The remaining chapters of this book are devoted to the study of each of these aspects of magick individually.

The Pagan concept of magick is built upon a series of beliefs concerning the nature of the universe and the role of consciousness. Some of these beliefs are set out in the Principles of Paganism, found in our introductory book and set out again below. These Principles are not drawn from any one Pagan tradition, but are our synthesis of commonly held beliefs and principles as we have encountered them in the Pagan community over the years. They are not Pagan dogma, but statements that point to the type of *relationship* with the universe and divine that Pagans envision. The seven Principles are:

1. You are responsible for the beliefs you choose to adopt.

2. You are responsible for your own actions and your spiritual and personal development.

3. You are responsible for deciding who or what Deity is for you, and forming a relationship with that Deity.

4. Everything contains the spark of intelligence.

5. Everything is sacred.

6. Each part of the universe can communicate with each other part, and these parts often cooperate for specific ends.

7. Consciousness survives death.

As the Principles indicate, Paganism generally affirms that all parts of the universe, whether in physical form or not, including subatomic particles, are alive with a spark of intelligence (or consciousness), are interconnected and can communicate and cooperate with each other. These beliefs are built upon other assumptions, such as the basic trustworthiness of the universe and the unflawed nature of consciousness, including its expression in human beings. It presumes a universe that is multidimensional, that exists in realms outside of space-time as well as within it. It presumes the ability of all parts of this multidimensional universe to communicate beyond the limits of space-time, a presumption which takes us beyond the purely mechanistic view suggested by Sir Isaac Newton. When we use the word "universe" throughout this book, we mean the entire multidimensional spectrum of all that is, both manifest and unmanifest, including potential multiverses—not just the physical universe that can be seen and touched with the physical senses.

We define magick as the *actions of many consciousnesses voluntarily working together within an aware and interconnected universe to bring about one or more desired results.* We believe that magick is a natural process, not a supernatural one, based on the structure and nature of the universe. We also believe it is a voluntary and cooperative process, hence our use of the term "cooperative magick" to describe our perspective. There are Pagans who believe that magick is based on the ability to bend spirits or energies involuntarily to their will. We call this view of magick "command mode." While command mode magick appeals to some Pagans, we promote the cooperative approach.

In our opinion magick works, not because of the beliefs or skill of the magician, but because everyone is immersed in the flow of an enfolding and unfolding universe. All are engaged in the movement and exchange of this flow together. In its unfolded state, the physical universe arises, and individuals and objects seem to be real and separate from each other. In its enfolded state, which is likely not one "state" but an infinite number of dimensions, the physical universe is not physically present but exists as potentiality and probability. Time and space have no meaning. The past, present, and future exist simultaneously, and perhaps multiple potential pasts, presents, and futures exist together as well. Consciousness has access to all of itself across the whole of this multidimensional fabric. We know that science confirms a type of ordering and communication that occurs beyond the speed of light, or let us say, beyond the realm where light exists and limits speed. If you wish to explore these perspectives in more detail, see the discussion of Bell's theorem and other scientific theories in chapter 5 of our introductory book. We also recommend that you rent and watch the movie *What the (Bleep) Do We Know?* as a fun and informative way to learn more about this scientific perspective of a conscious universe.

It is our position that everything and everyone on this planet experiences the multidimensional flow of the universe, and participates in the sharing of information and potential ordering of events regardless of age or belief system. Since all humans are a part of this process, they are probably going to have similar experiences with it. The cultural and religious beliefs of an individual, however, wrap these experiences in explanations that fit the individual's prevailing cultural ideas, dogma, or other belief systems. Such beliefs specify how the experiences are to be explained, what their origins are, whether they are natural or supernatural, whether such experiences are considered possible, and who is and isn't entitled to have them. What Pagans experience as "magick" in energy work, divination, conscious creation, and communing is probably experienced by non-Pagans but called by other names.

Since magick may be considered the primary form of spiritual expression for many Pagans, it is also the means by which their spiritual growth often occurs. Through prayer and communing, Pagans grow in their relationship with the multidimensional universe and the Divine as they understand it. Through energy work, the sensing and sending of subtle energies, such as healing, comfort, love, and justice, Pagans deepen their awareness of the needs of others and how to respond to them outside of the constraints of space and time. By listening for the truth within others and sensing the building-up of probabilities that are still in an enfolded state, Pagans deepen their ability to be a guiding and prophetic voice for individuals and society through divination. Through the work of conscious creation, Pagans develop their ability to manifest their desires in a concrete way, learn to cooperate in manifesting the desires of others in return, and grow in wisdom as they learn from the consequences of the realities they help create.

The goal of magick as we see it, in relation to personal and cultural growth, is to support openness to development generally, avoid arrested development, and encourage individuals and societies to move freely through the developmental spaces. This can be summed up as *maximum expansion* and *maximum healthiness* according to the capabilities of the individual and culture. Not everyone is capable of expanding to the furthest reaches of developmental space for a variety of reasons, including biological and social ones. But the encouragement of healthy growth within each person's capacity is a worthy goal, and one which Pagans can work toward within themselves, their Pagan communities, and society at large.

my journal

Pull out your personal timeline and take a look at the spiritual experiences you noted. If you didn't do so previously, make a note on your timeline of those spiritual experiences that stand out in your memory, including peak experiences and shifts in belief, times when the world suddenly looked different and you knew you were different, too. Notice at what ages these experiences happened, and whether they could be related to changes in developmental spaces, stages of faith, or colors on the spiral.

Make a note of your thoughts on these experiences based on the following questions:

My view of the Divine and spiritual authority before this event was . . .
    My view afterwards was . . .

Before this event I looked for confirmation of my beliefs, practices and
    lifestyle from . . . Ways this did or did not change were . . .

The parts of my life that changed, including friendships, and that gained or lost meaning because of this experience were . . .

Spiritual or personal needs I had that were not met before this experience included . . .

Since the experiences, my needs have changed in the following ways . . .

In what ways was this experience a positive or negative event in my life? What long-lasting consequences has it had, if any, and how do they make me feel? . . .

More on Magickal Pages

One of the ways the multidimensional realm gets your attention is by sending you what we call a "magickal page." A magickal page can arrive in the form of a piece of information, a question, a feeling, or sudden urge to do something. Usually the urges involve small things, or what appear to be small things, like the urge to call someone, drive home by a different route, or do something slightly out of the ordinary. Frequently such pages set off a series of events that are synchronous; that is, that seem to be coincidental but hold great meaning for one or more of the people involved. Pages can also alert you to the progress of other magickal work. Sometimes the significance of a particular page does not become clear until later.

Pages are certainly not the only way that consciousness communicates. Other examples include intuition, direct knowing, omens, the appearance of totems or power animals, dreams, and so on. All of these are examples of a connection and communication happening with you in the realm of space-time; it is possible that many also happen at deeper levels. However, since magickal pages are instances of communication happening in the physical realm, they are something you can work with in a deliberate fashion. You can make a conscious effort to hear them and not discount them. Working with magickal pages does several things to strengthen your magickal muscles. It improves your ability to listen and perceive, it increases your sense of participation in the universal flow, and it can make you think about your choices more carefully. Responding to pages makes you use your ethical muscles regularly as you choose whether or not to act, and as you

weigh the consequences of action or inaction. It helps you become more confi-
dent of yourself and your magickal abilities. As time passes and you see that
pages are not voices from a demonic, twisted part of yourself, you begin to trust
yourself more and shed the fear you may have picked up from elsewhere. You
may even begin to feel comfortable with Paganism's view that you are not an
inherently flawed being! Working with pages also helps you begin to trust the
universe, discover that it is responsive and supportive, and not a battleground
between the forces of good and evil with you located squarely in the middle.

If nothing else, improving your skill with magickal pages will bring you to a
greater appreciation of the creative genius of the universe and the vitality and gusto
with which it acts. You may gain a sort of quiet confidence that touches many
aspects of your life, and you may find that fear about things in general begins to
drop away.

Even if you have worked with magickal pages in the past, it's time to work with
them some more and develop an ongoing openness to them in your spiritual practice. If you still have the little notebook from the magickal pages exercise in our
introductory book, take it out and look over your last experience with it. Now is a
good time to look at the results again, especially if you did it some time ago. You
may spot things that did not grab your attention earlier and which you now find
significant. Take a look at the sorts of pages you got and their frequency. Were
there many you chose not to follow up on? For those you ignored or declined to
answer, what were the reasons? Was it a matter of interest and availability, or were
there more serious ethical issues involved? Was this a pattern and were the issues
similar?

If you experienced pages that were disturbing to you, especially on a recurring
basis, this is not a sign that the universe is untrustworthy or that you are evil.
More likely this is an indication that you have some psychological issues that are
trying really hard to get your attention. This may be something to seek counseling about; in fact, if it's disturbing you and is recurring, then go to counseling
immediately. See this as a golden opportunity to work on straightening out the
bottom floors of your skyscraper, as Wilber would put it. A disturbance at a basic
level of your self is interfering with your upper levels and putting a "tilt" into the
magickal pages coming to you. The fact that you are aware of it now may be an
indication that you are ready to work on issues you weren't ready to work on

before, or to take previous work to a new level. This is not a problem so much as an opportunity to advance in your spiritual and personal growth.

Although we are talking in the past tense to those of you who have worked with magickal pages before, everything said here applies with equal force to those of you trying this exercise for the first time. So, for the next two weeks, carry a small notepad and pen with you everywhere. Make a note each time you believe you receive a magickal page. Where were you, when did the page occur, and what was its content? Did you receive information? Did you get an impulse to do or say something? Note how you chose to respond and what the consequences were.

On the very first page of your notebook, write down the following questions. These are your ethical guidelines, which you should always consult before answering a page. Here they are:

"If I answer this magickal page, will I be doing something . . .

1. that is obviously harmful to myself or others, that disregards safety, that is offensive to me, or is unethical?

2. that will cause me to fail to perform a responsibility or job duty, cause me to break a promise, to be late, or unable to fulfill an obligation?

3. that is illegal?"

If you answer yes to any of these questions, don't answer the page. Make a note of it and study it later. Keep in mind that your interpretation of a page may be only partially accurate, and something may appear unwise or offensive that would be appropriate under other circumstances. For example, you may get a page that will cause you to miss another obligation if you answer it now. So you write this page off as "unethical" and permanently ignore it. Consider that *you* interpreted the page as one that must be answered *right now*, when the page as actually received was not time specific. Perhaps it would have been fine to follow through on it later, when you were available. Keep interpretation issues in mind as you make choices to act or not act, and later, study your results.

You may also find it helpful to begin each morning with a brief visualization to remind yourself to be open to pages during the day, and to encourage the universe to send them to you. At the end of the two weeks, study your notes for patterns. How many pages did you receive? What decisions did you make regarding them and why? What were the results and the consequences? Finally, has your view of magickal pages changed in any way due to your experiences with them?

Before ending this exercise, try sending a page of your own to the universe. What message would you like to send? Is it about this exercise or something else in your life? Perhaps you've experienced some synchronicities you'd like to explore further, or maybe some issues have surfaced for you. Your page can be a thought or message; it can be a wish or desire for something, but it doesn't have to be. Send your page for several days, and then make a note of what happens.

 questions to discuss

1. How would you describe your relationship with the universe currently? With what in the universe are you in relationship? How do you interact?

2. How do you feel about magickal pages? Do you think they are genuine and real?

3. How do you reconcile the Pagan view of an aware and interconnected universe with the prevailing mechanistic scientific view of a universe where everything exists in separate clumps of matter that are inert and unable to communicate? Are there parts of Paganism's view you accept and others you reject? Are there parts of the mechanistic view that you accept and others you reject? What led you to your current belief or position?

Magickal Integration

In the remaining chapters we explore each of the four "types" or applications of magick as we identify them: communing, energy work, conscious creation, and divination. We discuss what each of the types involves and offer exercises that build basic skills. We also look at each type of magick from within developmental space, since it is our contention that how you define magick, how you use it, and the importance you assign it depends on your developmental perspective. We will explore what Pagans might experience at different points of development for each of the types of magick. One of our chief interests in exploring these topics is to encourage the healthy development and integration of all aspects of your self in relation to magick. By "all aspects of your self" we mean your body, mind, spirit, emotions, interior experience, exterior expression, the objective, the subjective, the personal, and yourself in relation to culture.

To help you visualize this integration, Figure 3.1 shows the relationships we have drawn between Wilber's four quadrants, the four types of magick, and the four directions and elements familiar to Pagans.

We explain these interrelationships more thoroughly in the chapters that follow. But essentially, we believe the types of magick fall fairly naturally into the four directions: conscious creation in the north, divination in the east, energy work in the south, and communing in the west. They also relate well to Wilber's four quadrants, the internal and external aspects of the individual and the collective. Pagans can use a greater understanding of these relationships as a means to enhance their growth, especially by gaining a "big-picture" perspective of how Pagan spiritual practice impacts all aspects of themselves.

What Do You Want Magickally?

Sometimes one of the hardest parts of spiritual development is knowing what you want. Many people don't think much about what they want from their spirituality and relationships with the universe or the Divine. For those who do, their faiths often specify what kinds of relationships are and are not acceptable. The parameters of what they are allowed to experience are mapped out for them. Some were raised in faiths where religion did not require any input on their part except to show up, contribute to the offering, perhaps be on a committee, and of course agree

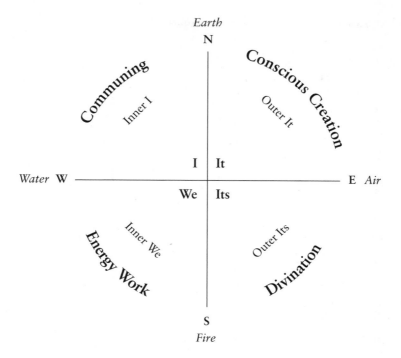

Figure 3.1
Correlation of the Quadrants, the Directions, and the Elements

to follow the rules. There are many people who come to Paganism expecting to be handed a program to follow. Many Pagans find this expectation is not met because there is no one Pagan program. While some covens and Pagan churches do have specific beliefs, training programs, or classes, not all do; even those which offer such training may themselves be in the process of forming and maturing. When classes and training are available, they can be extremely helpful. But because Paganism in its current form did not exist in the eras of Red and Blue dominance, it missed the development of dogma, structure, and rules that are essential features of most of the world's mainstream religions. Personally we think this is a strength of Paganism, but it does come with challenges.

So take a moment and ask yourself what you would really like magickally and spiritually. Either in your journal or on a fresh sheet of paper write a spiritual wish list for yourself. What experiences would you like to have? What skills would you like to develop? What sort of relationship with the Divine do you want to culti-vate? Where do you want to go in your magickal development and why? What skills do you feel comfortable with and which would you like to develop more? Don't forget to include spiritual goals that involve your body and emotions, as well as your mind. What about doing a bit more exercise, studying belly dancing, ecstatic ritual, or drumming? How about a class on drawing or pottery making? Also consider ways in which you can give back to others. In addition to your own personal development, be sure to include at least one item that relates to service to others, both to Pagans and to your larger community. Can you teach a class or workshop, volunteer at the next Pagan Pride day, help at the local shelter once a month?

How does your wish list compare to the areas of spiritual comforts and dis-comforts you identified earlier? Are there any connections? Look at the peak expe-riences you have had, noted in your journaling and personal timeline. If you were to grow to the level from which the peak experience came (as far as you can deter-mine it), what do you need to open or expand within yourself for this to occur?

Finally, ask yourself how you will know when you succeed in the goals listed on your wish list. Are the abilities obvious and external, or have you described an internal state of some kind? When you reach your goals, what do you think will be different about yourself and your life, or what do you hope is different?

Once you have finished your wish list, do the visualization below and let it speak to you about your goals, the challenges you have faced and have yet to face, and the gifts you possess that you are bringing with you. An exercise follows the visualization in which you will draw the labyrinth you walk during the medita-tion, which can represent your spiritual quest. The chapter ends with an exercise to help you create a plan for yourself for the coming year so you can begin to move forward in your goals in a concrete way.

visualization

Into the Labyrinth

Before beginning this visualization, take a look at the drawing of the labyrinth set out for the exercise which follows. This is the shape of labyrinth you will be walking in the visualization, which may be helpful to you, especially if you are unfamiliar with labyrinths in general. Also, be sure to have pens and paper at hand as soon as the visualization is finished.

Get in a comfortable position. If you are sitting, put your feet flat on the floor. If you are lying down, put your arms down beside you and your legs out straight. Close your eyes. Slow your breathing down . . . breathe in . . . breathe out . . . relax your muscles . . . breathe in . . . breathe out . . . feel the tension leave your neck and back . . . breathe in . . . breathe out . . . relax all the little muscles around your eyes . . . relax your spine . . . your legs . . . your feet . . . your hands and arms . . . keep breathing slowly . . . breathe in . . . breathe out. [*longer pause*]

You are very relaxed, and very light . . . you are so light you can float right over to the window of this room [*adjust to your setting*] . . . open the window and look outside . . . waiting for you just outside of the window is a large carpet that can take you anywhere. . . . See yourself floating right out of the window and onto the carpet . . .

When you are comfortable, the carpet begins to fly away . . . away from this building, over the street, and the roofs of houses around us [*adjust for your setting*] . . . the carpet knows how to return you to the place you began and will bring you back safely at the end of your journey. . . . You and the carpet are flying over the city . . . and soon you leave the city behind . . . ahead you see a forest of trees . . . the carpet takes you over the forest . . . soon it begins to descend and it heads for a clearing among the trees. . . . The carpet hovers on the edge of this clearing, a few feet off of the ground. . . . As the carpet pauses, you notice your surroundings. [*longer pause*]

The forest around the clearing is heavy with a soft moisture . . . you can smell the wet bark of the trees . . . and the thick cover of moldering leaves on the forest floor . . . you hear water dripping off of leaves. [*longer pause*] A mist rises from the ground and surrounds the trunks of the trees that are near you. . . . The mist covers the ground of the clearing also, and it gets thicker toward the center of the clearing, so that you cannot see completely across it. . . . You do see some waist high hedges in the clearing before the mist obscures your view completely. [*longer pause*]

The carpet begins to move again, staying several feet above the ground . . . it carries you into the clearing . . . the mist grows thicker as you go . . . soon you cannot see the forest anymore . . . you are enveloped in mist . . . but as you look down, you can make out the shapes of more hedges, and you realize you are flying over a labyrinth. . . . The carpet is taking you to the center of the labyrinth. . . . You reach the center and the carpet sets you down and you step off it. . . . The carpet will meet you at the end of the labyrinth, and flies away for now. . . . You stand in a small opening surrounded by waist-high hedges . . . you could see over the hedges if the mist were not so thick . . . still, the mist drifts in patches and you can see several feet in front of you, but no further . . . you breathe in the cool dampness of the mist. [*longer pause*]

You are about to walk this labyrinth . . . it is not a maze . . . there are no dead ends . . . there is only one path in and one path out . . . you cannot make a wrong turn. . . .

You notice a space in the hedge to your left, and so you enter there . . . you begin walking and soon you have a hedge on either side of you . . . they are only waist high, so you can see over them. . . . You can see toward the center where you began, but you cannot see in the direction you are headed, because the mist is so heavy. . . . You continue to walk and the path turns . . . just as you make the turn the mist clears and you see a being waiting for you, dressed in beige. . . . This being can be anyone or anything, and it represents you at your birth and infancy. . . . This is the part of you that could not tell itself apart from its environment very easily, and was completely dependent on others for care. . . . You and the being greet each other . . . it tells you that this period of your life offers you something, either a special ability or a challenge, that is still with you in your life now . . . you know what it is, you have only to look within to see it. . . . What is it? [*pause for 30 seconds*] The being gives you something, a message perhaps or some kind of gift or tool, and explains what it is for. [*pause for 30 seconds*] Then the being fades away. . . .

You begin to walk again and the labyrinth turns . . . as it does the mist lifts enough that you can see the path ahead of you to the next turn . . . as you reach the turn a being appears, dressed in purple. . . . This being can be anyone or anything, including yourself, and it represents your child-hood. [*longer pause*] This is the part of you that sees the world as filled with mysterious forces that obey your will . . . objects have special mean-ing and arouse deep feelings in you . . . you know yourself to be part of a social, family unit . . . and how important love and belonging are. . . . You and the purple being greet each other . . . it tells you that this period of your life offers you something, a special ability or a challenge, that is still with you now . . . you know what it is, you have only to look within to see it. . . . What is it? [*pause for 30 seconds*] The purple being gives you something, a message, tool or gift, and tells you what it is for. [*pause for 30 seconds*] Then the being fades away. . . .

You begin to walk again, and the labyrinth turns . . . as it does the mist lifts again and reveals the curving path ahead of you . . . you walk to the next turn and as you go around it a being appears, dressed in red. . . . This being represents your youth. . . . It represents the part of you that dreams and dares and gets a little wild . . . it loves power and pow-erful people. . . . It enjoys story and myth. . . . You and the red being greet each other . . . it tells you that this period of your life offers you something, a special ability or a challenge, that is still with you now . . . you know what it is, you have only to look within to see it. . . . What is it? [*pause for 30 seconds*] The red being gives you something, a mes-sage, tool or gift, and tells you what it is for. [*pause for 30 seconds*] Then the being fades away. . . .

You begin to walk . . . if you need to, put any objects you are receiving from the beings into a knapsack . . . the labyrinth is turning again . . . as it does the mist lifts further and reveals the path ahead of you . . . you come to the next turn, and as you round the corner a being appears, dressed in blue. . . . This being represents your late adolescence. . . . It is the part of you that wants fairness and relationships that operate safely within rules . . . you like order and relying on the world to be as it should . . . the roles that you and others play are very important . . . being right and having reasons for what you do matters a great deal. . . . You and the blue being greet each other . . . it tells you that this period of your life offers you something, a special ability or a challenge, that is still with you now . . . you know what it is, you have only to look within to see it. . . . What is it? [*pause for 30 seconds*] The blue being gives you something, a message, tool or gift, and tells you what it is for. [*pause for 30 seconds*] Then the being fades away. . . .

You begin to walk again and the labyrinth turns . . . as it does, the mist lifts even more and reveals the path ahead of you . . . you realize you're getting close to the end and so you turn and look back over where you have walked . . . you can see over the hedges to the center where you began . . . on the outer rings of the labyrinth the mist is still heavy and you cannot see outward beyond your current level, but you can see inward . . . you notice that you stand in an area free of mist that gets larger with every turn of the labyrinth that you make. . . .

You walk to the next corner and turn . . . as you do, a being appears dressed in orange. . . . This being represents your early adulthood. . . . It is the part of you that is independent and creative . . . the rule breaker, the seizer of opportunity . . . what makes rational sense to you is very important . . . you value expediency and exploring new frontiers. . . . You and the orange being greet each other . . . it tells you that this period of your life offers you something, a special ability or a challenge, that is still with you now . . . you know what it is, you have only to look within to see it. . . . What is it? [*pause for 30 seconds*] The orange being gives you something, a message, tool or gift, and tells you what it is for. [*pause for 30 seconds*] Then the being fades away. . . .

You begin to walk again and the labyrinth turns . . . as it does the mist clears before you and reveals the last segment of the labyrinth you will walk today. . . . As you make the final turn, a figure appears, dressed in green. . . . This being represents the compassionate part of you . . . the part that values community and belonging, that wants fair results for everyone . . . who feels past injustices deeply . . . and cares for the earth and the proper use of resources. . . . You and the green being greet each other . . . it tells you that this period of your life offers you something, a special ability or a challenge, that is with you now . . . you know what it is, you have only to look within to see it. . . . What is it? [*pause for 30 seconds*] The green being gives you something, a message, tool, or gift, and tells you what it is for. [*pause for 30 seconds*] Then the being fades from your sight . . .

As you walk out of the labyrinth, you notice that the mist that cleared before you as you stepped into each new level of the labyrinth still encircles you . . . the mist hides the regions into which you cannot see because you have not yet developed the eyes to see into them . . . unknown areas still lie before you to discover and grow into . . . you turn and look back over the labyrinth you have traveled and notice the space into which you have grown and expanded so far . . . honor and acknowledge who you are and what you have accomplished. . . . Then you step onto the carpet which is waiting for you, it lifts up and begins to fly away. . . . It carries you over the labyrinth and the forest, and back toward where you are now [*adjust for your setting*] . . . you see the buildings ahead of you, the houses around where you sit, and finally this building. . . . The carpet brings you to the window where you started . . . you step off the carpet and float back in the window, across the room, and to yourself where you are now sitting or lying. . . . Feel yourself come back into your body, and take a deep breath . . . move your fingers and toes and stretch a little bit . . . take another deep breath . . . and when you are ready, open your eyes.

Be sure that you are back. If you are leading a group immediately hand out pens and paper to all participants, and ask them to write down the names of the colors on the spiral that they visited in this meditation: beige, purple, red, blue, orange and green. While it is still fresh, have them make a note of the ability or challenge that they bring with them from each level, and the message, gift, or tool that the being from each level gave them. Also make a note of the beings they encountered at each level. Who or what were they, did they differ with each level or were they the same? When they are finished, invite all who wish to share their experience to do so.

Drawing the Labyrinth

Draw a labyrinth with seven turns. Feel free to draw the labyrinth pictured on the opposite page, either free hand or by tracing it. If you aren't comfortable with drawing, then photocopy the labyrinth in Figure 3.2. Some people work with labyrinths regularly and may have one they feel more comfortable with than the one we have provided. If this is true for you, draw the labyrinth you prefer, but be sure it has seven turns and space to write in each level. Feel free to use the simple spiral drawn in Figure 1.1 as a labyrinth also.

Write the color of each level of the spiral in the spaces of the labyrinth, beginning in the center and going outward. The colors are: beige, purple, red, blue, orange, green, yellow, and turquoise. See Figure 3.3 for which spaces correspond to which color. If you wish to add Wilber's names for developmental spaces or cultural types (see Figures 2.1 and 2.3), or a descriptive word or phrase for each color, feel free, but be sure you have room to write the rest of the information that follows as well. Later, if you wish to put everything on your labyrinth—Wilber's developmental spaces, cultural types, stages of faith, and colors of the spiral—you can take Figure 3.2 to a copy center, and have it enlarged to whatever size you wish. You can even color the spaces of the labyrinth if you choose.

In the meantime, in the Beige space write the name of the ability or challenge you identified as being with you today from the Beige part of

Figure 3.2
A Nine-turn Labyrinth

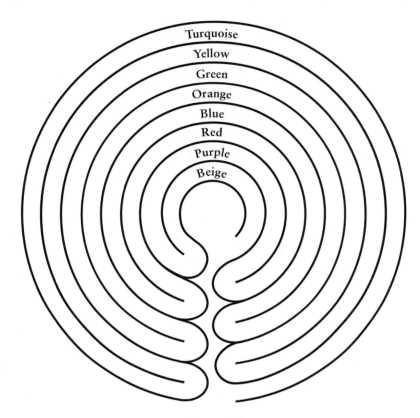

Figure 3.3
Correlation of the Labyrinth and Spiral Dynamics

you. Also write the gift, tool, or message which the Beige being gave to you. In the Purple space of the labyrinth do the same, and continue on for each of the colors. Although the labyrinth has turns for the Yellow and Turquoise levels, we did not take the meditation beyond Green. We left Yellow and Turquoise in the realms of mist to be discovered by you another day. You may do the visualization again in the future and add the last two levels if you wish, and see what comes to you.

Take a look at what you have written for the ability/challenge for each level and the gift/message for each. Are there any patterns, any recurring themes? Did you tend to identify more abilities or more challenges for yourself? Eventually we would like you to identify both an ability and a challenge for each level. The reason for this is that if you identify only challenges, then you may tend to emphasize the parts of yourself or your past that did not go smoothly, that did not get fed sufficiently, while over-looking your strengths. And if you identify only skills and abilities, then you may be overlooking areas that need some extra attention. Every space you occupy developmentally brings you both blessings and chal-lenges, and we believe it is a move toward balance to be able to acknowl-edge both.

As Beck and Cowan note, each of the first seven turns of the spiral tends to view itself as the best of the turns. It looks at the others and thinks, "well that was ridiculous, good thing I've advanced beyond that." Green, being at the outer edge of First Tier development, is able to do this to all the other levels of the First Tier and so needs to be the most careful. While it is true that each developmental space expands a person's capaci-ties and is therefore more adequate than the space that came before, that doesn't change the adequacy of the previous level. As mentioned at the very beginning of this book, crawling is a perfectly adequate skill for an infant. Although walking is more adequate, and more embracing of skill and capacity, it does not make crawling an object of ridicule. It is the skills learned in crawling that now enable you to walk. View each of the earlier levels of your development with honor and respect, for nothing you have gained since can stand without them.

If you need to do this meditation again in the future in order to iden-tify both a blessing/ability from each level, as well as a challenge, then do so by all means. In fact, we recommend you do this visualization once a year, say at New Year's, as a part of designing your plan for the year. You will discover that each year the beings give you a different message, tool or gift according to what it is you'd like or need to work on for the year. You may also discover that different blessings and challenges float up to your attention. The appearance and nature of the beings may change as well. Observing these changes in yourself over the years can be an inter-esting part of your growth process.

Write a stream of consciousness poem or narrative about your experience in the labyrinth. You do not need to write in complete sentences. Phrases, fragments, and single words are fine. Begin a new verse or paragraph for each color of the spiral, each turn of the labyrinth. In each, identify the being that came to you and the feelings it generated. What ability, blessing, or challenge did you identify for each level? What message, gift, or tool did the being give you? What are you supposed to do with what was given to you? Include your thoughts and emotions for each level, your desires for your self and your spiritual journey in the coming year.

Designing a Plan

Place your spiritual wish list and your drawing of the labyrinth in front of you. Also have a blank piece of paper and a pen at hand, and a calendar that includes the next twelve months. You might want to do this exercise around New Year's, or Samhain if you observe it as the new year, or at your birthday. Review your wish list and labyrinth and then breathe deeply and slowly for several minutes. Allow your mind to relax and open to ideas about what you would like to work on spiritually in the coming year. Compare your wish list and labyrinth. What two or three ideas, themes, or areas stand out to you as the most important? Write these on the blank piece of paper. You may write down more than three if you like, but then stop and open your mind again, and see if one or more of the things you identify can be combined with others, or perhaps be let go of for now. Having more than two or three goals in a year is too many for most people and we do not want you to get discouraged. It is better to pick one thing and do it throughout the year, and enjoy yourself while you're at it, than to choose several that you never get around to doing. As you make your choices, try to include at least one item that involves service to others, and one that is focused on yourself.

Out of your list of things to accomplish, work on, do, or study in the coming year, which one of them can you begin in the next month? Put a big star next to it.

What steps do you need to take to accomplish this item? Do you need to take a class, teach a class, attend a festival, go on a retreat, meet people, make phone calls, do research, go back to school, change employment or your residence? Make a note of the things you need to do to get started on this goal. Look at the other one or two items on your list and do the same for them. Since you didn't choose them as the item to do in the next month, what time frame do you need in order to get started on them?

Something we highly recommend you consider doing this year is working with the Virtuous Exercise set out in chapter 7 of our introductory book. Look through this exercise and see if any part of it can be brought into your plan for the year. Feel free to adapt it, or focus on the one or two virtues that relate most closely to your current spiritual goals.

On your calendar mark actual dates for doing the things you have identified. Make a note when classes are offered or festivals occur, which weekends you are free to make a retreat, what nights the drummers meet, which days you'd like to get in some exercising, meditating, or personal rituals, which evenings you are available to work in a soup kitchen, and so on. Hang your calendar in a place that will remind you of your goals and then get started! But be gentle with your-self. You will probably be overly enthusiastic in what you think you can achieve. If you can accomplish just a few things, you are off to a good start!

4

Communing

THE HEART OF MAGICK is *relational exchange*. It is *relational* because it involves interacting with others. Who or what you relate with may be others in your circle, others in the world, deeper aspects of yourself, the physical universe, spiritual beings, unmanifest reality, or your concept of the Divine. It is an *exchange* because something is being shared between you and those with whom you are relating. The exchange may be of information, thoughts, a sense of presence, devotion, energy, support, essence, emotion, or intention. The exchange and the relationship can be entered into for a variety of purposes, including no purpose other than deepening the relationship. But whatever the purpose or result, it is our contention that magick revolves around the principle of relational exchange, and that Pagan spiritual practice needs to be grounded in this exchange if it is to lead to spiritual growth.

For that reason, perhaps the most important of the four types of magick is communing. While other types, such as conscious creation and divination, can be more flamboyant, the meat of magick is right here. *Communing* is the heart of building relationship. The goal of communing is connection. The skills required are rather simple, actually, and consist of letting yourself listen and letting yourself be heard. The act of listening is a powerful one and in and of itself is very creative.

There is a vulnerability demanded by communing. Without the ability to listen, exchange and relationship at any level—physical, spiritual, emotional, or multidimensional—is extremely difficult if not impossible. At some level we think people know how powerful listening is, which is why they often go to such lengths to avoid it. It is so much easier, after all, to fill your spiritual space with chatter and rituals, formulae, chants, and gestures, than to be *still*, and listen.

 exercise

Listening

Find a time and a place where you will not be disturbed for half an hour to an hour. You may choose a place that is indoors or outdoors. Try to find a location where the surrounding noise and activity will not be a distraction. If you need to watch your time, take a portable alarm or timer with you.

When you are in the place you wish to be, pick a posture that is comfortable and that you can maintain. You can bring a portable chair or stool, or find a bench or curb. You can sit on the ground, a blanket, or a small pillow. You can lie flat on the ground or lean against a tree. Get comfortable in a way that is appropriate to your setting, safety, terrain, and weather conditions.

Once you are settled, spend several minutes just being present to yourself and your location. Spend several minutes listening to the environment around you. As you do, let yourself relax and gradually turn your attention to your breathing. Feel the rhythm of your breath and the blood pumping through your veins. Take several minutes to listen to your body and be fully present to it.

Then gradually step back and become the observer of your body. You are aware of its rhythms but you can stand back and observe them. Listen to see if your body has anything to say to you. Be silent and open to its presence; acknowledge it and let it acknowledge you. Gradually turn your attention to the contents of your mind and watch as thoughts rise and fall away. Notice that you can be an observer of your thinking as well as of your body. As a thought arises, label it "thinking" and let it pass on by. Don't try to stop the thinking, simply let it happen. Don't get caught up in individual thoughts, just notice them and let them pass on across your awareness. As you feel yourself becoming more quiet, begin to listen for the small, inner voice within you. You do not need to label what this voice is now, but you can feel that it is loving and supportive. Open yourself to its presence and simply listen for several moments. Let it know that you hear it and acknowledge it. Expand your attention to include the inner voice of your surroundings and see if you can hear what it has to say. How do the earth, sky, and your environment speak to you? Open your heart, be silent, and listen. What do you hear?

Continue with this until your time is up or you feel that you are finished. Do not go so long that you become fatigued. As you finish, bring your awareness back to yourself and stretch briefly.

Opening to Communing

The goal of communing is the building and deepening of spiritual relationships. The aim of communing is the communion itself—a sense of connection, flow, exchange, and acknowledgment. It is an experience both of a yearning and an embracing of whatever has ultimate meaning for you. There are many ways to reach this point of connection. Common methods include prayer and meditation of many kinds, but the experience of communion can come at any moment. While it can happen during prayer and meditation, it can also occur suddenly and unexpectedly. It can come upon you when you're in nature, hiking, or watching a sunset; while drumming, making dinner, having sex, or during a ritual. Moments of communion can be quiet, calm, even empty. Or they can be emotional, ecstatic, and full of sensory delight. When they occur, a connection happens and you and the universe become aware of each other in an immediate and intimate way.

While communing doesn't happen only when you decide to make time for it, it is still a good idea to make the time. This is because practices of meditation and prayer help you create a space in which to listen. There is a lot of noise and chatter in everyday life, and your sensitive inner ear can get rusty if it's not used. Since we believe that every other magickal skill is dependent to one degree or another on your ability to perceive and respond to deeper levels, then we believe your advancement in magick of any type rests heavily on what you do with communing.

Creating time to listen makes you a better listener. Setting aside time to develop deeper spiritual relationships will help deeper connections happen. Remember that relationships flow in both directions—you're not at risk of giving and receiving nothing back. At the same time, can you expect something from a reality based on exchange without giving of yourself, your time and energy, in return?

Prayer is a common type of spiritual communing, and therefore, a part of many Pagans' experience of magick. Many non-Pagans may find this a difficult concept to accept since prayer means very specific things to them, none of which include Paganism. However, we assure you that many Pagans do pray, and consider prayer to be an integral part of their magickal practice. The most common types of prayer are devotional, petitionary, and contemplative.

Devotional prayer is prayer that praises a deity, saint, spiritual being, or spiritual quality. This kind of prayer is generally word-oriented and usually involves the person addressing and praising the spiritual being or concept. From the Pagan perspective, devotional prayer includes, among other things, hymns and poetry in honor of the Divine and prayers of gratitude for blessings.

The second type of prayer is petitionary. Petitionary, or intercessory, prayer is prayer that asks for something. This is also a word-oriented prayer, with the talking again being done mostly by the one praying. From a Pagan perspective, petitionary prayer can be offered on its own or be combined with other types of magick. For example, prayers for healing may be combined with energy work for healing. Prayers for wisdom may be combined with divination. Asking for assistance with resources, people, and situations may be used in combination with conscious creation work.

Most people are familiar with devotional and petitionary prayer, as they are the types of prayer they experienced growing up, especially if they were raised Christian. Less well known, even among devout Christians, is contemplative prayer. Contemplation is most common within religious orders of monks and nuns of all faiths, but certainly is not limited to them. Contemplative prayer is an integral part of communing in that it is generally quiet and involves more listening than talking, and its focus is on the connection to spiritual realms.

However, on the more mentally "active" end of contemplative prayer are techniques that use mental imagery and emotion. An example from Christianity are the Spiritual Exercises created by St. Ignatius in which the one praying vividly imagines and enters into scenes from the life of Christ. Prayer that uses mantras—the repeating of words and phrases, which includes the praying of rosaries and prayer beads, and aboriginal chanting and toning—is also verbally active, but uses the repeated sound or phrase for the purpose of stilling and focusing the mind. Guided meditations, such as the visualizations we offer in this book, can also be viewed as a form of contemplative prayer that heavily utilize mental imagery.

As one moves away from the use of such imagery, a quiet, wordless form of contemplation begins. A form of modern contemplative prayer practiced by many people, Christian and non-Christian, was popularized by Basil Pennington and is known as "centering prayer." In centering prayer, a word or concept is chosen that acts as a focus (similar to a mantra) that can help re-center the person praying if his or her attention wanders. The word can be "love" or "God" or "forgiveness," among others, and may relate to an aspect of spiritual development the person wants to work on. You will have an opportunity to try centering prayer in an exercise later in this chapter.

The quietest type of contemplative prayer is one we call formless. Those praying this type of prayer turn their gaze toward their concept of the spiritual and desire simply to be present with it. There are no words, no phrases, or concepts which are said or thought by the one praying. The mind and body are brought to a point of stillness, and even the concept of the "Divine" may eventually be dropped entirely. At this point the person is beginning to approach what Wilber calls the "nondual" state of awareness, in which the one praying comes to the realization that nothing exists outside of the Ground of consciousness, and that everything is one with it.

In addition to types of prayer there are also many forms of meditation, some of which overlap with prayer to one extent or another. Western traditions of meditation are generally sedentary and range from the highly mentally active (as with the Ignatian Exercises and guided meditations), to the very quiet and formless. From the East comes a rich heritage of meditation from a wide variety of spiritual traditions.

Our studies of Eastern practices have convinced us that they are too numerous to cover with any justice in this book. They include those that use physical movement, such as martial arts, yoga and tai chi; that pursue ecstatic states such as Sufi dancing and tantra; that use imagery and mantras to focus the mind; and those which are more wordlessly and formlessly contemplative in nature.

Learning a prayer or a meditative tradition can be very beneficial to the development of your spirituality and your communing skills. Our earlier advice continues here, and that is to approach the formation of your communing skills with relaxed effort. Trying too hard or vigorously can burn you out and distract you from the point of the practice. Remember that the Divine is not contained in the practice. The practice is just a means to create a space for yourself in which to be mindful of a relationship that already exists, and of which you are becoming more consciously aware. We suggest to you that the universe wants to connect with you as much as you do with it. This is because a reality in flux seeks out places into which to flow. Consciousness enjoys mutuality and exchange. The universe indeed leans in your direction, and you also lean toward it.

Wilber notes that many religions and philosophies propose the idea of a love, desire, or caring that flows through every part of the universe. Lower level holons yearn, or reach out, toward wider, more developed holons, with a desire he terms "Eros." In turn, the higher holons express a care for the lower holons through a kind of embrace or support that he calls "Agape."[1] These concepts can be found in Neoplatonism, Christianity (especially in its mystics), Romanticism, and the works of Freud, Jung, and even Locke in the West.[2] In the East, Wilber notes that similar concepts are found in many tantric and yogic schools which teach that the "supermind" pulls people up to an identification with it to enable them to express compassion for all beings.[3]

Wilber terms this mutual exchange the Great Circle (a wonderful Pagan image!), and describes it as follows:

> . . . Eros is the love of the lower reaching up to the higher (Ascent);
> Agape is the love of the higher reaching down to the lower (Descent).
> In individual development, one *ascends* via Eros (or expanding to a
> higher and wider identity), and then *integrates* via Agape (or reaching

down to embrace with care all lower holons), so that balanced development *transcends* but *includes* . . .

Likewise, the love of the Kosmos reaching down *to us* from a higher level than our present stage of development is also Agape (compassion), helping us to respond with Eros until the *source* of that Agape is *our own* developmental level, our own self. The Agape of a higher dimension is the omega pull for our own Eros, inviting us to ascend, via wisdom, and thus expand the circle of our own compassion for more and more beings.[4]

exercise

Returning the Embrace

Find a time and a place where you will not be disturbed for half an hour to an hour. This may be someplace indoors or out of doors, but try to find a place that is not too noisy or distracting, and where you will not be interrupted. If you need to watch your time, take a portable alarm or timer with you. Don't forget to bring a chair or blanket if you need one. Once you are in the place you wish to be, get comfortable. Sit or lie down, find a bench, lean against a tree. Find a position you can maintain that is appropriate to your setting, safety, terrain, and weather.

Take several minutes to breathe deeply and relax. Think back over what you have read in this chapter, and notice if one particular concept or idea stands out to you. Allow yourself to sink into the thought or idea and let it speak to you. Why is it meaningful and powerful for you at this moment? Continue for several minutes.

When you feel ready, turn your attention to the sense of yourself experienced in the Visualization and Walking Meditation from the last chapter, where you felt yourself growing from a seed and nourished by the universe. Take yourself mentally back into that space. See yourself blossoming in the support that the universe provides you. Know that the universe is trustworthy. Open up to the power you feel coming from the multidimensional realms of manifest and unmanifest reality. Sit in this space for a few moments, and as you do, see how the thought or insight you had earlier fits into this sense of nourishment and support. The insight also comes from the vastness and wants to support you in your growth.

Feel the yearning of the universe toward you. Open yourself to it as fully as you can. Feel it surround you as an embrace. Let what you cannot hold simply flow on past you and let it go. Do not try to contain it all. Then feel yourself yearning toward the universe—toward spirit, the Divine, the Ground, the fullness and the emptiness of all that is. Open yourself to this yearning as fully as you can, without straining or being overwhelmed by it. Contain only as much as you comfortably can and let the rest go.

Drift into the rhythm of feeling your yearning going out, and the embrace of the universe coming back to you. Align your sense of this flow to your breathing if you wish, or let it move in and out of your awareness at its own tempo. Stay in this space for several minutes. If thoughts begin to intrude, watch them pass across the screen of your mind and return your attention to the sense of yearning and embrace.

As you near the end of the time you can give to this exercise, hold the sense of flow for a moment and acknowledge your experience. Recognize that you have listened and been heard, have seen and been noticed, have yearned and been embraced, and perhaps have embraced in return. Acknowledge and honor the exchange and sharing that you just experienced. Then bring your awareness back to your body and surroundings, and stretch briefly.

You can repeat this exercise several times in the near future as you wish. At moments when you don't have time to enter the experience completely, simply turn your attention in the universe's direction, give it a quick glance, and let it acknowledge you in return.

my journal

I feel that I am in spiritual relationship with . . .

My spiritual relationships satisfy me because . . .

My spiritual relationships leave me unsatisfied because . . .

The ways in which I listen spiritually are . . .

I wish my communing experiences were more like . . .

Five beliefs I was raised with about communing are . . .

Five beliefs I have now about communing are . . .

I feel or have felt the Agape, or supportive love of the universe (or the Divine) when . . .

The types of prayer and meditation that speak to me most right now are . . .

The types of prayer and meditation I want to learn more about are . . .

questions to discuss

1. Do you agree or disagree that magick is about relationship and mutual exchange?

2. Do you agree or disagree that the four types of magick comprise most of Paganism's spiritual practice? If you disagree, what do you identify as Paganism's main spiritual practices?

3. What is the value of communing to you?

4. What about listening do you find difficult? What about it do you find easy? Is it a part of your spiritual life now? Why or why not?

5. What experiences with prayer and meditation have you had? What types of prayer and meditation were they? What forms of communing and meditation do you prefer?

6. Have you ever had an experience of the Eros and Agape that Wilber describes?

 exercise

Centering Prayer

Find a place where you can be undisturbed for thirty minutes. If you are indoors and it is appropriate, feel free to use candles and incense, and to turn the lights low. Music is best left off unless you need to cover other sounds. In that case, keep the music soothing and the volume low. Get into a comfortable position, either sitting, reclining, or kneeling. Be sure you can maintain this position for the duration of the exercise. If you need to, bring an alarm or timer with you as you may lose track of time.

Once you are in a comfortable position, relax and breathe deeply and slowly. Gradually empty your mind of the concerns of the day. Allow your stream of thoughts to fade into the background. If a thought pops up demanding your attention, observe it, label it "thought" or "thinking," and let it pass on by. Do this for several minutes, until you feel relaxed and calm. Then gradually turn your attention to your concept of Spirit or the Divine. Allow this concept to fill your mind until one particular attribute stays in your mind. To you right now, the Divine is this attribute and embodies it perfectly. It could be "love," "forgiveness," "power," "joy," "healing," or some other concept. Choose one word that signifies Spirit or the Divine to you right now.

Then allow yourself to sink into this word and let it take you into the presence of Spirit as you know it. Turn your gaze toward the Divine as you conceive it and be present to it. Simply rest in this space. If you find your attention wandering, repeat the word silently and slowly and let it redirect your attention. Continue with this for fifteen or twenty minutes, but not beyond the time you are comfortable with it.

Before ending, bring the word into your heart center. Feel it fill your chest, and open yourself to the qualities of this divine attribute. Let it grow within you until it is glowing and expanding. Absorb as much of its energy as you can comfortably hold, and let it soak into the nooks and crannies of your body and spirit, especially those places that most need to be nourished. Then release the word and its energy. Let any excess energy flow down your body and into the floor or ground, as though you were in the shower watching it go down the drain. Gradually return your awareness to yourself and your surroundings, and end the exercise.

Communing and the Four Elements

As noted in the previous chapter, we correspond our four types of magick with the four elements and directions that are familiar to Pagans, and with Wilber's four quadrants. We place communing in the west, the home of the element of water, and in Wilber's upper left quadrant, his realm of the *Inner I*.

Communing is the most intimate, interior, personal, and subjective of the four types of magick, hence its relation to Wilber's quadrant of the interior of the individual. Your experiences of communion with the physical and nonphysical universe, Spirit and the Divine, are personal and private to you. They cannot be seen by a microscope, weighed, or measured, nor is their importance to you determined by cultural context.

In common Pagan practice, the archetype of the west is the realm associated with wisdom and intuition. Viewed on the wheel of the year, the west falls in the land of autumn, of fading life, and a withdrawal into dark, silent depths. On the wheel of the day it is the literal direction of sunset, where light fades and the day moves toward its close. On the wheel of human life it is the realm of aging, of crones and sages, a time of living that is less filled with work and more available for teaching and reflection. For these reasons the west for Pagans is frequently associated with times of quiet, withdrawal into interior spaces, and an increase of wisdom.

Water is the element usually associated with the west in Pagan practice, and is viewed as the element of acceptance, flow, and intuition. Water arises from the

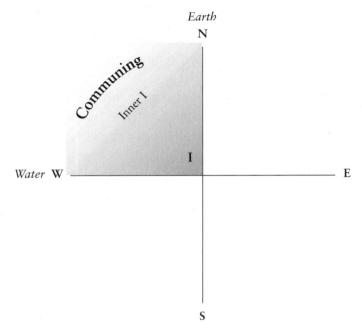

Figure 4.1
The Upper Left Quadrant: Communing, West, Inner I

hidden deep places of the earth, springing up with cold clarity. It settles in unexpected places and reveals aspects that were otherwise hidden. It is changeable and always moving, ebbing, and flowing, and so is also associated with emotion. Water is the element that flows, shifts, and penetrates quietly. Like the west, it is an archetype of wisdom and intuition.

Deepening your experiences with communing can help you move toward the goal of *maximum expansion* and *maximum healthiness* in your spiritual growth by opening you to an ever-broadening understanding of what is meant by spiritual relationship. It may give you insights into the other three quadrants and how to move toward an integrated spirituality. While Pagans need to honor their inner subjective experience, they also need to resist the tendency to focus exclusively on it. In this reality there are other consciousnesses and an external world with which to interact. By the same token, it is equally unhealthy to say that subjective experience doesn't exist or has no value, that the individual is subordinate to exterior or collective experience, or that tangible products are superior to interior phenomena. An integrated Pagan spirituality demands the equal embrace of all four elements and all the quadrants in every aspect of magick.

 **exercise**

Connecting to That Which Flows

This exercise focuses on experiencing flow through the element of water, though it does suggest some other aspects of flow. If you are fortunate enough to live near a body of water, such as a lake, river, or ocean, and the weather and other conditions are suitable, plan to do this exercise outdoors in the water. Please keep your safety in mind. Take another person with you who can swim, in case you lose track of time and distance, or need assistance. Don't go out in a storm or at night, and be mindful of tides and water creatures.

If you don't live near a body of water or can't go out due to the season or other reasons, you can use a swimming pool or tub. Again, be mindful of your safety, a point we are stressing here because you will likely be in an altered or trance state during the exercise.

Feel free to prepare a soothing environment, if possible, before you begin. Candles and soft music can be very helpful in creating an inviting space. Turn on a fountain if you have one, or play a recording of the sounds of water in nature. If you are in a natural environment, let the sights and sounds speak to you, though we recommend you find as quiet and undistracting a place as possible. Consider doing this exercise without clothing, or with the minimal amount that supports your comfort level and the appropriateness of your location.

Just before you begin, anoint yourself with the water you are about to enter. Anoint yourself on your forehead, throat, chest, stomach, groin, knees, and feet, and as you do say "I open myself to all that flows." Take several long slow breaths and then enter the water. Do so gradually if possible. Be aware of the feelings and sensations of the water as it slowly covers you. Submerge yourself in a position in which you can safely recline or float and be completely relaxed. We suggest that the time you spend in the water not exceed twenty or thirty minutes.

Continue to breathe deeply and slowly. Relax. Let the water support you. Open yourself to the rhythm of your breathing and gradually, to the rhythm of the water. Feel it ebbing and flowing around you. Meditate on how all things in the universe ebb and flow. Can you feel this ebbing and flowing within yourself? Occasionally swirl your hand through the water and feel the gentle resistance give way before your movement. Meditate on how things which flow gracefully give way and provide no resistance to their environment. In what ways do you flow in your life and in what ways are you resistive? Watch how the ripples spread out from your movements, or how the waves move toward the shore. Meditate on the unseen and far-reaching effects of what you do in this fluid universe. How is the universe rippling and responding to your movements and desires? How do you respond in return?

Mentally sink deeper into the watery element. Hear it whisper to you of the deep hidden places in which it lives, the aquifers and ocean abysses, underground rivers and wells. What has this element seen, what does it know, what is its wisdom? How does it speak to the deep and hidden places within you, your underground rivers and abysses? When you spring up anew in cold, fresh springs, what wisdom do you bring with you from the depths?

Allow yourself to become aware of all the things around you which flow, in addition to water. Feel the flow of the blood in your veins, and if you are a woman, of your monthly cycles past or present. See the flow that exists in your breath, your thoughts, your day, and on further into the flow of time itself, and the enfolding and unfolding universe. Notice that even constructed things have a flow, like language, economies, electricity, and traffic. See that flow permeates everything. Open yourself to it, blend into its energies, let it become you and you it. Notice that flow is always happening, even when you are not consciously aware of it.

Gradually bring your attention back to your surroundings. Express gratitude for your experience. Leave the water and dry off and journal a bit if you wish. If you are doing this exercise with a group or class, spend a few minutes sharing.

Building Relationships

If communing is about the building and deepening of spiritual relationships, then we must ask, what are Pagans relating to spiritually? Most of the Pagans we know develop relationships in more than one of the following areas across the course of their life. These areas are: spiritual relationships with the physical world; with archetypal or energetic representations of the physical world; with the physical self; with archetypal or energetic representations of the self; with the deeper, multi-dimensional self; with all of consciousness; with spiritual beings, such as angels and saints; and with the Divine as they conceive it.

Many people are raised to believe that spiritual relationships exist only between "humans" and "God," and the nature, identity, and qualities of this God are strictly defined. Also strictly defined are the types of relationships permitted to exist between humans and God, and the ways in which communing can happen. Such people most certainly would not accept that communing is possible between humans and anything other than this God. They certainly cannot envision having a spiritual relationship with physical matter or the collective unconscious. For others this strict view is softened somewhat by including additional spiritual beings with which they are allowed to relate, such as the Holy Spirit, saints, angels, devas, or ancestors. But rarely is the full spectrum of spiritual relationships that is accepted within Paganism found in other mainstream faiths.

Let us summarize the spiritual relationships we identify as common in Paganism, and then briefly discuss each one. They are:

- Building relationships with the physical world, and archetypal and energetic representations of it

- Building relationships with your physical self, not only as it exists in this world but also at deeper levels, including archetypal and energetic representations of the self

- Building relationships with all of consciousness; or stated another way, with the entire multidimensional universe in its manifest and unmanifest reality

- Building relationships with the Divine, however it is conceived, which can include deities and various spiritual beings or essences

Spiritual relationships with the **physical world** are those which embrace nature, the body, and physical phenomena. The physical world can also be abstracted to psychological, archetypal, and energetic constructs such as Mother Earth, Gaia, the four elements, the four directions, elementals, astrology, deep ecology, some aspects of shamanism, power animals or totems, faeries, devas, earth spirits, and environmentalism. Many mainstream faiths do not allow spiritual relationships with either the physical world or an archetypal expression of it. Because Pagans do permit it they are sometimes accused of "worshipping creation and not the creator." This statement is based on a view of spiritual relationships that is obviously narrower than Paganism's and does not view the physical world as being an appropriate part of spirituality. It also overlooks, either willfully or through ignorance, the other three types of spiritual relationships Pagans embrace, as though Pagan spirituality is limited only to the physical.

Rabbi Gershon Winkler beautifully expresses the sort of spiritual relationship with the physical world which Pagans have in mind in his book *Magic of the Ordinary: Recovering the Shamanic in Judaism*, where he writes: "When I walk in the wilderness around my home and I pass a stone, and the stone catches my eye, I can simply notice it and keep walking, or I can acknowledge a still small voice deep deep inside me that beckons me toward that stone, that is communicating to me the desire of that stone to have me engage it. If I pay attention in that moment to that ever so gentle, almost dormant 'pull' toward the stone, and then sit by the stone or lie down beside it, I will enter into relationship with its spirit. Because that stone exists only because it is enlivened by the same breath of Creator that is willing me, too, into being."[5]

Spiritual relationships with one's **self** are those which embrace deeper knowledge of the physical self in this existence, including one's thoughts, emotions, motivations, dreams, the body, and the spirit. They also involve levels of the self which are expanded, multidimensional versions of what is known at the physical level, including such things as past and future lives, the "higher self," or the "over-soul." Relationships with the self can also be abstracted to psychological or archetypal constructs, such as those encountered in the tarot, astrology, psychic phenomena, regressions, and various out-of-body experiences.

Spiritual relationships with **all of consciousness** can begin with what people usually think of as "conscious" or "sentient" beings (which includes other humans), but pushes deeper to find the consciousness in matter usually considered "inert." Nor do relationships stop here but press on into unmanifest levels of reality. These relationships seek a wider embrace, perhaps expanding to the very ground of consciousness and the fabric of all that is.

Spiritual relationships with the **Divine** are those which embrace one's concept of ultimate cause and meaning and the realm of Spirit. They can include relationships with deities, gods and goddesses from a variety of traditions, spirit beings, spirit guides, totems and power animals, angels, faeries, devas, saints, sages, honored teachers, ancestors, messengers, and so on. Many mainstream religions focus on one deity or set of deities (deity is used here to mean any being or essence ascribed with power), while Pagans are free to explore all images of the Divine regardless of the culture or religion from which they are drawn. See chapter 3 of our introductory book for a more complete discussion of Pagan views about God. Pagan concepts of the Divine can also be very abstract, even to the point of leaving behind all "traditional" concepts of the Divine, or into realms in which no concepts exist.

We think that most Pagans benefit from becoming more spiritually well-rounded, and should consider being open to building spiritual relationships from each of the categories. We believe you will be drawn to develop the sorts of spiritual relationships that suit your developmental needs at the moment. As you grow your needs will change, so be open to changing your ideas about spiritual relationships also.

 my journal

The experiences with communing I've had that have had the biggest impact on me are . . .

The impact they still have on me today is . . .

These experiences were or were not peak experiences for me because . . .

The types of spiritual relationships I have developed so far are . . .

What I find most challenging about building spiritual relationships is . . .

I would describe my relationship with the four directions as . . .

I would describe my relationship with the west as . . .

Experiences I have had with the west are . . .

My relationship with the element of water is . . .

Experiences I have had with the element of water are . . .

 exercise

Choosing a Relationship

Take a look at the common spiritual relationships we describe above: the physical world, the self, all of consciousness, and the Divine. If there are others you would like to add or emphasize, make a note of them. Study this list and identify which relationships you are most comfortable with, those you have already spent time developing, and those to which you have given less attention. If you were to pick an area of relationship to work on now, what would it be? Which type of relationship would you be the least likely to choose now, and why?

For this exercise we suggest you work with a relationship you do not already have a great deal of experience with, so that you can develop something new. You may also want to consider choosing the type of relationship that holds the least attraction for you at the moment, as it may represent a particular challenge that would be helpful to your growth.

Find a time when you will have about twenty uninterrupted minutes and a place that is quiet. You can be indoors or out, as you choose. Feel free to sit, stand, kneel, or lie down, but choose a position that you can comfortably hold. Light candles and incense if you wish. Turn off the phone and turn down the lights if you choose. Get into a comfortable position and take several deep breaths. Spend several minutes relaxing, breathing, and letting go of tension. Let the concerns of your day float by or drain out of you into the floor. Give yourself time to feel clear and calm.

Then turn your attention to the spiritual relationship you have cho-sen to work with today. Set it front of you as though it were an object sitting on a table, and take a good look at it. Walk all the way around it and see what it looks like from several angles. What do you know about this aspect of spiritual relationship now? What experiences have you already had with it? What does it mean to you? If you chose an area that is not attractive to you, what about it bothers you? Go right up to it and ask it, "why don't I like you?" or "why do I find you unin-teresting?" See what it has to say. Spend a few minutes in this dialogue.

Then ask, "if I were to have a relationship with you, what would that mean?" Listen to what you hear and respond back. You may want to ask, "if I form a relationship with you, what effect will you have on my spiritual growth right now?" Ask what gifts this relationship has for you, and what challenges. Continue this conversation until you feel it has run its course.

After this exchange is ended, stand back for just a moment and notice what you have been chatting with. Have you given a shape, form, or appearance to this spiritual relationship? Are you speaking to a person, animal, tree, color, emotion, sense of energy, or a mental concept? You do not have to give it a form, but if an image suggests itself, allow it to take shape.

If you are comfortable doing so, allow yourself to merge for a few moments with this image. If it is a color or energy, step into it. If it is a being with a physical form, embrace it. Or, if you'd rather, just sit next to it for a few minutes and watch the clouds go by. If you have no image, then merge with your idea or sense of what this spiritual relationship or interaction would feel like. Share whatever emotions, messages, and con-versation you feel moved to share, and continue until it feels finished.

When you are ready, end the merging and acknowledge the experi-ence. Express your thanks for the encounter. Do you want to continue building a relationship with this spiritual being or aspect? If not, why not? If so, what can you do next to continue what you began today? Say farewell to your experience and let your awareness return to your-self and your surroundings.

Communing in Developmental Space

In this section we discuss communing in the context of the developmental sequences set out in the first two chapters. Pagans often fall into the mode of thinking that magick is one thing which functions more or less the same for everyone. They presume that what they experience is what other Pagans experience. Instead, we suggest that magickal experience really and truly differs depending upon one's developmental capacities. The magickal experiences a person has and the interpretations given to them are a function of that person's beliefs and developmental space. The magick experienced by a person with an egocentric worldview and moral embrace, for example, is fundamentally different from that experienced by a person with a shamanic worldview and moral embrace. In our introductory book we emphasized the importance of belief, the power to choose one's beliefs, and the impact beliefs have on your experiences and the world you help create. This book adds developmental capacities as a further variable to consider when discussing issues of personal and spiritual growth.

Think back to the discussion of holons presented in chapter 1. As human capacity grows, new abilities emerge that transcend and include all prior capacities. So in the case of motor development, to choose one example, most people agree that the skills of walking and running embrace a larger capacity than those of toddling and crawling; and crawling transcends the ability to turn from side to side in a crib. The difficulty in looking back on earlier capacities is that people see them from their present developmental position. From where you are today you see a baby in its crib, and watch it learn to sit up and crawl, from the point of view of one who already walks and runs. It is easy to forget that while in a particular developmental space the world is no greater than that space. To the infant in the crib, the crib and the caretakers are its world. The crawling infant knows nothing of walking; though it observes it in others, its world is a crawling world. It is not experiencing the same world you are, and it will not understand the world you know until it grows to embrace the capacities you now possess. If growth is halted or arrested at a certain point, then the individual will be limited to the capacities found in that developmental space unless he or she becomes "unstuck" and is able to continue growing.

It can also be easy to forget that issues of developmental capacity, and the differences in ethics and worldview each capacity brings, applies to spirituality as well. A lot of time and energy is expended fruitlessly between people debating spiritual issues who occupy different developmental spaces. Teachers and leaders in Paganism need to be developed enough themselves to recognize the spaces others occupy and adjust their approach accordingly. Doing so will help more effective communication occur.

Paganism as a whole is in a unique position to appreciate and foster spiritual development through all spaces while not being threatened by their variety. Paganism's strength in this regard comes from its being a postmodern movement, that is, one which is nondogmatic and explores a variety of paradigms. It embraces a range of perspectives rather than offering one as the final solution. Pagans are learning how to support each other in this process and sit comfortably in the seeming contradictions without giving in to the urge to resolve them through dogma. What we hope to demonstrate in this section, and similar sections in each of the next three chapters, is that many of the differences found in Paganism are an expression of expanding worldviews. They are not a chaotic jumble, nor are they cause for alarm. They are part of the invisible but organizing pattern of human development. A working knowledge of these patterns can be helpful to you, not only for your own growth but also in your work with others if you serve as a teacher, counselor, priest, or priestess in your community.

Communing, then, is going to be experienced in fundamentally different ways by Pagans in different developmental spaces. Prayer, meditation, spiritual relationships, and connection with the Divine are going to look very different from various points along the spiral. For the purposes of this discussion here and in the next three chapters, we eliminate the earliest level of development, the archaic or beige, since its capacities are normally limited to the first year or so of life, and its impact on magickal development is more difficult for us to ascertain.

Beginning with the **egocentric** self, which is Purple and early Red on the spiral, we see that the individual in early childhood confuses inner symbols and outer reality, believing them to be the same. The world is filled with mysterious forces which revolve about the self and tend to do its bidding. Communing at this level will likely involve contact with these mysterious forces for the purpose of obtaining something the self desires. As the egocentric self moves into the early Red phases of the spiral, it becomes more impulsive and interested in power. It lets go of believing that the powers of the universe revolve around itself, and transfers these powers to parents, gods, kings, and leaders instead. As the self matures, it expands its worldview such that it no longer identifies primarily with this level, but it will always carry its Purple and early Red self within it.

The healthy communing experiences of Purple and early Red are filled with a sense of wonder, magick, and awe. The self uses these experiences to help it build its identity. Early experiences may take the form of wish fulfillment, with spiritual forces doing the self's bidding and meeting its every desire. However, as it matures, the self begins to shake loose of its early narcissistic view of spiritual relating and grapples with deeper issues of power and authority, including both the scope and limit of its own power and that of its environment.

Before we discuss unhealthy or "stuck" aspects of the egocentric space, we want to emphasize that behaviors we enumerate here and in the next three chapters are not limited to Pagans by any means. Many of the examples we share from our personal experience are similar to those we've had with members of other faiths. Getting stuck, or having trouble processing a developmental space, is a human condition and is not limited to any particular faith.

To an individual in an egocentric space, communing is generally going to be "all about me." The moral embrace of the self usually does not extend beyond itself as the ego is the center of power. We expect this of young children, but we do not expect it in teenagers or adults. A Pagan stuck here may approach communing with the belief that the gods and goddesses are their personal servants, that prayer and spiritual relationships consist of giving instructions to beings who respond to their whims. Beliefs that they command the forces of nature, life and death, and wield great power are not unusual. We have met adult Pagans who told us that seasonal birds migrate because they told them to, that they can imprison angels and spirits, that several goddesses are fighting over who gets to be "pulled down" into them as priestess at the next ritual, and that they will dispatch a particular goddess to keep the utility company from turning off their gas service.

If you are in a teaching or leadership position you can offer your opinion of such statements, and minimize the effect such egocentric comments can have on other students and group members. But expect your gentle correction not to have much effect; the narcissistic person probably isn't listening. You can, however, offer a different perspective or model a behavior you believe may be helpful in the situation.

The **mythic** self, late Red and Blue on the spiral, usually appears in adolescence and is concerned with rules and roles, order and fairness. The grandiose view of the self is abandoned and the center of power is transferred to powerful Others. The roles which the self and others play is very important. The mythic self's level of tolerance of other views is low and it sees other beliefs as a threat. This self loves to create stories and myths, but is caught in them and cannot see that they are just stories. Religious stories and symbols are literal to this self, and the sacred is contained in the symbol. The moral embrace of the mythic self expands beyond itself to include family, nation, and close groups.

Mythic Pagans will likely view communing as an expression of devotion for a powerful god or goddess. There is a sense that spiritual relationships involve reciprocal fairness, in that the self says "I will play the role I have been assigned to play, and now you play yours." As a Pagan deepens in growth, he or she may begin to feel that the Divine is its friend, and may relate to Spirit as to a divine lover who knows them intimately and deeply. This development can lead to powerful emotional experiences with communing.

A self which gets stuck in the mythic phase may find itself suffering from neurosis and guilt, a feeling of not being able to please powerful Others, and a repression of its feelings and bodily urges. A Pagan stuck here may become rigid in his or her beliefs, think in black and white terms, and have little tolerance for other Pagans and religions. Concerning communing, only those Pagans who pray to the "right" gods or do the "correct" ceremonies will be deemed worthy to have their prayers answered. Some Blue traditions descend through a lineage traced from a powerful teacher or leader, who is treated as an absolute, or near absolute, authority. Pagans who are not a part of this lineage may be viewed as false Pagans who will not be able to commune with the highest levels their tradition recognizes. Rigidly Blue Pagans can become very upset if precise norms are not followed, even at large gatherings and public events where their tradition is not predominant.

As a teacher or leader, be aware of potential negative behaviors and do what you can to minimize the impact of rigid Blue behavior. You may also wish to accommodate the wishes of a Blue participant in areas that don't detract from the overall experience, such as a meditation or ritual, while encouraging them to participate in those segments drawn from other perspectives.

The **rational** self typically begins to emerge during the Blue phase of adolescence, and unless the individual never leaves Blue (which, according to Fowler, was approximately 40% of those studied),[6] it will unfold to Orange by young adulthood. Orange is reflective and holds all its prior beliefs up to the scrutiny of reason. If the beliefs don't pass muster they are abandoned. The self is finally able to step outside the stories it created or was told earlier, and begins to create its own personal mythology. It also begins to separate the sacred from the symbol that represents it, whether the symbol is a story or an object.

For a Pagan in a rational space, communing may take the form of conversations and discourses either with spiritual beings or archetypal qualities. Prayer may tend to the intellectual side as the individual sorts out his or her beliefs. Communing experiences may lose the emotional power they had in the previous level, leaving the Pagan feeling just a bit out in the cold.

A self which gets stuck in the rational phase will find itself surrounded by the creations of its rational mind, with an abandonment of intuition, myth, ritual, ceremony, and perhaps spiritual relationships of any sort. Pagans who find themselves in this situation may abandon Paganism, or if not, they may find that previous observances and practices have lost much of their meaning. This can be a difficult transition, especially if the Pagan is surrounded by a strongly mythological peer group. Pagans may struggle with demythologizing symbols previously meaningful to them, with breaking free of the stories and roles they were caught in before, while avoiding being trapped within the creations of their rational mind.

We have met few adult Pagans with large doses of unhealthy Orange, since if their expression of it tends to competition and entrepreneurialism, for example, they probably don't have time for any spiritual path. If their difficulties stem from not being able to ground their Pagan views in reason, and they have given up trying, then they are probably not going to be at Pagan events either. The handful we have met who seem to be stuck here are almost obsessed with rational debate and critique. They tend to "bash" individuals or groups who still mythologize story and rituals. They frequently refuse to participate in ritual or magickal work, or at the least hold themselves apart and do not share in the energetic experience with others. But they will sit back and pick apart what you and others are doing and how you're doing it wrong in some detail. Their overall dissatisfaction and hunger to resolve their issues may lead them to your classes, open rituals, and discussion groups. They can be good additions to a group as long as they don't take over a discussion or class, or dwell on their disillusionment. If this happens, gently take back control and be sure to let others have a chance to speak. Insist that they participate in all energy or ritual work, if you can appropriately do so, as in a class you are teaching. The way out of their difficulties is through intuitive and ecstatic experience, so participation may help open this door for them.

The **vision-logic** self, which is Green on the spiral, begins in adulthood if transitions are successfully made through the other levels. Paganism has many healthy Green aspects, including a strong sense of community, shared values, consensus decision-making, concern for justice, recognition of the global community, concern for use of resources and the earth, and heightened self-awareness. The moral embrace of the Green Pagan expands to include all humans on the planet. Communing experiences will likely be holistic, contemplative, emotional and intuitive. There may be a strong sense of belonging and interconnectedness. Communing may expand to include a more "global" representation of gods and goddesses, and also to include other human beings, living or deceased. A sense of connection to ancestors, "soul families," or the collective unconscious may become a part of the self's communing.

A self which has difficulty navigating the vision-logic space may experience cynicism, or a lack of purpose and meaning. This is because the diversity of perspectives leave it wondering if anything matters and has enduring value. Unhealthy Green can also exhibit arrogance if it declares its view superior to other views, while claiming it favors no view over another. A Pagan with this tendency is quick to judge the sincerity of someone's faith based on how well the person conforms—whether they shop in the right places, eat the right foods, vote the right party, recycle, and so on.

As a Pagan teacher or facilitator witnessing unhealthy Green behavior, try to minimize the effect of it on others, particularly those who appear likely to be punished for not conforming to a group norm, or who happen to belong to an out-of-favor group. Discourage labeling and the judgmentalism and ostracism that can come with it. Focus on the global aspects of communing skills which they are now beginning to experience, and emphasize the ability to hold a variety of perspectives at once without the need for judgment or dogmatic labeling.

The **psychic** self, which we place at Yellow and Turquoise on the spiral,[7] expresses itself if the individual successfully integrates the development of the rational mind. At this point, the self opens up to psychic phenomena and experiences that are coming from "other realms," certainly not from the rational faculties. These experiences are full of sensual detail and feeling and can be quite powerful and ecstatic. The self opens to an experience of mysticism that Wilber calls Nature Mysticism, and sees the fundamental unity of the physical realm.

Pagans certainly work with psychic and nonrational phenomena, though it is easy for narcissism to masquerade as true psychic-level abilities, so be cautious here. A psychic Pagan's experiences with communing, prayer, and meditation will focus on experiencing the greater web of life; his or her spiritual relationships will likely expand to include the physical world, the earth, Gaia, a power animal, the energies of plants, and so on. As an outgrowth of this development, Pagans may be attracted to shamanism and other similar practices.

The moral embrace of psychic Pagans expands to include all earthly beings, and as a part of this wider embrace they will begin to experience the interconnectedness of the physical world. Communing will expand to include spiritual relationships with the physical world, even to physical objects previously considered "inert," as their concepts of intelligence and consciousness expand beyond prior limits. It is our position that interconnectedness doesn't end with the physical world but extends into spirit and the ground of consciousness itself. However, psychic Pagans are not ready to take interconnectedness so far. At this point in their development the focus is on the physical level, as interconnectedness is a new concept and capacity for them, and they are not yet ready to concern themselves with how far it may extend.

Many Pagans we know seem to experience moments of Nature Mysticism, although it is possible that they are occurring as peak experiences. If so, this means that although they normally operate from another developmental space, they temporarily travel to the psychic level as part of a powerful ritual or meditative experience. As Pagans continue to grow they can eventually integrate this level such that it becomes their primary spiritual level. We should not expect this to happen for everyone, however. According to Fowler, only 7% of his study population reached an equivalent faith state in their lifetime. Pagans need to remember that growth is not a contest to see which "level" they can reach. It is about developing to their full potential, whatever that means for each individual.

A self which gets stuck at this point of development will find it has trouble breaking free of psychic experiences and living in the "real world." It will feed off the rich sensory and ecstatic energy of psychic experience and become somewhat addicted to it. It may romanticize nature as part of its mystical connection to it. If it has unresolved narcissistic tendencies, its ego can grow to be quite large, especially now that it has psychic powers at its disposal. It is our experience that narcissism can masquerade as true psychic development. Discerning the difference is one of the trickiest tasks for those in Pagan leadership positions. Generally speaking, narcissism boasts of its abilities. The stories it tells of what happens with its psychic powers are usually dramatic, emotional, full of crisis, and often involve attacks and pursuit by all sorts of beings and powers. The narcissist figures prominently in these stories and usually saves the day. Pagans that are truly at the psychic level rarely talk about it; you may not know they have such skills unless a situation arises in which they feel it is a necessity to use or discuss them. When they do, their self takes a back seat to the needs of the situation, and the psychic intervention happens without frantic emotion. Indeed, the energy surrounding such individuals at this time is often quiet, calm, and assured. If there is emotion, it is often compassion.

As the self moves into the **subtle** realm, its communing experiences frequently involve visions and illuminations. The rich sensory and ecstatic aspects of psychic level experiences fade away, however, and subtle experiences are more intuitive. The self begins to have brief moments of union with Spirit. Its moral embrace expands to include all sentient beings, whether incarnate or discarnate, which means a wide variety of spiritual beings or essences. Developing relationships with these beings becomes the primary focus of the self's spirituality. Wilber calls the mysticism experienced here Deity Mysticism and the path of saints. Working with deity, energies, angels, guides, and archetypal representations of them is the primary mystical goal of this developmental space.

Although it is our experience that the number of Pagans operating at this level is currently low, there is no reason Pagans cannot grow to this level. We think the lack of Pagans in this developmental space has more to do with the youth of

Paganism as a religious movement than the ability of Paganism as a belief system to lead people to this point. Pagans who reach this level will need to beware of delusions and hallucinations, and the appearance of deeply repressed issues. A good counselor or spiritual advisor may be able to help with this process. Wilber also recommends working with tantric yoga as a way to keep balanced and energetically healthy at this stage. We agree, since it seems to us that a lot of repressed material focuses on sex and the body, and tantra deals directly with both as a means to illumination.

The self which progresses to the **causal** level will find itself letting go of all the concepts of deity and spirit it developed in the previous level. The type of mysticism experienced here is described by Wilber as Formless. Images are abandoned. The moral embrace expands to include all manifest and unmanifest reality. Pagans working with communing at this level will be delving into those spiritual relationships we describe as relating to consciousness in whatever form, including multidimensional and unmanifest realms, proceeding right to the ground of consciousness. An awareness that everything is the Ground, Wilber tells us, eventually leads the self to the **nondual** developmental space. If a Pagan at these levels becomes overly attached to his or her experiences of formlessness, and overly detached from the world, then he or she needs to be encouraged to get re-involved in the world and be active in some form of service to others.

In this survey of developmental sequences relating to the magickal skill of communing, we have outlined how Pagans might progress in their development of spiritual relationships, beginning with those focused primarily on the self and moving on to those focused on a deity or other powerful authority figure, then the physical world, and finally to all of consciousness, manifest and unmanifest reality. This brief discussion highlights the fact that Pagans can and should expect to experience a wide variety of spiritual relationships throughout their lives, as their spirituality grows and deepens.

questions to discuss

1. What view of spiritual relationship and exchange were you raised with? How do you feel about Paganism's views?

2. What kinds of spiritual relationships feed you now? What fed you in the past? What do you think is responsible for the change?

3. Does Paganism emphasize the building of spiritual relationships sufficiently? If so, why and how? If not, what more do you think it should be doing?

4. What developmental issues have you faced in regard to communing? To the west and water? Are you facing any now?

5. Have you observed others struggling with developmental issues relating to communing? What did they do to try and resolve them?

visualization

Communing and the Labyrinth

Get in a comfortable position. If you are sitting, put your feet flat on the floor. If you are lying down, put your arms down beside you and your legs out straight. Close your eyes . . . slow your breathing . . . breathe in . . . breathe out . . . relax your muscles . . . breathe in . . . breathe out . . . feel the tension leave your neck and back . . . breathe in . . . breathe out . . . relax all the little muscles around your eyes . . . relax your spine . . . your legs . . . your feet . . . your hands and arms . . . keep breathing slowly. [*longer pause*]

You feel yourself becoming lighter and lighter . . . you are so light you can float right over to the window of this room [*adjust for your setting*] . . . open the window and look outside . . . waiting for you just outside the window is a large carpet that can take you anywhere . . . see yourself floating right out of the window and onto the carpet. . . .

When you are comfortable, the carpet begins to fly away . . . away from where you began this meditation, over the houses and away from your neighborhood [*adjust to your setting*] . . . it is taking you to your labyrinth, the one you walked before . . . you see the forest approaching . . . then the clearing among the trees. . . . The carpet enters the clearing and sets you down at the beginning of the labyrinth. . . . You step off the carpet, which will be waiting for you when you are finished. . . . As you enter the beginning of the labyrinth you notice that the hedges have grown since your last visit . . . they are as high as your head now and you cannot see over them . . . but you remember that this labyrinth is not a maze, there are no dead ends and no wrong turns . . . there is only one path in and one path out and the hedges will guide you. . . .

As you enter the labyrinth, you notice that two rows of hedges form the walls between which you walk . . . you walk deeper into the labyrinth and the path stretches out ahead . . . in this journey through the labyrinth you will acknowledge your growth in the skills of communing, the ability to listen to inner guidance, and to form spiritual relationships . . . you will meet with the Keeper of Water, who has a gift or bit of advice which you need. . . . The labyrinth soon begins to turn . . . as it turns it opens into a small clearing . . . in the center of the clearing is a fountain, made from the most beautiful alabaster . . . water pours out of the fountain into a small pool filled with cream colored stones . . . Walk up to the pool of water and look into it. . . . There you see yourself as an infant . . . this was a time of trust and dependency, when your expectations of relationship and mutuality began to form . . . let this time of your life speak to you. . . . What does it say? [*longer pause*] Before you leave this space, offer a blessing to this period of your life, to yourself as an infant, and to all those who cared for you. [*longer pause*]

You begin to walk again, down the path . . . soon the labyrinth begins to turn . . . as it turns it opens into a small clearing . . . in the center of the clearing is another fountain, made of amethyst . . . water pours out of the fountain into a small pool filled with purple stones. . . . Walk up to the pool of water and look into it. . . . There you see yourself no longer as an infant, but a toddler and preschooler, busy exploring your world . . . it is full of mysterious forces . . . love and belonging are important to you and you know you are part of a family unit . . . let this time of your life speak to you about what relationship means . . . and how you related to the mysterious forces in the universe. . . . What did you learn during this time about spiritual relationships that is still with you today? [*longer pause*] Before you leave this space, express gratitude for the development you experienced here . . . and bless the part of yourself you have brought with you from this space. . . .

You begin to walk again . . . the path stretches out before you . . . soon you approach another turn . . . as you turn the labyrinth opens into a small clearing . . . in the center of the clearing is a fountain, cut from the reddest rubies . . . water pours out of the fountain into a small pool filled with dark red stones. . . . Walk up to the pool of water and look into it. . . . There you see that you are no longer a preschooler, you are a youth . . . you have begun school and you are impulsive and head-strong . . . you have no real sense of danger or caution, and you love adventures . . . you like powerful cartoon characters, as power of all kinds intrigues you . . . you like stories and playing out stories . . . let this period of your life speak to you. . . . What was prayer to you then? . . . How did you visualize what you prayed to? . . . What kind of powers did spiritual forces have? . . . What relationship did you have with them and what were your expectations of them? [*longer pause*] What did you learn during this time about spiritual relationships that is still with you today? [*longer pause*] Before you leave this space, express gratitude for the development you experienced here . . . and bless the part of yourself you have brought with you from this space. . . .

You begin to walk again . . . soon the labyrinth begins to turn . . . as it turns it opens into a small clearing . . . in the center of the clearing is a fountain made of sapphires . . . water pours out of the fountain into a small pool filled with blue and lapis stones. . . . Walk up to the pool of water and look into it. . . . There you see that you are about to enter adolescence . . . fairness is important to you . . . the roles you and others play matter . . . you want to rely on the world to run predictably . . .

you are beginning to think through the reasons for things and you want the world to make sense. . . . Spiritual forces feel like friends to you. . . . Let this time of your life speak to you. . . . What was your relationship to spirit? [*longer pause*] Did you have any experiences with water or the west? . . . Did the concept of flow mean anything to you? . . . What did you learn during this period about spiritual relationships that is still with you today? [*longer pause*] Before you leave this space, express gratitude for the development you experienced here . . . and bless the part of yourself you have brought with you from this space. . . .

You continue to walk the labyrinth, down the path . . . soon it begins to turn and as it does it opens into a small clearing . . . in the center of the clearing is a fountain made from tiger eye . . . water pours out of the fountain into a small pool filled with orange stones. . . . Walk up to the pool of water and look into it. . . . There you see yourself as a young adult. . . . You are ready to leave home and the restrictions of childhood . . . you want to be independent and challenge the rules a bit, maybe leave your mark. . . . You may feel that you don't have a lot of time for relationships at the moment. . . . Let this time of your life speak to you. . . . What was prayer to you then? . . . How did you conceive of spiritual forces? . . . What relationship did you have with them and what were your expectations? [*longer pause*] Did you have any experiences with water or the west? . . . Where did you experience flow in your life and where did you experience resistance? . . . What did you learn during this period about spiritual relationships and communing that is still with you today? [*longer pause*] Before leaving, express thanks for the development you experienced here and may still be experiencing . . . bless the part of yourself you have brought with you from this space. . . .

There is only one turn left in the labyrinth, and you walk toward it. . . . As you make the turn, a clearing opens before you . . . in the center of the clearing is a fountain made of malachite . . . water pours out of the fountain into a small pool filled with green stones. . . . Walk up to the pool of water and look into it. . . . As you continue to grow in your life, community becomes important to you . . . teamwork matters, as does the fair distribution and use of resources . . . you care about the earth . . . injustice deeply disturbs you. . . . You want to express how you feel and you want to give others room to express themselves. . . . Let the green part of you, whether present, past or future, speak to you about spiritual relationships. . . . What are your expectations for these relationships? [*longer pause*] Have you had any experiences with water or the west? . . . Where do you experience flow in your life and where do you experience resistance? . . . What have you learned about communing from this period of development that affects you now? [*longer pause*] Before leaving, express thanks for the development you experienced or are still experiencing in this space. . . .

You are now at the end of the labyrinth . . . waiting for you at the end of the path is the Keeper of Water . . . she stands in a stream that flows across the exit of the labyrinth . . . she wants to speak to you about spiritual relationships . . . how you commune with the world, yourself, the universe, and the Divine. . . . She wants to talk to you about that place where you and the Divine intersect. . . . She has things to say about where you flow in your life and where you resist. . . . Listen to her. [*longer pause*] Ask her questions if you wish. [*long pause*] When your conversation is near an end, the Keeper of Water tells you that to leave the labyrinth you must walk through the stream of water, and she steps aside to let you pass . . . she tells you that when you walk through the water she will give you a gift . . . it could be a message, a promise, a challenge, or the opportunity to develop a skill . . . whatever it is, it is something that you need right now in your growth in communing and your relationship with flow. . . . Walk through the stream . . . as you do, the Keeper of Water tells you what gift she is giving you. . . . What is it? [*longer pause*] Thank the Keeper of Water and say whatever more needs to be said between you, if anything. . . .

You then turn and leave the labyrinth behind you, and ahead see the carpet waiting to take you home. . . . You step onto the carpet and sit down, and it slowly begins to lift and fly away. . . . You bid farewell to the labyrinth . . you will return to it again. . . . As you sit on the carpet, you think about your experience in the labyrinth. . . . What parts stand out in your mind that made an impression on you? [*longer pause*] Can you observe how your ideas and experience of spiritual relationships has changed throughout your life? . . . How have they changed? [*longer pause*] What do you expect from those relationships now as compared to earlier? [*longer pause*] What do you believe now about prayer and communing, as compared to earlier times in your life? [*longer pause*] How do you feel about your encounter with the Keeper of Water? . . . What do you want to do with what she gave you? [*longer pause*]

The carpet is carrying you back toward the city where you began your journey [*adjust for your setting*] . . . you see the buildings ahead of you, the houses around where you sit, and finally this building. . . . The carpet brings you to the window where you started . . . you step off the carpet and float back in the window, across the room, and to yourself where you are now sitting or lying. . . . Feel yourself come back into your body and take a deep breath . . . move your fingers and toes and stretch a bit . . . take another deep breath . . . and when you are ready, open your eyes.

If you are leading a group in this visualization, be sure everyone is back and then encourage those who wish to share their experiences, including their conversation with the Keeper of Water and what they received from her. Be sure to stress that no genuine spiritual encounter will ever ask them to do anything dangerous, harmful, disrespectful to self or others, or anything that is unethical. Occasionally students will be disturbed by their encounters, which is often due to their own issues surfacing and overlaying the experience. If this should happen, help them as best you can in the moment and then encourage them to seek counseling, as whatever needs addressing will continue to surface until they process it. This is not something you as a friend, teacher, or group leader should attempt to do; instead encourage the student to seek out a professional therapeutic environment.

Blessing Ritual

Pick a space you can dedicate for use as an altar, preferably one that can be left undisturbed as you work through the rest of the book. Each blessing ritual in the last four chapters focuses on the quadrant, direction, element, and type of magick discussed in that chapter, as well as what you experience in the labyrinth.

Arrange your altar space so that it is pleasing to you, decorating it however you wish, and leaving room for items to be put in each of the quadrants. We recommend that you place the drawing of the labyrinth or spiral you created in chapter 3 where you can see it during the ritual, perhaps hanging or leaning on a nearby wall. You may also wish to have your journal nearby during the ritual, as it is a written record of your hopes, fears, and experiences with spiritual development. You will need a candle for each of the four directions, and in the last ritual, one for the center as well. Also have your knotwork cord at hand. For this ritual you will need a small bowl of water. You will also need to find or make items that represent your experience in the labyrinth, if you so choose. You may wish to draw a picture of the Keeper of Water, make an abstract painting of emotions you felt as you traveled the labyrinth, or create a collage that represents the experiences you've had with communing, for example. If the Keeper of Water gave you an object as a gift, find a similar object if you can or create a representation of it. If she gave you a quality or ability, create a symbol of it and place this symbol in the western quadrant. You may play music softly during the ritual if you choose, especially if you have a tape of water or other sounds that remind you of the west. You may also set the mood with incense and lowered lighting if you wish.

Place one candle in the western or upper left quadrant. The other candles do not need to be on the altar at this time. Put the bowl of water in the west, and all the items you found or made that represent your experiences with this element and in the labyrinth.

When you are ready, take several minutes to relax and cleanse your mind. Breathe deeply. Deliberately tense and relax your muscles beginning with your feet, moving upward through your body, breathing slowly and deeply the entire time. Sit and listen quietly for a while. When you feel you are ready, you may cast a circle, call the directions, and ask your concept of the Divine to be present if you wish and if it is part of your spiritual practice. Light the candle in the western quadrant, and if you have not already done so, invite the energies of water and the west, of spiritual communion and your deep, private inner self to be present for your ritual. If you wish, also invite the Keeper of Water from the labyrinth.

Then take your knotwork cord and acknowledge the you that it represents at this time. You may say something like "this is my self, my body, mind, emotions, and spirit. This is who I am here and now as I continue in my journey of self-discovery and spiritual growth." Sprinkle water from the bowl onto the cord and place it in the western quadrant. Take a few moments and acknowledge the self you bring to your work with communing, and your relationships with water and the west. Dip your fingers again into the bowl of water and bless yourself as you wish—perhaps on each of your chakra points—and as you do say words which honor the intuitive, emotional parts of you, the inner, private experience of consciousness you enjoy, the parts of you which flow and merge.

Then bless each of the items you placed in the western quadrant with water from the bowl, and as you do describe aloud what the item means to you. Why is it on your altar? What challenge, gift, or ability does it represent and what do you think you are to do with it? How do these things relate to your goal of spiritual growth, and the experiences you have had in your life that have brought you to where you are now?

Express aloud the value of this quadrant's gifts to you, how it helps you commune spiritually, and how you wish to continue to grow in this communion. Give thanks to the deities you honor, to the vast ground of potentiality, to all the creativity and vitality in the universe, and to all other consciousnesses that support you in your journey and your growth in communing. Bless them and your growing relationships with them.

When you are finished, sit quietly for several minutes and be present to the feelings and thoughts this ritual has raised for you. Give yourself five or ten minutes. When you feel ready to end the ritual, thank the west, the element of water, the Keeper of Water (if invited), and dismiss the directions and deities you invoked, if any, according to your tradition. Blow out the candle in the west but leave it and the items on your altar if possible. Let their presence there remind you of your gratitude for the gifts of this quadrant and your work in deepening your spiritual relationships in communing.

Checking in with Your Magickal Plan

Take a look at your magickal plan for the year. What parts of it relate to communing? How have you incorporated prayer, meditation, spiritual relationships, the west, water, and the principle of flow? If your plan does not contain many of these aspects, why do you think that is so? Is communing something you want to work on this year, and to what extent? Feel free to adjust your plan as you wish to integrate more aspects of communing into it, but again, don't try to do too much at once. Rather than make sweeping changes, look to see if your existing goals can have more elements of prayer and meditation added to them. Do your goals involve the forming or strengthening of spiritual relationships, and if so, in what ways and with which ones? Make a note on your plan or in your journal about any thoughts you have concerning your spiritual development and communing.

5

Energy Work

THE SECOND TYPE OF magickal practice we identify is *energy work*. Its focus is the sensing and directing of energies for various purposes. Where energies are seen as "coming from" will likely depend on the type of spiritual relationships an individual develops. As discussed in the previous chapter, these relationships may involve the physical world, the self, all realms of consciousness, and the Divine.

The most personal source of energies is of course yourself. Energies of the self include thought, emotion, desire, intention, and memories, as well as electromagnetic forces, chi, chakras, and auras. Pagans may focus on their own or another's internal energy state and work on mental and emotional issues, empowerment, self-esteem, grief, and healing. They may focus on their own or another's physical well-being, and do energy work to facilitate healing from accident, illness, or other trauma. In some instances, Pagans sense the thoughts and emotions of others and interact with them for a specific purpose. Some Pagans are able to sense auras and the state of another person's health based on body energies.

Another source of energy with which Pagans interact is that of the physical world. This type of energy can sometimes be measured, as in the case of kinesthetic, gravitational, electromagnetic, and strong and weak nuclear forces. When Pagans refer to energies of the "earth" and "sky," or energies they sense in storms, tides, migrations of animals, moon cycles, and so on, they are usually blending a description of actual physical forces with an archetypal concept. Examples of archetypal energies include the Four Directions and the Four Elements, each of which we are examining in turn as we go through Wilber's four quadrants.

Energies may also be perceived as arising from all of consciousness. These energies may be experienced as the collective unconscious, macro-patterns of development—as in morphogenetic fields—and also thoughts, emotions, will and intention, when they arise from cooperative and large-scale events. There may be a sense of groupings of consciousness that form combinations of energy for various purposes.

Finally, energy can be perceived as arising from one's concept of the Divine and spirit beings. Such energy workings might involve the laying on of hands, shamanic journeys, the assistance of angels, spirits, the Holy Spirit, archetypal currents (such as the Trickster, Great Mother, or Wise Woman archetypes found in many cultures), devas, deities, faeries, elementals, ancestors, guardians of the directions, prophets, and saints.

As we noted above, these sources of energy correspond to the types of spiritual relationships Pagans are open to developing. Again, not all religions permit the recognition of each of these types of energies, or believe they are appropriate for spiritual working. Some may argue they don't exist at all, or if they do, have nothing to do with spirituality. Others may declare all energies evil except those which emanate from a specific deity, and limit humans to certain interactions with it. Most Pagans we know believe that energies are essentially neutral, and that "goodness" or "badness" is not found in the energy but in the intentions of the person working with it.

 exercise

Sensing Energy

This is an exercise you can fit into your daily routine. Choose a day in which you decide to be more consciously aware of the energies around you, preferably a day you are not rushed or overwhelmed. If you find your day becoming more hectic than you expected, and you cannot give time to this exercise, simply try again another time.

As your day begins, take a few moments to breathe deeply and calmly, and say, "Today I open myself to noticing the energies around me." You might write this phrase on a notepad and keep it near you during the day as a reminder. Begin by taking a few minutes to go outside, if possible, and notice the weather, the light, and the feeling of the day. If you travel to work, take your time as you go to your car or the bus stop, and notice the energies of the world around you. Is the wind blowing through the trees, has snow covered the ground, can you hear birds, children, traffic? Take a moment to breathe it in and notice how it feels.

If you work in a city, notice its energies as you arrive. Slow your walking if you can and notice how the concrete feels beneath your feet. Briefly touch the stone, glass, wood, or brick of the place you work. All of these materials came from natural sources and were shaped by human design. Can you feel the energies of the materials or of the people who fashioned them?

Once or twice during the day, take a moment to notice the energies of the people and places around you. As you return home, go for a brief walk and sense the energy of your own neighborhood and house. Connect with the grass, trees, and wind in your own backyard. End by breathing slowly and deeply for several minutes and acknowledge the things you experienced throughout the day. Get out your journal if you wish, and record your impressions.

Some people are very sensitive to energies and can feel overwhelmed by them quickly. Keep in mind that you are completely in control of this exercise and you do not have to feel anything you don't want to feel. Imagine your energy sensor as a volume dial on your personal radio receiver. If someone's energy is too much for you, or a place feels overwhelming, turn down the volume. If it's still too much, turn the volume completely off. If you find you are "buzzing" too much from leftover energy or are having trouble turning the volume down, then end the exercise for now. You can come back to it another day and try again, remembering that you—not what you are sensing—are in control of how much you take in.

To rid yourself of excess energy, try having something to eat while imagining yourself standing in the shower while all the extra energy goes down the shower drain. You can also try taking a brisk walk, working out vigorously, having sex, lying flat on the floor or the ground, placing the palms of your hands on the floor or ground, drumming, or dancing. If you continue to have difficulties with regulating your energy, talk to a teacher or healer who has experience in these matters, and build your skills gradually.

Opening to Energy

The goal of energy work is the sensing and directing of energies for a particular magickal purpose. The process of opening to this type of magick involves learning how to sense energies, and then how to move and direct them.

Learning to sense energies begins with the desire to sense them while keeping an open mind. You will likely have many new and unfamiliar experiences as you begin developing your energy skills. You may not have a language or belief system currently in place that knows how to explain or categorize these experiences, so let go of the need to label for now and simply be present to your experiences as they occur.

Many people sense energies of one sort or another every day but discount what they are feeling. They may write their experiences off as the result of some external cause, like noise, fog, or lighting, or decide their energy experiences are just their imagination. Remember that from the Pagan perspective imagination is a powerful tool. In its broadest sense, imagination encompasses most internal events such as sensation, thought, emotion, desire, and even spiritual sentiments. As we saw in the last chapter, your interior experience occupies an entire quadrant of spirituality all by itself, and is a valid measurement of what is happening to you. Certainly it is not the only measurement, but resist the urge to dismiss your internal impressions, including your imagination.

Ways in which you might sense the energies of the body include seeing or feeling the flow of energy, as with chakras and auras. You may sense the flow of energy through physical sensation, such as tingling, warmth, lightness, heaviness, blockage, or pressure. You may hear other people's thoughts or get a strong impression of their emotions and intentions. Concerning energies of the physical world, you may have impressions or physical sensations about a place or thing. Upon touching an object belonging to someone else, you may see images, smell odors, or feel emotions. Perhaps you get strong impressions during storms or certain cycles of the moon, or you may have a sense of being able to communicate with animals and the natural world. Concerning energies from all of consciousness, you may be able to sense stirrings in the collective unconscious, the building of patterns and probabilities, and the unfolding of individual and large-scale events. You might encounter groupings of consciousness, or encounter yourself in other probabilities. Regarding energies of the Divine, you may discover you sense spirit beings, guides, angels, devas, or faeries. You may get strong impressions of the presence of deities, archetypal figures, or various spiritual currents.

A good place to begin to practice the sensing of energies is with yourself. Take some time to listen to your body, thoughts, and feelings whenever you have a few moments. Learn about your body's energy centers and do the exercises in this chapter. You might wish to take some classes or workshops on chakras, energy meridians, chi, or energy medicine. There are many books on these topics that you may find helpful. Attend rituals featuring energy work as their primary purpose, or where it plays a prominent role. Because the sensing of energy is so experiential, you cannot fully taste it without experiencing it. We think it is worth your time to look for a teacher or class that can give you some hands-on experience and a chance for feedback.

questions to discuss

1. How do you define energy?

2. How would you explain energy work to a non-Pagan?

3. Have you had any notable energy experiences? What were they and what happened?

4. What kinds of energies do you sense easily? Are there some kinds of energies you do not sense at all or only with difficulty?

5. What personal and spiritual value does energy work have for you, if any? Why?

exercise

The Past and Future You

You may do this exercise either indoors or out of doors, but choose a place that is fairly quiet and where you will not be disturbed for twenty minutes or so.

In the first part of the exercise you will be sending energy to yourself in the past during a difficult time of your life. It is not our intention for this exercise to be upsetting. If a particular experience from your past is too traumatic to hold in your mind, even lightly, then choose another one not as painful.

Feel free to light candles and play music during the exercise if you wish. Turn down the lights if you like. Get in a comfortable position, one which you can maintain until the exercise is finished. Close your eyes and breathe deeply for several minutes. Gradually begin to imagine that as you breathe in, energy from the greater universe is streaming into you. It comes into your body through your feet, and also through your head, flowing up from below and down from above until it meets in your chest. As you breathe out, exhale all this energy from your chest and into the room, sending your tension, cares and concerns with it. As you breathe it out, this energy settles onto the floor like faery dust, and then dissolves back into the ground. Meanwhile, breathe in another breath that pulls fresh, clean energy into you from above and below, from earth and sky together, and then breathe it out again, releasing all that you want to rid yourself of. Continue breathing in this manner for several minutes, until you feel calm and refreshed.

Now turn your attention to a time in your past that was difficult for you. Picture yourself as you were then, remember how you felt, what concerned you, and what happened. You are only observing yourself as you were then. You are not that person anymore; you are removed from the situation now and can view it with dispassion. If this event or period is extremely distressing, be very gentle in your approach to it. Get no closer than you feel comfortable. If you are in therapy or under a doctor's care for this incident, do not choose it as the event for this exercise without their permission and supervision.

Holding the image of this "past you" in your mind, breathe in the clean pure energy of earth and sky, and with each out-breath send love, support, strength, forgiveness, and courage to your self in the past. See the energy you are sending gather around the past you as a cloud or shield, which stays with you throughout your ordeal. Continue sending energy for five minutes or so. When you feel ready, let the past you acknowledge your presence and the energy and support you are sending it. If there is something you want to say to each other, share it now.

Let the image of yourself in the past fade, and begin to imagine yourself at some point in the future. This is a time that will again be challenging for you. You don't know the nature of this challenge now, and you don't know when it will happen, but you know that some day you may find yourself in such a situation. Create a picture of yourself in the future—it doesn't have to be specific, or show you at a certain age or living in a certain place. It can be a vague sense of self without shape or form.

Hold this sense of yourself in your mind, and on your next in-breath inhale the bright, vibrant energies of the earth and sky, and mingle them in your heart. As you breathe out, exhale them to this future you. Send this energy along with thoughts of love, support, and courage to yourself. See the energy building up around you, perhaps as a cloud or shield, as a source of strength and comfort you can draw on. Continue sending energy in this way for five minutes or so. Then let the image of the future you acknowledge your presence and thank you for your loving support of it. If there is anything you want to say to each other, share it now.

Let the image of your future self gradually fade and bring your attention back to your surroundings. Begin to let go of pulling energy into your body with each breath, until you are breathing normally again. See any excess energy flowing out of your body and into the floor. Bring your focus completely back to yourself, stretch your muscles, and open your eyes.

You can repeat this exercise from time to time as you feel moved to do so. You can focus on yourself at different times in the past, in the future, or a combination of both. You can also do this exercise for the benefit of other people individually or as members of a group. They can be people you know or people you've never met, such as historical figures who faced momentous decisions, or groups who went through tragedies or other experiences together. We suggest that whenever you send energy to others in this manner not to force its acceptance. Simply offer the energy as a gift and leave it there in case it is wanted. Remember that for many Pagans the outer physical world is only the tip of the iceberg that is reality, and that the universe unfolds from deeper levels. These levels are outside of space and time and not limited by them. Therefore it is possible at these deeper levels to send energy to the past or future, since they and the present moment exist together simultaneously.

my journal

I think energy is . . .

Energy work is or is not important to me spiritually because . . .

Three beliefs I held about energy growing up were . . .

Three beliefs I have now are . . .

Directing Energy

Opening to the sensing of energy is the first step in developing skills with energy work. Learning to direct this energy for a particular purpose is the second. Both aspects frequently occur together, as the worker senses an energy and then begins to interact with it in a conscious fashion.

What we call the directing of energy actually involves a variety of skills including centering, raising, focusing, circulating, projecting, sending, clearing, shielding, blocking and unblocking, releasing, and grounding. Each of these skills may be used to a greater or lesser degree during any one working depending on the work being done, the needs of the situation, and the abilities of the energy worker. Most Pagans we know have at least a passing knowledge and some training in each of these energy skills. Some Pagans are not drawn to energy work as their primary spiritual or magickal practice, and so they may choose not to focus their development in this area. Others are quite skilled in one aspect of energy work or another. You will know if you are drawn to developing your energy skills as you grow spiritually. Even if you are not, we believe acquiring some basic skills will be of benefit to you since most Pagan rituals and practices have some aspect of energy work in them. The more energetically engaged you can be in these rituals and practices, the more meaningful they are likely to be for you.

Most energy work begins with the raising or calling up of energy. The source of the energy depends on which type of spiritual relationship you are working with— that is, the self, the physical world, the realm of manifest and unmanifest consciousness, or the Divine. Some Pagans always work with one type of energy or another, others with a variety. Some prefer to use energy they visualize as coming from the earth. Others are only comfortable using energy that comes from their concept of the Divine. Many non-Pagans certainly fit into this latter group, such as those who work only with Jesus, the Holy Spirit, or spirit guides. Energy can also be raised from multiple sources simultaneously. As an example, a Pagan may balance his or her chakras internally, "plug" into earth energies to keep the chakra flow going (to avoid the depletion of their personal energy), and then call upon a deity or spirit guide to assist them in their working. Types and sources of energy certainly are not mutually exclusive, and the use of sources often overlaps.

Centering refers to the process of placing the energy—from whatever source it is drawn—into a certain region of the worker's energy body. Most often the regions used are the chakra points or some part of the aura. Centering is a mental process, although it is frequently accompanied by distinct physical sensations and effects. Its general purpose is to bring the energy into a certain "frequency," or vibration, which in effect links it to certain types of intentions. Each of the chakras, for example, is associated with specific powers, abilities and vibratory energies. Centering one's energy in a particular chakra point is believed to flavor the energy with the attributes associated with it. Figure 5.1 features a diagram of the body's main chakra points.

The first, or root, chakra sits at the base of the spine and its color is red. Its vibration is considered to be long and slow, corresponding to the denseness of matter, and it connects you to your body and the physical world. The second chakra is orange and located near your sexual organs, and is associated with passion, fertility, impulses, and sexuality. The third chakra is located in the solar plexus and its color is yellow. It is associated with willpower, energy, ego, and personality. The fourth chakra is the heart chakra, and is sometimes described as green and other times as pink with gold. It is associated with love, selflessness, forgiveness, and nurturing. The fifth chakra is located in the throat, its color is blue, and it is associated with communication, self-expression, and self-esteem. The sixth chakra sits in the forehead between your eyebrows and is known as the "third eye." Its color is indigo, or purple with silver, and is associated with wisdom, as well as psychic and intuitive powers. The seventh and highest chakra sits above your head, and connects you to spirit and the energies of the universe. Its vibration is considered to be quite high and fine and its color is white.

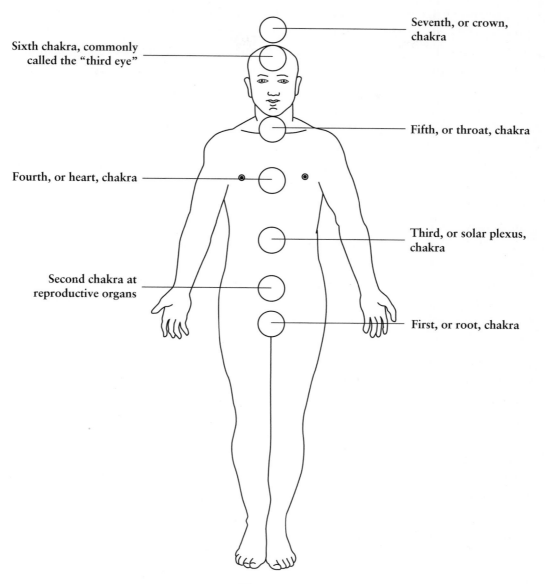

Sixth chakra, commonly
called the "third eye"

Seventh, or crown,
chakra

Fifth, or throat, chakra

Fourth, or heart, chakra

Third, or solar plexus,
chakra

Second chakra at
reproductive organs

First, or root, chakra

Figure 5.1
The Chakras

Energy work is most often centered in the heart chakra, as the intention of many energy workers is to approach their magick from a point of selfless compassion. Pagans often "center" themselves by first pulling physical or "earth" energies up through their feet, and then pulling down spirit or "sky" energies through the top of their head, mingling both through the entire body and resting with them in the heart chakra. It is often believed that mingling the energies in this way in the heart center leads to greater balance, which is why to many the expression "to be centered" is synonymous with "being balanced." Many Pagans view "earth" energy as feminine, and "sky" energy as masculine, and believe that centering and balancing these energies is one way to bring their masculine and feminine aspects into harmony.

Not all workings are done from the heart chakra. A person who wants to be more assertive, for example, and gain the courage to speak out may center their working in the throat chakra. A woman struggling with her sexuality or wanting to have a child may center energy in the sex chakra. We have met healers who center the majority of energy either in their heart or solar plexus chakras, but move large portions into their hands as they do healings. This not only serves to increase the sensitivity of their hands for sensing energy, but also helps them direct energy as needed during the working.

Once a working begins, energy can be moved and directed in a number of ways. It can be circulated among a group of people, an experience we hope you will try in the following exercise. It can be circulated through a room, person, or object in order to clear out something that needs to leave. It can be set as a shield around a person, room, or object in order to block unwanted energies from coming in. The casting of a circle at the beginning of many Pagan rituals is often done for this purpose. A bundle of energy can be focused in one spot and then projected to an intended receiver. This method is frequently used with long-distance healings or any working where a recipient asks that energy "be sent" to them. Sometimes energy can be focused into an object that is later used for a specific purpose. We have observed this done with stones and crystals for use in healings, and with ritual tools to attune them to specific energies, deities, or to the worker who will be using them. Such objects can also slowly radiate the energy out over a period of time for a given intention, as we have observed in the use of prayer feathers, talismans, dream catchers, and a prayer mandala sent to an abused women's shelter.

Those who work with deities and other spirit beings such as angels, saints, the Holy Spirit, or gods and goddesses, may see themselves in a more passive role in which they facilitate the receipt of energy emanating from the Divine source. They may also use prayer to ask that energy flow from the Divine to the recipient, or as a means of delivering the energy, as when prayer is used during a laying on of hands.

While energy workers often have desired results in mind for a given working, they usually do not specify details. Energy that is projected outward for a given purpose is frequently left to "do its thing" on its own, or be applied by those receiving it as they will. An energy working can have a discrete beginning and ending in time, or it can persist over an indefinite period of time. In either case, once the magickal work is done, the worker needs to release the energy and let it go to do what it's being sent to do. This takes trust, especially trust that the universe really is supportive, is listening, and is capable of responding. This is why the building of spiritual relationships we discussed in the previous chapter is so important, since trust generally increases as a relationship matures and deepens.

Part of the releasing process includes the worker grounding excess energy from his or her body. As the word suggests, grounding frequently involves visualizing the energy flowing back into the earth, usually down and out the lower chakras of the body. You may have noticed that most of our exercises have a grounding at the end of them. Whether an exercise has one or not, always ground if you feel you need it, even if some time has passed since you ended the exercise. Grounding can be effective at any time.

 exercise

Opening the Chakras

This exercise can be a lot of fun with a small group of people. If you can arrange for a few friends to join you, then do. It will be better if the group consists either of other Pagans or people who are familiar with, or open to, the concept of chakras and energy circulation. The first part of the exercise dealing with the opening of the chakras can be done alone or in a group. The second part, which focuses on the circulating of energy, requires a group.

A group doing this exercise should begin with several minutes of quiet, deep breathing. A member of the group can be chosen to lead the exercise. The group should then break into pairs. One person lies on the floor and the other person passes his or her hands above the reclining person's body. Their hands should be held one to two inches above the body and should not touch it. Moving from the head downward and then from the feet upward, the active person tries to sense the other's chakras. Can the active person feel each of them? Do any chakras feel blocked? Give this part of the exercise about three minutes, and then the partners should trade off. There should be no chatting or talking while the sensing is occurring. If the group is very small, say four people or less, then each person can lie down one at a time while all the others take turns sensing his or her energy. This part of the exercise will be repeated after the following meditation to see if the energy flow has changed in any way, and if others can detect it.

Opening the Chakras. Get in a comfortable position, either sitting or reclining, but one you can hold for about ten or fifteen minutes. Close your eyes and relax. Breathe slowly and deeply for a minute or so.

Now imagine that your body is a tube full of energy. The lines of energy crisscross your body from top to bottom and in places from side to side. In several areas a number of these lines intersect and create glowing balls or spheres of energy, known as the chakras. The lowest chakra is located at the base of your spine. It is a dense, slowly vibrating wheel of dark red energy. Take a moment and sense this energy center—how does it feel?

Now move upward to your lower abdomen, in the area of your sex organs. This is your second chakra, a slowly vibrating wheel of orange or red-orange energy. This is your center of passion and desire. Take a moment to sense this chakra—how does it feel? Move upward to your solar plexus, or third chakra. This energy center is less dense and vibrates more rapidly, and its color is yellow. It is your center of willpower and vitality. Take a moment to sense this chakra—how does it feel? Continue to move upward, to your heart. This is your fourth chakra, the heart chakra, a less dense, faster-vibrating wheel of green or pink-gold. It is your center of love, compassion, and selflessness. How does it feel energetically?

Further up is your fifth chakra, located in your throat. The energy here is much finer and the vibration much faster. The color of this chakra is sky-blue. It is the center of your self-expression and communication. Take a moment to sense this chakra—how does it feel? Moving up is your sixth chakra, which sits in the middle of your forehead between your eyes. It is known as the "third eye," and its energy is very fine and fast. Its color is indigo to purple, sometimes combined with silver. This chakra is the center of your psychic powers, intuition, and wisdom. How does it feel energetically? Lastly is your seventh chakra, found above the top of your head. Its energy is so rapid and fine you can barely sense it. The color associated with it is white, and it is the center of your spiritual self. Take a moment to sense its energy—how does it feel?

On your next several in-breaths, imagine that you are gathering the energy and vitality of life and the universe together and pulling it into yourself through your feet. Pull this energy up to your first chakra at the base of your spine, and let it gently expand. Let the first chakra spin freely and glow red brightly. Feel it pulse with energy and clear out any blockages. Do this for about thirty seconds and then take several more in-breaths that are full of the energy of the universe, and pull this energy on up to your second chakra. Let this chakra expand and open. Let it spin freely and its orange color glow brightly. Feel it pulse with energy and clear out any blockages.

After a short while, pull in more energy from the universe and lift it higher in your body, to your solar plexus. Feel this chakra open and expand and spin freely. See it glow bright yellow and pulse with energy. Clear out any blockages. With several more in-breaths, pull the energy from the universe up to your heart chakra. See a burst of green or pink-gold light as this chakra opens and expands. See it spin freely and grow brighter. Clear out any blockages. After several seconds, pull the energy yet higher, into your throat. Relax your throat, almost as if you are yawning, and feel the energy there spin freely. This chakra expands and glows a beautiful sky-blue. Clear out any blockages, and as you do, exhale a sound—a tone, a sigh, a groan, a scream. Do this several times.

Take a moment to pull more energy into yourself as you breathe it in, and move higher, to your third eye. Feel this chakra open and glow a deep purple streaked with silver. Feel your intuition and psychic abilities expand and be energized. Clear away any blockages. Take in a few more breaths and pull the energy clear up to your crown chakra, above the top of your head. Don't stop the flow of energy here, but let it continue to move right through the top of your head, through the chakra, and then cascade like a fountain back over your body. As this is happening, feel the crown chakra open and spin in dazzling white. Clear away any blockages.

Take a couple of minutes and enjoy the feeling of your chakras being open and full of the vitality you have breathed in. After a few minutes, gradually turn the energy fountain off and pull the energy back into your head. Let it slide down your body, past your throat, chest, stomach, spine, and hips. Your chakras relax and return to their normal size and energy as you reduce the extra flow. When the energy reaches the base of your spine let it flow on down your feet and into the ground. Continue this until you feel that all excess energy has been drained away. Then stretch and open your eyes.

If you are with a group, go with the same partner you had at the beginning and repeat the exercise of sensing the energy of your partner. Has anything changed in the energy flow since the chakras were opened? Compare notes and share your findings with the group.

Circulating Energy. This part of the exercise requires a group. It can be done immediately following the chakra-opening exercise as long as group members are not energetically tired. Members should sit together in a circle, in chairs or on the floor, close enough to link hands comfortably. One person in the group may lead with instructions.

Begin with a minute or two of slow and relaxed breathing. Gradually turn your attention to where you are sitting on the floor or chair. Imagine that your feet and legs are extending through the floor and into the earth, like long tree roots anchoring themselves into the soil. As your roots spread into the earth, feel the earth's energy around you and allow it to flow up your roots. Feel this energy rise up your roots and into your body, up your feet and legs, to the base of your spine, on up through your stomach, chest, and neck. Pull this energy through your throat and head. Then let it flow down your arms and into your hands. Imagine the energy pooling in your hands like little balls of light. Can you feel this energy in your hands? It may feel like heat, pressure, or tingling. Take a minute or two to sense this energy.

Then group members should join hands, and with a collective in-breath, pull energy up their roots, through their bodies, down their left arms and hands, and into the hand of the person next to them. As this is happening, they should allow energy to flow into their right hand from their other neighbor. The energy will come into their right hands, pass through their bodies and out their left hands. This can be timed with breathing, so that energy is pulled into the right hand on the inhale, and pushed out the left hand on the exhale. All the while, energy continues to flow upward through everyone's roots to feed the energy exchange.

Let the flow continue for five to ten minutes. The leader should alert the group when there is about a minute left, then ask that the flow of energy through the hands be stopped. The group should then release hands and let the energy drain out of their hands and back into their body. It should then flow down their body and out their legs and feet, into the roots. All remaining excess energy should be drained through the person's roots and back into the earth. Then pull the roots back into the body, and allow everyone's awareness to return to themselves and the room.

The group can then share its experience—did everyone feel energy circulating? What did it feel like? Was anyone not able to feel it?

Energy Work and the Four Elements

Looking again at Wilber's four quadrants, we place energy work in the lower left, which is the south and home to the element of fire.

The lower left quadrant is Wilber's realm of shared inner meanings, where individuals interact in a cultural or group context. In this quadrant the self's experience moves from one that is completely private, as found in the upper left, to one that is shared with others. Such experiences still cannot be seen by a microscope, weighed, measured, or built out of wood or stone, but they are real nonetheless. Energy work can be a connection between you and others that exists on the level of shared meaning, whether you are connecting in this reality or in unmanifest reality. Energy work marks the point where your internal thoughts, feelings, desires, intentions, and energies intersect with the intentions and energies of others and of the entire multidimensional cosmos. Justice, peace, love, support, forgiveness, and healing are deeply shared values even though they may occur only internally. This doesn't mean that energy experiences cannot have real world counterparts. Many times they do. When energy experiences cross into physical manifestation—as when healing energies result in a medical change—then you will find yourself on the right side of Wilber's quadrants, in the realm of outer effects. The inner and the outer, though able to stand independently, do not stand in isolation from each other. As we have noted earlier, none of the quadrants exists in a vacuum, and the healthiest spirituality is one that is able to integrate all of them.

In common Pagan practice, the south is an archetype for willpower, desire, creativity, and passion. Viewed on the wheel of the year, the south falls at the height of summer (in the Northern Hemisphere), when life is at its most abundant, productive, and fertile. The sun is at its strongest and the world feels lush and bursting with vitality. On the wheel of the day, south is represented by high noon. On the wheel of human life, it is the realm of full maturity, adulthood, and parenting. This is a busy and active time, not particularly reflective, but one which seeks to express itself.

Fire is the element usually associated with the south in Pagan practice because it is considered the element of power, will, intention, passion, sexuality, fertility, and creativity. As it burns, fire releases energies from its source that previously existed only as potential, an energy that lay dormant until hit by its spark. Fire is a

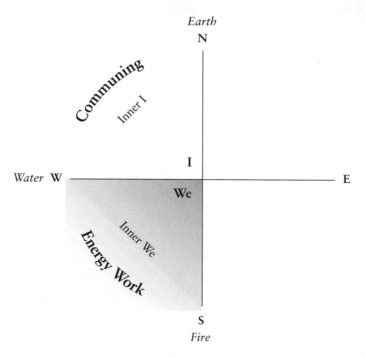

Earth

Figure 5.2
The Lower Left Quadrant: Energy Work, South, Inner We

very extroverted sort of element. It's not shy or quiet or hard to notice. It does its thing with a roar; its presence is clear for everyone to see. Fire is the element that illuminates and advances, transforming as it goes. Like the south, it is an archetype of passion, vitality, and power at its height.

Developing and deepening your skills in energy work can help you move toward the goal of *maximum healthiness* and *maximum expansion* in your spiritual development as it broadens the focus from "only me" to embrace the existence of "we." This also mirrors human development, as the infant moves from an awareness of itself to an awareness of others, and sees that it exists in the context of a family, culture, and society. This awareness provides the opportunity to take individual drives and intentions to a new level and express them in a shared context.

Connecting to That Which Empowers

This exercise focuses on experiencing power through the element of fire. You can do this exercise indoors or out of doors as you choose. The only requirement is to have a source of fire on hand, one that is appropriate for your setting. We prefer that you pick a place where you can comfortably sit or lie down and be surrounded by fire, as in a a circle of candles, torches, or lanterns. A campfire will do if you are out of doors and able to build one. Please be safety conscious in your use of fire, and be sure you have appropriate means at hand to extinguish it.

Prepare a meditative space before you begin. Feel free to include music, lighting, and incense. Arrange the torches or lanterns ahead of time and be sure they have fuel. Build the campfire in advance so that it is ready to light.

When everything is ready, take several minutes to sit and breathe slowly and deeply. Relax from your efforts in preparing a beautiful space. When you feel calm and open, take your matches or lighter and begin lighting the sources of fire you have chosen. As the wick catches for each candle or torch, pass your hand over the flame very quickly (do not burn yourself and watch out for long sleeves), and as you do so say "I open myself to what inspires and empowers me." When all have been lit, take several long, slow breaths and sit or lie down in your circle of fire, or before your campfire. Be positioned so that you can see some or all of the flames if you choose to keep your eyes open.

Continue to breathe deeply and slowly. Relax. Open yourself to the rhythm of your breathing, and gradually to the flickering of the flames. See how the flames arch up from the wick or firewood, reaching, striving. Feel the parts of you that reach and strive, that drive you to meet your desires, to take action, and to burn. What feeds your fire? What enflames you?

Meditate on how all things in the universe are vibrant and enlivened with an inner, radiant, creative fire. Look into the flames and connect with the flame of your own life. Can you feel the creative power of life at work within you? See how the fire consumes the wood, how the wick burns down and the wax drips. What are you willing to burn for, to use yourself up for? Stir the fire or blow lightly past a candle. Watch the flame dance and move and adapt while always staying connected to its source of fuel. The fire only lives as long as it stays centered in its point of power, its connection point. In what ways do you stay in your point of power no matter what happens to you, and in what ways do you let yourself get unconnected? What *is* your point of power? How do you balance your use of power?

Fire blazes forth from the sun above and churns restlessly in the deepest core of the earth. The two realms on which you are most dependent for life, the earth and sky, are alive with fire. In a sense, fire sustains this globe and allows life to flourish. It empowers the entire planet with itself. If it burns out and dies, life here dies. Too little and life ends; too much and life ends. The warmth and heat of life is a balance of power that fire strikes and holds. Sink deeper into this fiery element and let it speak to you. What has this element seen, what does it know, what is its wisdom? How does it speak to the powerful and hot places within you?

Allow yourself to become aware of all the things around you which burn, spend themselves, illuminate, and create. Feel the fire in your cells that burns up calories, the plants that absorb the power of the sun, the energy of anger, passion, sexuality, nuclear forces, fission and fusion, solar collectors, and lightning. Open yourself to this fiery, powerful energy, and know that it is a part of you even when you are not consciously aware of it. Absorb as much of this energy as you comfortably can and allow it to flow through you for several minutes. When you are ready, gradually bring your attention back to your surroundings. Express gratitude for your experience. Blow out the candles, extinguish the torches or campfire, and journal a bit if you wish. If you are doing this exercise with a group or class, spend a few minutes sharing.

The most memorable energy work experiences I have had are . . .

The impact they had on me was . . .

These experiences were or were not peak experiences because . . .

The parts of energy work I find most challenging are . . .

The parts I enjoy most are . . .

I would describe my relationship with the south as . . .

Experiences I have had with the south are . . .

My relationship with the element of fire is . . .

Experiences I have had with the element of fire are . . .

Energy Work in Developmental Space

As with communing, energy work is going to be experienced in different ways that are dependent on the developmental perspective of the person working with it. The sensing and directing of energy and the purposes for which it is used will take different forms depending on the developmental space the energy worker occupies. As a reminder, each level of growth brings new capacities to the individual, new gifts, and new perspectives. We do not want our discussion of "stuck" aspects of different spaces to leave you with the impression that certain ones have only negative qualities. Indeed, each developmental space has its healthy aspects which Pagans can and should bring forward with them as they continue in their growth.

Energy work done by the **egocentric** self (Purple-Red), will be filled with a sense of awe and wonder, and perhaps a bit of fear of the spirit beings that are believed to be in control and the source of energy used in energy work. The role of the energy worker is to determine what the will of these spirits and beings is, and to appease and satisfy them through the use of elaborate rituals, words, and gestures. An energy worker who lives in a Purple-Red society and is successful at doing this will be viewed as very powerful. This adds to the worker's sense of narcissism that is normal for this level.

The moral embrace of the egocentric self extends only to itself and perhaps its immediate circle. Energy work will be viewed as ethical if it favorably impacts one's self and immediate group, and assists in a right relationship with the spirits and beings acknowledged by the group. Adult Pagans who get "stuck" at this level, permanently or temporarily, live in a world in which they are the center of power. Their energy experiences can be quite dramatic, featuring great cosmic battles between themselves and evil beings, or the forces of life and death. By way of example, a Pagan once told us about her child who was taken to the emergency room for strep throat, and while waiting in the emergency room "died four times" before the doctor could see her. Luckily our storyteller was there, and through her astounding healing powers brought this child back to life all four times. Strangely, no one else in the emergency room noticed this was happening (we asked). In another instance, some Pagans interrupted a dinner party they were hosting to exorcise a demon from one of the dinner guests, naturally accomplished with many dramatic words and gestures offered in front of their captive audience.

If you are in a teaching or leadership position when flamboyant Purple-Red appears, approach the situation calmly and rationally. Stop the narcissistic activity at once, dispel the high emotions and anxiety that are frequently generated, and do a simple energetic exercise that is positive and affirming. This will help everyone calm down, get back in touch with their rational adult, and rebuild a sense of trust in a safe universe.

Healthy aspects of the egocentric self that all energy workers can bring along with them in their development include that important sense of awe and wonder, a love of ritual, tools, garb, and ceremony, a dash of drama, and a large, healthy dose of self-confidence.

For the **mythic** self (Red-Blue), energy work will follow set customs and formulae, with participants playing very specific parts. These roles and customs will be set out specifically in the prevailing mythology which the mythic self adopts wholeheartedly. Most likely, the mythology is a continuation of the stories that concern the spirits and beings experienced at the egocentric level, now codified in a more rigid structure or story. The source of energy will likely be attributed to these spirits and beings, since the mythology generally teaches that they are all-powerful. Energies from other sources, including beings and spirits of other mythologies, will be seen as false or dangerous. Energies will be experienced in precise ways and under approved circumstances. If approved energy work is not done just so, then the spirits and beings may not respond and the magickal work may fail. As the mythic self continues to develop it will gradually let go of its need for this degree of structure and order and its reliance on authority figures, and gain new perspectives on prevailing myths.

The moral embrace of the mythic self expands from itself to include its ethnic group or country, if the country shares its mythological view. Energy work done by mythic Pagans will be viewed as ethical as long as it helps preserve the group and the supremacy of its mythology. Pagans who get stuck at this level may suffer from guilt and anxiety as they try to live up to the demands of their powerful Others. Their energy experiences are usually quite orthodox and structured. They may become rigid in their beliefs about the "right" way to do a healing, or to raise energy, or project it, and not be willing or able to tolerate any other views. Such a Pagan may cause a great deal of tension during a group working and make harsh judgmental statements about the work to be done and the people doing it. We have seen Pagans walk out of rituals and energy workings if the structure varied from their standards of orthodoxy, and who had tantrums during workings because someone inadvertently touched a ritual tool at the wrong time, or otherwise committed an "error." If you are in a teaching or leadership position when rigid Blue makes an appearance, try to minimize the impact on others, encourage an attitude of cooperation and tolerance for the duration of the working, or suggest a compromise that partially accommodates the mythic Pagan, such as letting them be responsible for the part of the working that is causing them the most discomfort. Processing what happened when the work is done can be helpful also, since if the mythic Pagan can hear how and why the experience was meaningful for others, he or she may begin to open to the idea that other approaches are also effective.

Healthy aspects of the mythic self that all energy workers can bring along with them in their development include respect for authority and rules of conduct for groups and festivals, a love of myth and stories, customs, and the enjoyment of playing roles in ritual.

If all prior developmental transitions are made successfully, the **rational** self (Orange) will emerge by young adulthood. The rational self subjects all its prior beliefs to the scrutiny of reason and abandons those it cannot reconcile. The moral embrace of the rational self is still ethnocentric but leaning toward world-centric, so the rational Pagan may begin to view energy work in a broader context. Energy work will tend to be viewed as ethical if it makes rational sense and positively affects one's society. Rational energy workers may be experimental and creative in their ritual work and be very interested in the practical effects of what they are doing. They may want a rationale to explain why magick and energy work make sense and are effective. They may be unsure of what the source of energy is, as they are beginning to separate from a complete reliance on mythology but do not yet have anything with which to replace it. A solid philosophical base for their magickal practice becomes practically a necessity at this point.

Pagans who get stuck at the rational level live in a world that has lost much of the emotional richness they felt at earlier levels and they are left in a dry world of their mental creations. No mythology may hold meaning for them anymore, so energy work that is set in any mythological context may be painful and hollow to them. Their dissatisfaction can lead them to be argumentative and cynical, criticizing any form of energy work a group wants to do. If you are in a teaching or leadership position, encourage such Pagans to participate in the working and ask for their input on what might make it a more meaningful experience for them. They may surprise you and themselves with the suggestions they come up with; most likely they will break with any mythological base at all, but if it's a sound idea, incorporate it into the working.

Healthy aspects of the rational self that all energy workers would do well to integrate include its skills of mental evaluation and processing, debate and questioning, and its strong emphasis on personal responsibility and self-reliance.

Energy work done by the **vision-logic** self (Green) will be increasingly concerned about the feelings of those both sending and receiving energy, and the fairness of its effects. Vision-logic energy workers look to their own internal set of ethics, rather than external authority, to determine the rightness of their workings. The moral embrace of the vision-logic Pagan expands to include all humans on the planet. Energy work at this level will be viewed as ethical as long as it fairly impacts all human beings. This expansion of perspective will likely bring with it an expansion in spiritual relationships. Energy work will not be seen as an exercise done exclusively with powerful spirit beings, but will begin to include one's inner self and collective groupings of consciousness. An awareness of being in spiritual relationship with the physical world will also begin to make an appearance.

Pagans who get stuck at this level, either permanently or temporarily, may feel confused and cynical. Confusion may result in paralysis as they do not know what decisions to make. After all, there are so many more perspectives to take into consideration now that they may feel frozen and not know what decisions are correct. Or such Pagans may become judgmental about points of view that do not match their own. We know Pagans who have refused to do energy work for someone who is involved in something they disapprove of, say an unpopular political party. We've also encountered Pagans who want every person to be so completely happy with every aspect of an energy working that hours are spent discussing each part of the ritual to the point that they became overwhelmed and no energy work occurs at all. If you are in a teaching or leadership position, do not let either judgmentalism or confusion take over a group. Gently bring the group back on-focus and offer suggestions that help move things forward, and remind the participants of tolerance and a global perspective.

Healthy aspects of the vision-logic self that all energy workers can benefit from include a sense of community and common values, consensus decision-making, and concern for humanity and the natural world.

The **psychic** self (Yellow-Turquoise) opens itself to psychic phenomena and other nonrational experiences which are frequently ecstatic, emotional, and sensual. Energy work done by the psychic self will likely also be ecstatic and powerful, with a truly global perspective and a sense that all things are one. Energy workers may be able to feel things happening at deep levels they've never experienced before. If they have not expanded their spiritual relationships to include the physical world, they will now. Their workings will expand to include the earth, animals, plants, ecosystems, physical matter, and phenomena such as weather, perhaps in a shamanic fashion.

The moral embrace of the psychic Pagan expands to all earthly beings, which includes animals and plants. Such Pagans move from only talking about interconnectedness to really feeling it and knowing it to be true, at least among all of physical reality. Energy experiences will call upon this new sense of interconnectedness and may frequently focus on it. Energy work will be considered ethical as long as it doesn't detrimentally affect living beings or the physical world. Psychic Pagans may get stuck in this phase if they become attached to the intensity and sensuality of the psychic realms. Staying grounded in the needs of the physical world can help avoid this tendency, as can doing energy work for very practical purposes, and in a simple fashion that avoids emotional excess.

Energy workings at the **subtle** level become more intuitive and lose their ecstatic punch. The subtle self may feel a union with the realm of Spirit that comes and goes. Its moral embrace now includes all sentient beings, including spirit beings. The subtle energy worker will likely be very attracted to working with spirit guides, saints, deities, and angels. Energy work will tend to be viewed as ethical as long as it does not detrimentally impact any being in the physical or spiritual realms. Visions can also be common, and the Pagan at this level needs to be careful of obsessing on these visions or allowing them to turn into hallucinations. A good counselor or spiritual advisor may be able to help with this discernment. Unresolved issues may pop up in these visions and be disturbing to the worker and others around them, and if so, should be addressed by a professional.

If a Pagan at the **causal** and **nondual** levels chooses to do energy work, it will likely be very fluid and formless. The worker may find him or herself more interested in the nature of the consciousness behind the energy than in the working, especially as the moral embrace expands to include all manifest and unmanifest reality. A Pagan may become overly detached. If this begins to happen, he or she needs to be encouraged to stay involved in the world and active in some form of service.

In this section we have briefly outlined how Pagans might progress in their development with energy work through each of the developmental sequences. As energy workers grow from being focused primarily on their selves, families, and groups, they have the potential to expand their scope and abilities until energy work embraces all of physical reality, the Divine, and manifest and unmanifest reality.

questions to discuss

1. What view of energy and energy work were you raised with? What do you believe about it now?

2. Does energy work feed you spiritually? Why or why not?

3. Do you think Paganism does enough with energy training? What aspects would you like to see improved?

4. Does Paganism do enough with energy work in its rituals and other practices? If not, what more would you like to see done?

5. What developmental issues have you faced in regard to energy work? With the south and fire? Are you facing any now?

6. Have you known anyone who has struggled with developmental issues in regard to energy work? What happened?

visualization

Energy Work and the Labyrinth

Get in a comfortable position. If you are sitting, put your feet flat on the floor. If you are lying down, put your arms down beside you and your legs out straight. Close your eyes . . . slow your breathing . . . breathe in . . . breathe out . . . relax your muscles . . . breathe in . . . breathe out . . . feel the tension leave your neck and back . . . breathe in . . . breathe out . . . relax all the little muscles around your eyes . . . relax your spine . . . your legs . . . your feet . . . your hands and arms . . . keep breathing slowly. [*longer pause*]

You feel yourself becoming lighter and lighter . . . you are so light you can float right over to the window of this room [*adjust for your setting*] . . . open the window and look outside . . . waiting for you just outside the window is a large carpet that can take you anywhere . . . see yourself floating right out of the window and onto the carpet. . . .

When you are comfortable, the carpet begins to fly away . . . away from where you began this meditation, over the houses and away from your neighborhood [*adjust to your setting*] . . . it is taking you to your labyrinth . . . you see the forest approaching . . . then the clearing among the trees. . . . The carpet enters the clearing and sets you down. . . . You step off the carpet, which will be waiting for you when you are finished. . . .

You approach the opening of the labyrinth and enter . . . in this journey through the labyrinth you will acknowledge your growth in energy work, the ability to sense and direct energies . . . you will meet with the Keeper of Fire, who has a gift or bit of advice which you need . . . you begin walking into the labyrinth, and soon the path starts to make its first turn . . . as it turns it opens into a small clearing . . . in the center of this space is an altar on which sits an orb of glowing light. . . . The color of the light is beige . . . step up to the orb and look into it. . . . Go back in time and get in touch with yourself as an infant . . . your energy world then was your body, and the warmth, food, and nourishment that were given to you. . . . Take a moment to get in touch with your basic life energy. [*longer pause*] Before leaving, offer a blessing for this period of your life, for your body, and the life force energy that has sustained you to the present. . . .

You begin to walk again, down the path . . . soon the labyrinth begins to turn . . . as it turns it opens into a small clearing. . . . In the center of this clearing is an altar on which sits an orb of glowing light. . . . The color of this light is purple . . . step up to the orb and look into it. . . . You are no longer an infant, but a preschooler . . . you are a bundle of energy that is busy exploring its world, which seems to you to be full of magickal and mysterious forces, and powerful grown-up Others . . . you want to please these forces and grown-ups and be accepted in the family unit in which you live . . . let this time of your life speak to you about the natural joy and exuberance you were born with . . . about how you use your energy to please Others in your life and make a space where you feel you belong. . . . Before you leave this space, express gratitude for the development you experienced here . . . and bless the parts of yourself you have brought with you from this space. . . .

You begin to walk again and the path of the labyrinth stretches out before you . . . soon you approach another turn which opens into a small clearing. . . . In the center of this clearing is an altar on which sits an orb of glowing light. . . . The color of this light is red . . . step up to the orb and look into it. . . . You see that you are no longer a preschooler, but a youth . . . you are impulsive and headstrong . . . you have no real sense of danger or caution, and you love adventures . . . power of all kinds intrigues you and you like playing superheroes and other fantastical characters . . . let this period of your life speak to you about what power is. . . . In what ways is your power creative and imaginative? . . . What makes you feel spiritually powerful? . . . What did you learn during this time about energy and the use of your own energy that is still with you today? [*longer pause*] Before you leave this space, express gratitude for the development you experienced here . . . and bless the part of yourself you have brought with you from this space. . . .

You begin to walk again and the path stretches out before you . . . soon the labyrinth begins to turn . . . and as it does the path opens into a small clearing. . . . In the center of this clearing is an altar on which sits an orb of glowing light. . . . The color of this light is blue . . . step up to the orb and look into it. . . . You see that you are becoming an adolescent . . . relationships matter to you . . . you want to rely on the world to run predictably . . . you want to know you are doing the right things and that those in authority approve. . . . Let this time of your life speak to you. . . . What was your relationship with energy? [*longer pause*] Did you have any experiences with fire or the south? . . . Did you ever do any energy work? . . . Did you get impressions about people or objects? . . . How did you feel out in nature? . . . What did you learn during this period about willpower and spiritual energies that is still with you today? [*longer pause*] Before you leave this space, express gratitude for the development you experienced here . . . and bless the part of yourself you have brought with you from this space. . . .

You continue to walk the path of the labyrinth . . . soon the path begins to make another turn . . . and as it does the path opens into a small clearing. . . . In the center of this clearing is an altar on which sits an orb of glowing light. . . . The color of this light is orange . . . step up to the orb and look into it. . . . You are now a young adult. . . . You are ready to leave home and the restrictions of childhood . . . you want to be independent, creative, and push the envelope a bit. . . . The reasons for things matter to you, and you don't want to accept someone else's word that something is so . . . You want to experience it for yourself. . . . Let this time of your life speak to you. . . . What was energy to you then? . . . Did you have intuitive experiences, see auras, get impressions from things? . . . Did you have any experiences with fire or the south? . . . What was your view of sexuality? . . . What things were you passionate about? . . . What did you learn during this period about energy and energy work that is still with you today? [*longer pause*] Before leaving, express thanks for the development you experienced here and may still be experiencing . . . and bless the part of yourself you have brought with you from this space. . . .

There is only one turn left in the labyrinth, and you walk toward it. . . . Make the last turn and step into a small open clearing. . . . In the center of this clearing is an altar on which sits an orb of glowing light. . . . The color of this light is green . . . step up to the orb and look into it. . . . As you continue to grow in your life, community, fairness, and justice become important to you . . . you care about the earth and the proper use of its resources. . . . You want to be heard and you are willing to listen to others. . . . Let the green part of you, whether present, past, or future, speak to you about energy . . . the energy of your self and your body . . . the energy of the earth, the sky, all creatures, and the physical world . . . the energy of consciousness and realms that are deep within . . . the energy of the Divine and of spirit. . . . How do you relate to these energies in your life, spiritually and otherwise? [*longer pause*] How do you want to relate? . . . Have you had any experiences with fire or the south? . . . What are you currently learning about power and its proper use? [*longer pause*]

Before leaving, express thanks for the development you experienced and may still be experiencing in this space. . . .

You are now at the end of the labyrinth . . . waiting for you at the end of the path is the Keeper of Fire . . . he stands waiting for you in a ring of fire that marks the exit out of the labyrinth . . . he wants to speak to you about what enflames you, empowers you, and illuminates you . . . how you stand in your point of power and strike the balance between what is too much and what is too little. . . . He wants to talk to you about how you touch and connect with others, including unseen realms. . . . What does the Keeper of Fire say to you? [*long pause*] Ask him questions if you wish. [*long pause*] When your conversation is near an end, the Keeper of Fire tells you that to leave the labyrinth you must pass through his ring of fire . . . he steps aside to let you walk through it . . . he tells you that when you pass through the flames he will give you a gift . . . it could be an object, a message, challenge, or opportunity to develop a skill . . . whatever it is, it is something that you need right now in your growth in energy work and the use of your inner fire . . . walk toward the ring of fire and pass through it . . . and as you do the Keeper of Fire tells you what gift he is giving you. . . . What is it? [*longer pause*] Thank him and say whatever more needs to be said between you, if anything. . . .

You turn and leave the labyrinth behind you, and ahead see the carpet waiting to take you home. . . . You step onto the carpet and sit down, and it slowly begins to lift and fly away. . . . You bid farewell to the labyrinth . . . you will return to it again. . . . As you sit on the carpet, you think about your experience. . . . What parts stand out in your mind and made an impression on you? [*longer pause*] Can you observe how your ideas and experience of energy have changed throughout your life? [*longer pause*] What do you believe now about energy, power and will, and energy work, as compared to earlier times in your life? [*longer pause*] How do you feel about your encounter with the Keeper of Fire? . . . What do you want to do with what he gave you? [*longer pause*]

The carpet is carrying you back toward where you began your journey [*adjust for your setting*] . . . you see the buildings ahead of you, the houses around where you sit, and finally this building. . . . The carpet brings you to the window where you started . . . you step off the carpet and float back in the window, across the room, and to yourself where you are now sitting or lying. . . . Feel yourself come back into your body and take a deep breath . . . move your fingers and toes and stretch a bit . . . take another deep breath . . . and when you are ready, open your eyes.

Be sure you are back. If you are leading a group in this visualization, encourage those who wish to share their experiences, including their conversation with the Keeper of Fire and what they received.

Blessing Ritual

You will again be using the altar you created for the blessing ritual in the prior chapter. You will need another candle to set in the southern (or lower left) quadrant. You may use the candle to symbolize the element of fire, or you may use a smudge stick, incense, or lava lamp. Feel free to use music, incense, and lighting to set the mood as you wish.

Decorate the southern quarter of your altar as you like, and again leave room for one candle and other items you choose to represent your experience in the labyrinth. As before, you may wish to draw an image of the Keeper of Fire, write a poem, paint a picture, or make a collage that represents the experiences you had in the labyrinth and with energy work. If the Keeper of Fire gave you an object as a gift, find a similar object if you can, or create a representation of it. If he gave you a quality or ability, create a symbol of it and place this symbol in the southern quadrant.

When you are ready, take several minutes to relax and cleanse your mind. Breathe deeply and let go of your thoughts. Tense and relax your muscles beginning with your feet, moving upward through your body, breathing slowly. Sit and listen quietly for a while. When you feel you are ready, you may choose to cast a circle, and call the directions and any deities you work with if it is part of your spiritual practice. Light the candle in the southern quadrant, and if you have not already done so, invite the energies of fire, the south, and energy work to be present at your ritual. If you wish, also invite the Keeper of Fire from the labyrinth.

Then pick up your knotwork cord which you placed in the western quadrant in the prior blessing ritual, and acknowledge that it represents your self and your many aspects at this time. Take a few moments and acknowledge the self you bring to your experiences with energy work, and your relationships with fire and the south. Pass the cord quickly over the flame of the candle—do not catch your sleeves or hair on fire!—or through the smoke of smudge or incense if you are using it. If you are using a lava lamp, wrap or place it at the lamp's base. Set your cord onto your altar in the southern quadrant. Pass your fingers quickly near or through the candle flame again, being careful not to burn yourself or your clothes, or smudge yourself with the smudge stick or incense, and bless yourself as you wish. Again, you may wish to touch each of your chakra points, and as you do say words which honor your fiery, passionate, empowered aspects, and the connection you share with others in your culture and society.

Then bless each of the items you placed in the southern quadrant with the candle flame or smoke, and as you do describe aloud what the item means to you. Why is it on your altar? What challenge, gift, or ability does it represent and what do you think you are to do with it? How do these things relate to your goal of spiritual growth, and the experiences you have had in your life that have brought you to where you are now?

Express aloud the value of this quadrant's gifts to you, how it helps you attune energetically, and how you wish to continue to grow in energy work. Give thanks to the deities you honor, to the vast ground of potentiality, to all the creativity and vitality in the universe, and to all other consciousnesses that support you in your journey and your growth in energy work. Bless them and your growing relationships with them.

When you are finished, sit quietly for five or ten minutes and be present to the feelings and thoughts this ritual has raised for you. When you feel ready to end the ritual, thank the south, the element of fire, the Keeper of Fire (if invited), and dismiss the directions and deities you invoked, if any, according to your tradition. Blow out the candle in the south but leave it and the items on your altar if possible. Let their presence remind you of your gratitude for the gifts of this quadrant and your work in deepening your spiritual relationships in energy work.

Checking in with Your Magickal Plan

Take a moment to review your magickal plan for the year and look at the items you have chosen to work on presently and in the near future. Most likely every one of them has some kind of energetic aspect to it. Examine each item with an eye to whether it involves a higher or lesser degree of energy work. Identify which energy skills each item will tend to use, and ask yourself what kind of energy experience you want to have with each. If you can detect little to no energy work in your plan, why do you think this is so? Is energy work something you want to work on now, or something you want to avoid? What are your reasons? Have you incorporated any aspects relating to the south and fire, passion, creativity, drive, and empowerment in your plan? Feel free to adjust your plan as you wish to add energy work into it, but rather than make too many changes, be aware of the energetic aspects already present in the work you have chosen to do. If you wish, take some time to journal about energy work and its relation to your spiritual development.

6

Divination

DIVINATION IS THE THIRD type of magickal practice we identify. Divination focuses on the receipt of information. Frequently this information concerns the sensing of probabilities developing in unmanifest reality. Divination can also concern events in the present and the spiritual meaning or lessons contained in them. It can address the past and the manner in which past events have led to present issues. Any magickal work that involves the receipt of information not obtained through ordinary, rational means likely involves divination.

Most commonly recognized psychic abilities also utilize divination, such as the seeing of past or future events (clairvoyance), the hearing of sounds or information (clairaudience), and the direct knowing that something is true, has happened, or will happen (clairsentience). Information can also be received empathically, through smells and the touching of objects (psychometry). Divination essentially consists of two parts: being open to receiving information and then receiving it, and the use of the information in some fashion.

Information flows from any of the spiritual relationships Pagans are free to develop. One Pagan may believe information comes from the multidimensional universe, and sees him- or herself as plugged in to the cosmic "hologram." Another may believe information comes from the Divine, and is a part of communicating with God and angels. A third may believe that information comes from the self's own inner wisdom and collective repositories of it. All of these perspectives are a part of Paganism, and an individual may embrace one or several of them.

Not only do a Pagan's spiritual relationships and views of divination vary, but so does the preferred manner in which the diviner receives information. In our years of teaching we have noticed that some Pagans are very visual, others are kinesthetic, and yet others are auditory. That is, some Pagans "see" information, some "hear" it, others "smell" it, some feel emotions or bodily sensations, while others receive information in packets of "knowing." None of these ways is better than another. What matters is that you work with the ways that come naturally to you and build on those skills over time. We believe that if you wish to develop your divination skills, it can help if you first discover your natural preferences when it comes to how you receive information. To help our students discover their preferences, we led them through a visualization designed to use every sense and mode of perception, and then talked about which came easily for them and which were difficult. Often the way they described what happened during the visualization would make their preferences clear, and we would encourage them to continue developing their skills in this area.

The exercise below provides you an opportunity to design such a visualization for yourself or others. You may find the exercise to be more fun if you can gather a group of friends together to do it with you.

 exercise

Campfire Meditation

The purpose of this exercise is to help you identify the primary ways in which you experience information and mental imagery. This exercise is essentially a guided meditation and you may want to ask a friend to help guide you through it, or tape it for yourself and listen to it later. This exercise also gives you the opportunity to create your own guided meditation within the framework we provide and, if you do assemble a group, to practice leading others in a meditation if you wish. Be sure that you have a chance to experience the meditation yourself at some point, even if you lead others in it.

The words you choose for the meditation need to create a sensually rich experience in which the participants are encouraged to walk through a forest at night to a campfire that is burning in a clearing, to sit and experience the campfire, and then leave the forest to return to the point of beginning. The goal is to create as many opportunities for sensing the forest and the fire as there are ways to sense. In addition to visual imagery, be sure to include listening, smelling, touching, intuition, and emotions.

Lead the participants (or yourself if you are doing this alone) in imagery that walks them into the forest, noticing the sights, sounds, and smells as they go. Bring them to the clearing where a campfire is burning, and have them sit near it. Once they are seated by the fire, have them visualize the fire, feel the heat on the front of them and the coolness on the back of them, listen to the crackling of the flames, and smell the smoke. Take your time in creating these images, sensations, and feelings. Try to engage all of the senses and modes of perceiving, and don't forget emotions and impressions that are more abstract.

Find a quiet place for the meditation where you will not be disturbed. You and any other participants may sit or lie down, but choose a position which can be held comfortably. Take several minutes to quiet the mind and body, and breathe slowly and deeply. When you design the meditation you can choose to use the flying carpet from the labyrinth to take you to the forest and campfire, if you like. You can try another means if you'd rather, but some image of journeying to and from the destination is usually helpful. We recommend that the meditation last for fifteen or twenty minutes, with many pauses to give yourself or group members plenty of time to experience the forest and fire with all their senses and modes of perception.

Be sure to journey back to the point of beginning and return fully to your body. If you are in a group setting, be sure everyone is back after the meditation has ended. You may want to have food and drink at hand to help with grounding. A group setting is ideal for processing what is experienced during the meditation. Be sure that each person in the group has a chance to speak and share what they experienced. You and the group may want to help them interpret how they tend to perceive internal information. Did they have good success with visualizing, or with tactile, emotional, or abstract imagery? If you do this exercise on your own, you may wish to journal about your experience.

You may find that you have a predominant way of receiving input, with one or two other ways that are present but secondary. For example, you may determine that you tend to hear information better than see it, with occasional flashes of abstract "feelings," or a sense of knowing. If you are unsure of the results, you may wish to do the meditation again and then discuss it with a friend or teacher.

Receiving Information

Successful divination begins with the willingness to perceive information. An attitude of openness flows from a person's belief that this sort of information exists and is capable of being perceived, and that it is spiritually permissible and desirable to do so. Some belief systems conclude that information of one type or another doesn't exist, or may limit its reception to a priestly class or to certain approved situations, such as a charismatic prayer service. A belief system may cloak the receipt of information in warnings or fear, often for the purpose of limiting its appearance to those persons and circumstances that are permitted. If received under these controlled circumstances, both the receiver and the information are declared to be "safe" and free of whatever spiritual dangers the belief system embraces.

Pagans generally do not believe there is anything dangerous about divination or the information received during it. Most Pagans do not adopt the worldview which holds that the physical world is a battleground between the forces of good and evil. Only a handful of the hundreds of ancient and modern mythologies paint the world in this fashion in any event. Most Pagans have no theological basis to believe in an unsafe or unsupportive universe filled with evil spirits out to get them. We explore the Pagan view of evil and the nature of the universe more fully in our introductory book. The Pagan view of magick, which includes divination, cannot be readily understood without a knowledge of Pagan philosophy on these issues.

Most Pagans, therefore, tend to draw the boundary around the use of divination pretty broadly, with ethics—not dogma—as the limiting factor. Pagans tend to be open to the practice of divination in a variety of circumstances and encourage each other in their development of this magickal skill.

While Pagans are open to receiving divinatory information, the question remains: where does the information come from? The answer to this question is the same as for the other types of magick. All magick is based in relational exchange, and the relationships which Pagans experience range from relationships with the self, to the physical world, to other people, to all of consciousness, and to the Divine. Information can flow from any or all of these sources to and from the receiver, assuming the receiver is willing to engage in the exchange. Since Pagans have such a broad view of permissible spiritual relationships they may receive information from a variety of sources, including their subconscious, plants, trees, animals, Gaia, the collective unconscious, a person who is living or deceased, past or future selves, probable selves, atoms and molecules, unmanifest reality, gods and goddesses, angels, spirit guides, and ancestors.

One of our favorite ways of visualizing this process is through the metaphor of the iceberg. As explained in our introductory book, the iceberg is a model we developed for Paganism classes as a metaphor of our view of the interconnected nature of the universe. The parts of icebergs that you can readily see, the tops that stick above the water, represent physical reality. This is reality as you know it, readily perceived by your five senses. From the perspective above the water, the physical world appears to be composed of separate chunks of matter that seem to be independent. And yet you know that only a small fraction of icebergs are visible above the water. When you shift your perspective below the water, or in our metaphor, below the surface appearance of things, you discover that the vast majority of an iceberg is not visible from the top. Under the surface the icebergs are gigantic, and in an ice field may meld to form a solid interconnected mass. Like an iceberg, your deeper nature and the deeper nature of others and physical reality are interconnected. When you engage in divination you move your point of focus below the surface of things and connect with the deeper levels of other consciousness to exchange information. Pagans certainly do not view divinatory information as originating from evil spirits, as suggested by some other religions. Instead, Pagans view divination as one of the ways in which the profound interconnectedness of consciousness naturally expresses itself.

As with energy work, it can be easy to dismiss information you receive during divination as imagination or wishful thinking. While discernment is very important, we think most people discount their reception of information too much rather than too little. It is our experience that reliable information frequently comes without emotion, with calm, clean impressions that "feel" right, and often at times when the receiver is in a relaxed or open state. Many Pagans who work with this form of magick report getting some of their best information while driving, taking a shower, or doing some other repetitive action that puts them in a daydreamlike state. Others receive insights and solutions to problems in night-time dreaming. Receiving information through magickal pages is another way you can receive divinatory impressions. Be open to the possibility that information may come to you in a variety of ways, and that these ways may shift over time.

Also remember that as with any form of magick, you are in control of whether or how much information flows into you at any time. Your divination receiver does not have to be turned on or left on unless you choose. You can turn the volume of your receiver down or off whenever you like. Even if you turn your receiver off, you can ask the universe to send you a magickal page if a critical piece of information is headed your way.

 questions to discuss

1. What does divination mean to you?

2. Have you ever experienced receiving divinatory information or impressions? If so, how does information tend to come to you?

3. When do you tend to receive such information?

4. Where do you believe the information you receive is coming from?

5. What personal and spiritual value does divination have for you, if any? Why?

 exercise

The Window of Time

In this exercise, we want you to begin to experience the deeper levels of the iceberg where physical reality blends into the realm of spacelessness and timelessness. We do this by having you establish an energy presence of yourself with which you will connect across the apparent barriers of time and space. You will need to choose a window from which you can clearly see yourself coming and going from your home. If there is no such view at your home, then you may choose a window at work from which you can see where you come into the workplace. For this exercise we are assuming you are at a window at home.

Spend several minutes in deep slow breathing. Pull energy into yourself from the earth and into your feet. With each in-breath, pull more energy into yourself until it flows into your back, chest, and head. Let it cascade out from the top of your head and flow over you like a fountain, then back into the ground.

See yourself as an energy being, which like all the energy in the universe, flows in and out of multidimensional realms. The energy of your consciousness is not limited by space and time. In this exercise, you will find a multidimensional perspective from which you can cross through time and see yourself in two places simultaneously.

When you feel ready, stand in front of the window you chose. From there you can see your street, or driveway, or bus stop, or your entrance to work. Imagine yourself tomorrow, at a time you know you must leave for work or an appointment. See yourself leaving your home and passing in front of the window where you now stand. Take several moments to imagine this and get a strong image or impression in your mind. This does not have to be a visual image; use whatever senses or mode of perception works most easily for you. Then imagine your self of tomorrow stopping deliberately and turning to look directly at yourself in the window. Make eye contact, make energetic contact. Feel yourself connecting with your self of tomorrow.

Gradually end eye contact and observe yourself continue on your way. Watch yourself until you are out of sight and then withdraw your awareness from tomorrow. You are simply standing in front of your window in the here and now. Move away from the window and sit or lie down. Gently turn off your energy fountain and stop pulling energy from the earth into yourself. Let the excess energy gradually subside and slide down your body, out your feet and into the floor. Be sure all excess energy is released from your body. Take several more breaths and end the exercise.

The next day, leave for work or your appointment as planned. As you prepare to leave, take several slow breaths and put yourself in touch mentally with the open energy state you felt the day before. You will not fully enter that state now because you need to walk or drive and not be in an altered state of consciousness. When you are ready, leave your home just as you imagined the day before. In about the place you saw yourself stop, come to a halt and turn and look at the window where you stood yesterday.

Open yourself to feeling the energy presence you established at the window. You may or may not have a visual image of yourself. Even if you do not get a visual image, imagine that you are making energetic or eye contact with yourself and allow a strong sense of connection to flow between you. After a moment or two, break the contact and continue on your way. Know that your past self is watching you until you pass out of view. End the exercise and proceed on with your day.

We suggest you do this exercise four or five times over the course of two weeks. Give yourself some practice at creating an energy presence of yourself. Setting this presence and sensing it are skills you have likely never developed until now, so be patient if you aren't successful with the exercise immediately. As you become sensitive to your own energy presence you may discover that you begin to sense energy presences or gaps in time in and around others, or in particular locations. Make a note in your journal of these impressions, and whether or not you find your sensitivities improving.

my journal

For the next thirty days, have your journal at hand first thing in the morning. You can do this journaling before getting out of bed, but definitely do not turn on the TV or radio, or read any news of the day beforehand.

With your journal open before you, close your eyes and take several deep breaths. Allow yourself to float away in a daydreaming sort of state to a place where you can access all the information in the universe that you wish. You may choose to imagine a library, or a busy intersection where the cars are packets of information and probabilities passing by, or you may go to a deeper part of the iceberg.

Then open yourself to receiving impressions about what is setting up as probable for the day. This information can relate to yourself, your family, local or world news, weather, or the stock market. Your impressions can be partial and do not have to be detailed. They can be one or two words, like "baseball fight, balloon launch, market up" and so on. Write the date in your journal and then make a note of your impressions as they come. Do not second guess the images you get or try to interpret them. The exercise will likely take less than five minutes. At the end of the day, compare what you have written to what is happening in your life and the news. As the month progresses notice whether you tend to pick up on events of that day or a few days ahead.

Journal about your experience as you go along. Note your feelings about this work. Do you enjoy it? Do you struggle to get impressions? If you get them, do you argue with yourself about whether they make sense? Do you dismiss your impressions and feel you are imagining them? Throughout the month notice whether you feel differently on days you did this exercise and those where you forgot or didn't have time. Note whether you feel a different sense of connection to yourself and the world depending on whether you did the exercise or not. At the end of the month go back and review your entire experience and notice if there are any patterns in the type or nature of information you received. Also notice whether your feelings about the information and your ability to receive it changed as the month progressed.

Working with Divination

The second aspect of successful divination is the use or application of the information received. This involves several skills, beginning with the interpretation of the information, and then discernment surrounding how to communicate or act on it.

The interpretation of information especially comes into play when the diviner is using a specific symbol set or divinatory tool to help him or her receive information. Examples of symbol sets include tarot cards, palm reading, aura reading, runes, dreams, pendulums, I Ching, tea leaves, and so on. In all of these systems, the diviner is presented with a symbolic image which has certain meanings ascribed to it. The diviner must first learn what these meanings are and then how to interpret them in a divinatory "reading." This can take a great deal of practice.

It has been our experience that over time the diviner finds that the process of learning the meaning of the symbol and applying it to a reading often results in a level of communication that runs deeper than the symbol. The runes or cards become merely evocative of information that begins to come of itself. The reader is often in an altered state before the reading begins and is already getting information or impressions which are then clarified or confirmed by use of the symbols. Some readers may stop using the symbol set altogether and go to a direct knowing or intuitive approach. Others continue to use cards or other tools because their symbology helps trigger the flow of information.

One of the biggest misunderstandings non-Pagans have about divination is the misconception that information is coming from the symbol or tool itself. Observing a reader in action may strengthen this misunderstanding since it appears their comments are generated by the card or rune or other tool. However, it is our position that all tools—whether tarot cards, runes, palms, tea leaves and so on—contain no divinatory information. The information emerges from the exchange experienced between the diviner and his or her source of information, not the tool. The tool can be useful in triggering a thought or image, or even by keeping the conscious mind busy while the intuitive mind drops down to interact with deeper levels of consciousness. Here, at these deeper levels, is where the vastness of the iceberg spreads out, where enfolded reality rests in its unmanifested state, and probabilities are designed by a conscious universe that is ever creative and in flux.

It is the task of the diviner to step into the flow and listen. Depending on which spiritual relationships the diviner has developed and is working with, this flow may be seen as originating from the earth and its creatures, natural forces, angels, God, spirit beings, ancestors, the personal or collective unconscious, the Ground of Being, atoms, molecules, thought, or the unmanifest realms. This same flow is also occurring within the person receiving the divinatory reading. Sometimes the role of the diviner is simply to point the way to this flow and help the receiver connect to it directly.

The more the diviner can connect to the natural flow of the universe, the more clearly the information will be perceived. The symbols of tools can sometimes help this process, but at other times they may hinder it. If you find that most of your divination time is spent with a book trying to interpret a tool's symbology rather than hearing and sharing information, then consider allowing yourself to open directly to the information. Allow the tool to be a tool instead of your primary focus and see what happens. The interpretation of information starts to get easier when you begin to trust receiving information directly, because less interpretation is needed. As the diviner, you can then share the information you are receiving exactly as you're receiving it. Keep in mind that information does not have to make sense to you to be valid. It is quite all right to begin a remark with a comment like, "I don't understand what I'm getting, but here it is—does this make sense to you?" You may be surprised how often such information is directly on point and has meaning for the person receiving it.

Some kinds of information are difficult to share. Use your common sense, your discernment and compassion in these situations. It is not the diviner's role to alarm or offend, and even the most sensitive or personal information can usually be offered in a gentle and constructive manner. Concerning future events, it is our position that diviners cannot predict the future. They may pick up on probabilities that are being arranged in enfolded realms; they may hear the chatter of many consciousnesses pulling events and people together, but probabilities are always subject to change. An individual can always choose a different course or abandon a probability he or she has been diligently creating. Therefore, present information about probabilities in their real light—as a direction that can always be changed. This is especially true of information you receive that is troubling or sensitive.

exercise

The Flow of Probabilities

This exercise can be done indoors or out of doors, but choose a place where you will be undisturbed for fifteen or twenty minutes. Choose a comfortable position, either sitting or lying down. Feel free to play music, burn incense, and light candles to help with the meditative mood.

When you are ready and comfortable, take two or three minutes to relax and breathe slowly and deeply. Gradually turn your attention to some decision you made during the day. It doesn't have to be a momentous or life-changing decision; it can be as ordinary as turning left or right at the intersection. But pick one in which a choice was made and your course continued onward. Imagine yourself floating toward this decision point and hovering above it while you look it over. From this perspective examine your choice—what do you see? What were your options?

As you float above this decision point, imagine the probabilities flowing out in the direction of one of the choices you did not make. See yourself making that choice instead, and then watch the probable results spread out from it like lines, or waves, or a spiderweb. Each one of these additional probabilities has choices within itself, and each of those choices has its own set of probabilities stretching out from it and into the future, resulting in yet more choices, and more probabilities, to infinity.

Hold this image lightly in your mind and come back to your initial decision point. This time pick a second choice you could have made, and again see the probabilities flowing outward from it. Some of these probabilities might intersect with those from the first alternate choice.

Each decision you make for each of the probabilities creates further decision points, and these choices create further probabilities, and so on to infinity.

Continue with this exercise for as long as you care to, coming back to your initial decision point and looking at all the potential choices you could have made but didn't. When you have visualized all that you can, hover above your initial point of decision and observe the amazing, infinite, interwoven web of the choices you could have made and all of the probabilities and future choices each of them could have created. Each one of these potential choices and probabilities leads to a different probable you, a different personal landscape, a different future. See how powerful your choices are.

Notice that where you are now poised, above the decision point you chose for this exercise, is your point of power. It is from here that you choose your future, and create your self and your reality. From this point of power you steer your way through the past and future and the myriad of probabilities you see spread out around you. Take a deep breath. Feel this point of power and the vitality that sustains you as you choose from the unmanifest what you will make manifest. Let this power and vitality flow through you for several minutes, and then release it. Take several more deep breaths, allowing any remaining excess energy to flow out of your body and into the earth. Then open your eyes and end the exercise.

As you go on with your day, see if you can feel this point of power as you come to a decision point. See if you can catch a glimpse again of the probabilities that are branching out to infinity from even the most ordinary of your choices.

Divination and the Four Elements

We place divination in Wilber's lower right quadrant, which is east and home to the element of air.

The lower right quadrant is Wilber's world of the *Outer Its*, where groups of individuals give physical expression to the shared inner meanings they created in the lower left. In this quadrant cultural expression moves from that which is interior, such as values and the meaning of language and symbols, to one that is primarily exterior. As noted in our introductory book, this is where belief systems are translated into belief structures. Values are given physical form such as institutions, governments, armies, churches, universities, hospitals, corporations, monasteries, and so on. The nature of the beliefs and values determines the nature and shape of the structures built from them. By the same token, if you study a culture's structures you can determine what values and beliefs underlie them. The lower right quadrant is the realm where groups choose from among multiple probabilities those which they wish to make real. This process of discernment and choice is also at the heart of divination.

In common Pagan practice the east is the archetype for cleansing, freshness, new beginnings, and mental inspiration. Viewed on the wheel of the year, the east heralds the beginning of spring, the return of life, growth, and hope. The sun is not yet at its zenith, temperatures are milder, many species are mating, and plants are blooming. Spring brings with it a unique invigoration that seems to invade everything. On the wheel of the day, east is the sunrise, the point of beginning and new opportunities. On the wheel of human life, it is the land of birth and youth, of innocence, freshness, and enthusiasm. This is a busy time of life, full of rapid growth, experimentation, and curiosity. Groundwork is laid both physically and mentally for the years of maturity that lie ahead.

Air is the element usually associated with the east in Pagan practice because of its cleansing properties. It is also associated with communication, information, and the flash of knowledge and insight. Air is associated with all mental faculties, clear thinking, planning, organizing, and decision-making. Like the east, it is associated with spontaneity, freshness, and rapid communication. As with divination, it is the element of information and messages.

Deepening your experiences with divination can help you move toward the goal of *maximum healthiness* and *maximum expansion* in your spiritual develop-

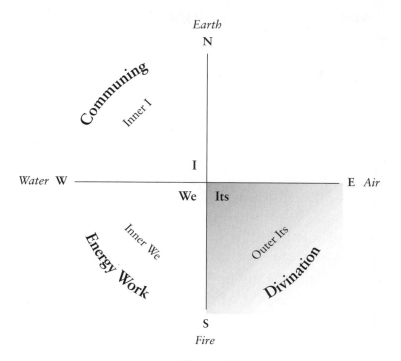

Figure 6.1
The Lower Right Quadrant: Divination, East, Outer Its

ment by involving you in the communication of the goals, intentions, and desires of yourself and others. Through divination you may become increasingly aware of potentialities and probabilities that are developing and preparing to move into manifest reality. The more sensitivity to this information you gain, the more you become consciously aware of the choices that you and others face, and the more experience you can gain in choosing what you will help to make real and what you will leave in potential. This process of discernment and decision-making helps individuals grow by moving them away from a solely private, interior experience of spirituality and compelling them to put their beliefs and values into action and experience the results.

exercise

Connecting to That Which Discerns

This exercise focuses on experiencing knowledge, discernment and choice through the element of air. You may do this exercise indoors or outside, but have incense or smudge available if possible. If you are outside perhaps you can pick a location where there are many birds or butterflies, or a day that is windy. Bring a kite to fly if you wish. If you live where there are drum circles, and you would be welcome to meditate during the drumming, you might try this exercise there. A tape of bells or singing bowls might also be effective.

Take a few minutes to relax and breathe deeply. Feel the air coming in your lungs, revitalizing your tissues and blood, and then passing back out. Acknowledge the life-giving power of air as it sustains your breathing. Light the smudge or incense you have with you, and let the smoke surround you. Pull the smoke toward you with sweeping motions. If you are outside on a windy day, throw your arms wide, dance around, and let the wind blow across you. As you open your arms or sit in the smoke of the smudge, say "I open myself to that which knows, discerns, and chooses."

Continue to breathe deeply and watch the smoke dissipate in the air, or the wind blow, or the birds fly. Mentally relax further into the airy element. Hear it whisper to you of the places in which it lives. What has this element seen, what does it know, what is its wisdom? Find the parts of you that soar and move without restriction. Where does your consciousness live? Feel the swiftness of your thoughts and the exchange that exists between you and all the intelligence in the universe. Meditate on how all things, manifest and unmanifest, are alive with knowledge and intelligence, the spark of life that is consciousness.

Knowledge is the gift of air and of divination. How do you use your gifts of knowledge? What do you do with multidimensional information that comes to you? Discernment and choice are also gifts. Which you are you choosing to make real? Which world? Which future? As you feel the air moving around you, meditate on what invisible forces connect you to the greater whole. What sweeps across your landscape and cleanses you? Identify places within where you may need freshening and cleansing. What makes you joyful and enthusiastic? What can you do to bring more joy and enthusiasm into your life?

Open yourself to the energy of communication, knowledge, and intelligence that surrounds you. Feel and acknowledge your exchange and relationship with this intelligent universe, which goes on even when you are not aware of it. Own your mental gifts and powers of discernment and choice.

Gradually bring your attention back to your surroundings. Express gratitude for your experience. Put out the incense or smudge, and journal if you wish. If you are with a group, spend a few minutes sharing.

my journal

The most memorable divination experiences I have had are . . .

The impact they had on me was . . .

These experiences were or were not peak experiences because . . .

The aspects of divination I find most challenging are . . .

The aspects I enjoy most are . . .

I would describe my relationship with the east as . . .

Experiences I have had with the east are . . .

My relationship with the element of air is . . .

Experiences I have had with the element of air are . . .

Divination in Developmental Space

As with the other forms of magick, divination will be experienced in ways that are unique to the developmental perspective of the Pagan working with it. The nature of the information received, the circumstances of its reception, and the purposes to which it is put will take different forms depending on the developmental space the diviner—and possibly the recipient—occupies. What is considered ethical, both in terms of the information received and how it is used, will also vary.

For the **egocentric** Pagan (Purple-Red), divination will almost assuredly be seen as a communication with the powerful and mysterious forces that control the universe. Many superstitions may surround the receipt of divinatory information. Rituals are likely elaborate and must occur at specified times or seasons. Early Purple may believe that the continuation of the world, and certainly the continuation of the spirit world's friendliness toward humans, is dependent on these rites. With the move toward Red and the issues of power and control it raises, acts of divination may become more violent. At least historically, sacrifices to the gods became more common during Red periods, and divination took the form of reading entrails and other signs. The moral embrace of egocentric diviners extends no further than themselves and their immediate circle, so divination that is bloody or destructive is still considered ethical since it is designed to preserve one's self and family by keeping the gods happy.

It is unclear whether adult Pagans who get stuck at the Red level will be drawn to blood rituals or similar practices, as were their historic counterparts. It has been our experience that such a tendency is rare, and when it occurs it may mark other and deeper disturbances. Most Pagans who get stuck in Purple to Red likely exhibit it through irrational and superstitious beliefs about divination, along with grandiose ideas of their divinatory powers. Perhaps the difference between "stuck" Red divinatory practices now and in the historical past is due to the developmental space occupied by the surrounding culture, especially in terms of what that culture believes to be acceptable and unacceptable expressions of Red.

Because individuals whose growth is arrested at this level have trouble separating their emotions from others' emotions (they do not know where they end and others begin), an egocentric diviner may project his or her feelings and desires onto others as they do readings. If a diviner is not particularly popular and doesn't get much attention from the opposite sex, for example, and does a divinatory reading for someone who is handsome and popular, he or she may predict the end of the receiver's relationships, followed by the onset of deadly cancer, and the nightly attack of evil spirits. We have witnessed incidents similar to this example and have seen people leave in tears or be terrified for months, all because the diviners projected their issues and resentments onto someone else. If you are in a teaching or leadership position and encounter such behavior, end the divination session if you are able and it is appropriate, and discuss your concerns with the reader at an appropriate time. Also talk to the receiver of the information, discuss what authentic divination does and does not consist of and relieve his or her fears.

Healthy aspects of the egocentric self that diviners can bring with them as they grow is a sense of the importance of their work, and of awe and appreciation for the creative power of the universe and the individual.

As Pagans enter the **mythic** level (Blue), divination is still experienced as a communication from powerful spirit beings. Rather than feeling at the mercy of these beings, however, the mythic self relates to them through roles and myths. If the self behaves correctly, then the deity is also bound to behave in determined ways, which in divination is to communicate information. Depending on the belief system, approved divination may take the form of prophecies, visions, warnings, apparitions, and other signs. Divinatory rituals are codified and cannot be varied, or the deities may not respond.

Since mythic individuals tend to have difficulty tolerating beliefs other than their own, it is common for them to condemn another culture's or religion's experience of divination. These other cultures or religions may even be demonized despite the fact that both groups are engaging in identical behavior, such as prophecy. The moral embrace of the mythic self expands to include its ethnic group. A divinatory practice will be viewed as ethical if it helps preserve the group, especially from all other (and therefore hostile) mythologies, or helps to eradicate other mythologies. A particular divinatory practice may also help distinguish one's group from other groups, in which case it is morally acceptable to praise your own divination practices while demonizing that of others.

Pagans who get stuck at the mythic level will be very concerned with the details of divinatory practice, which must be done precisely. Divination will not be seen as legitimate if diviners do not come from a specific tradition, receive certain training, use specific tools or symbol sets, cleanse and empower their tools in specified ways, or fail to prepare themselves precisely before doing a reading. If you are in a teaching or leadership position when rigid Blue expresses itself, try to minimize any negative impact and encourage cooperation and tolerance among all present. Accommodate some or all of the requirements of the mythic Pagan if it is feasible and appropriate. If you cannot, explain your reasons clearly and be understanding if the person does not wish to participate.

Healthy aspects of the mythic self that diviners can bring with them in their divination practices include a love of ritual and custom, respect for divinatory tools and the process of divination itself.

The **rational** (Orange) Pagan leaves behind his or her former mythic view and will begin to look for rational reasons that explain what divination is and why it works. It may be useful to introduce scientific concepts that suggest the transmittal of information outside of space and time, as in Bell's Theorem, discussed in our introductory book. Exploring the wide range of spiritual relationships Pagans are free to embrace may also be of help.

The moral embrace of the rational self is still ethnocentric, that is, focused on its own group or country. Divination will be viewed as ethical if it supports the preservation of the society and makes rational sense. The fairness of divination or its impact on others' feelings and access to resources is generally not considered unless it impacts one's own group. Divination based solely in superstition or which is irrationally destructive, however, will be rejected as unworthy and phony.

Pagans who get stuck in the rational level will likely not retain the ritual or mythic richness from prior developmental spaces. They may have no interest in divination, or any magickal practice, unless a rational basis can be clearly shown to support it. They may be critical of divinatory work and anyone who engages in it, and may be too uncomfortable with it to participate on any level. If you are in a teaching or leadership position, encourage the rational Pagan to try different divination techniques and to participate in group exercises. Then help them process their experience from a rational perspective.

Healthy aspects of the rational self that diviners can bring forward with them include clear thinking and an emphasis on authenticity.

Vision-logic (Green) Pagans will make sensitive diviners who are as concerned about the feelings of the recipient as of the content of the information shared.

They do not need approval from an authority figure when it comes to divination. If the information feels right to them and is not damaging to others, they will share it. Their moral embrace expands to include all of humanity. Divination will be viewed as ethical if it supports the growth and fair treatment of all human beings. The source of divinatory information is likely seen as coming from deep levels of the self, as well as other human archetypal energies.

Pagans who get stuck at this level may find themselves disapproving of those on other levels of the spiral. As with the egocentrist, they may be tempted to color their divination with their own perspective, in this case with sermonettes about being a politically correct Pagan. Somehow they manage to weave in subtle messages about politics and where to shop and acceptable lifestyle choices, that may leave the recipient feeling uncomfortable without quite knowing why. If this happens to you during a divinatory reading, you may wish to end it, and then discuss your observations with the reader. If you are in a teaching or leadership position you will want to discuss the situation with both the reader and the receiver when it is appropriate. If the diviner's statements are extremely upsetting to the recipient you may have to take immediate action.

Healthy aspects of vision-logic that diviners can benefit from are a truly global vision, a concern and caring for others and the advancement of human development to its fullest potential.

When a Pagan reaches the **psychic** space (Yellow-Turquoise), a world of psychic phenomena opens up that is sensually rich and emotionally powerful. Diviners are able to tap into deeper layers of information than ever before. They now grasp the interconnectedness of physical reality and can develop a variety of spiritual relationships, particularly with that of the physical world. They may find themselves receiving information from the earth and animals, and experience a level of communication with them that was previously unknown.

The moral embrace of psychic diviners expands to include all life on the earth, including nonhuman life. Divination is considered ethical if it supports or is not detrimental to any life form. The prophecies and oracles from earlier levels which may have encouraged sacrifices, the smiting of enemies, the advancement of one culture at the expense of another, or the self-serving use of animals or resources will be absent from this and any future level of divinatory development.

Psychic Pagans may get stuck in this level if they become attached to their enhanced divination skills, especially the attention and fame such skills may bring them. Letting go of this attachment can be difficult.

At the **subtle** level, Pagans will occasionally experience union with spirit during divination and other magickal practices. They may continue in the practice simply hoping for another moment of ecstatic union. Their moral embrace expands to include spirit beings, and divinatory information now is viewed as proceeding from all the sources recognized by earlier levels, plus angels, saints, deities, and spirit guides. Divinatory information and practices will be considered ethical if they do not detrimentally affect humans, animals, and plants, and are not disrespectful of spirit and spirit beings. The diviner may begin to experience visions and illuminations which may or may not be appropriate to share while performing a divination. A good spiritual advisor with strong discernment skills can be of great help to the Pagan struggling with these issues.

At the **causal** and **nondual** levels, Pagans may find themselves so absorbed in their experiences of union with spirit that they lose interest in divination. This is somewhat ironic since they have attained the realization that separateness is an illusion and they have direct and immediate access to the whole of multidimensionality. The moral embrace of such a person expands to include all of manifest and unmanifest reality. It is rare to find anyone, Pagan or otherwise, developed to this point. But if you should ever meet someone, encourage him or her to stay involved in practical, everyday concerns, and to share their unique spiritual insights and gifts with others.

 questions to discuss

1. What view of divination were you raised with? What do you believe about it now?

2. Is divination spiritually meaningful to you? Why or why not?

3. Does Paganism do enough with divination in its rituals and other practices? If not, what more would you like to see done?

4. What developmental issues have you faced in regard to divination? To the east or air? Are you facing any now?

5. Have you known anyone who has struggled with developmental issues in regard to divination? What happened?

 **visualization**

Divination and the Labyrinth

Get in a comfortable position. If you are sitting, put your feet flat on the floor. If you are lying down, put your arms down beside you and your legs out straight. Close your eyes . . . slow your breathing . . . breathe in . . . breathe out . . . relax your muscles . . . breathe in . . . breathe out . . . feel the tension leave your neck and back . . . breathe in . . . breathe out . . . relax all the little muscles around your eyes . . . relax your spine . . . your legs . . . your feet . . . your hands and arms . . . keep breathing slowly. [*longer pause*]

You feel yourself becoming lighter and lighter . . . you are so light you are able to float right over to the window of this room [*adjust for your setting*] . . . open the window and look outside . . . waiting for you just outside the window is a large carpet that can take you anywhere . . . see yourself floating right out of the window and onto the carpet. . . .

You settle yourself onto the carpet and it begins to fly away . . . over the houses and streets where you live [*adjust to your setting*] . . . the carpet is taking you back to the labyrinth . . . you can see a forest growing closer . . . you fly over it and see a clearing where the labyrinth awaits. . . . The carpet enters the clearing and sets you down. . . . You step off of it, knowing it will be waiting for you when you are finished. . . .

You see the entrance of the labyrinth ahead of you and you enter it . . . in this journey through the labyrinth you will acknowledge your growth in the skills of divination, the ability to communicate with all levels of reality and to share information with others . . . you will meet with the Keeper of Air, who has a gift or bit of advice which you need. . . . You walk into the labyrinth, and soon the path begins to make a turn . . . as it turns it opens into a small clearing . . . in the center of the clearing is an altar on which sits a bowl filled with hot coals . . . next to it is a feather fan and a container of white incense powder . . . pour the powder into the censer and use the feather fan to help the incense catch . . . it smells like daisies . . . keep fanning the incense until billows of smoke surround you. . . . As you breathe it in, you are transported back to the time of your infancy . . . the information you could receive and process then related solely to your body, food, and warmth, the meeting of your immediate needs. . . . Take a moment to get in touch with your infant self. [*longer pause*] Before leaving, offer a blessing for this period of your life and the gifts of physical development and knowledge that has brought you to the present. . . .

You begin to walk again, down the path formed by hedges . . . soon the labyrinth begins to turn . . . as it turns it opens into a small clearing . . . in the center of the clearing is an altar on which sits a bowl filled with hot coals . . . next to it is a feather fan and a container of purple incense powder . . . pour the powder into the censer and use the feather fan to help the incense catch . . . it smells of lilacs . . . keep fanning the incense until billows of smoke surround you. . . . As you breathe it in, you see that you have grown beyond infancy . . . you are now a child . . . you can hear the trees, birds, and animals talking . . . and you communicate with them . . . the world seems mysterious and everything around you seems alive and filled with power . . . let this time of your life speak to you about the mystery of spirit . . . the rituals surrounding communication with these powerful forces. . . . Before you leave this space, express gratitude for the development you experienced here . . . and bless the parts of yourself you have brought with you from it. . . .

You begin to walk again and the path of the labyrinth stretches out before you . . . soon you approach another turn which opens into a small clearing . . . in the center of the clearing is an altar on which sits a bowl filled with hot coals . . . next to it is a feather fan and a container of red incense powder . . . pour the powder into the censer and use the feather fan to help the incense catch . . . it smells of roses . . . keep fanning the incense until billows of smoke surround you. . . . As you breathe it in, you see yourself as a youth, communicating swiftly and impulsively. . . . You use information to help you express your power and perform feats of daring. . . . Spirit beings seem to be very powerful indeed, and so you communicate in order to learn how to behave toward them. . . . Most likely you prayed to them, and let authority figures tell you what the spirits were saying in return . . . let this period of your life speak to you about what power is. . . . What did you learn during this period about how the spiritual realms works, about communicating with spirit, that is still with you today? [*longer pause*] Before you leave this space, express gratitude for the development you experienced here . . . and bless the part of yourself you have brought with you from this space. . . .

You begin to walk again and the path stretches out before you . . . soon the labyrinth begins to turn . . . and as it does the path opens into a small clearing . . . in the center of the clearing is an altar on which sits a bowl filled with hot coals . . . next to it is a feather fan and a container of blue incense powder . . . pour the powder into the censer and use the feather fan to help the incense catch . . . it smells like berries . . . keep fanning the incense until billows of smoke surround you. . . . As you breathe it in, you see yourself as an adolescent . . . information is exchanged between certain parties because of the roles they play . . . and because certain procedures and rules are followed . . . if you were "good," then spirit might communicate with you . . . divination must be done under only the most careful of circumstances in order to be proper. . . . During this period of life did you have any experiences with divination? . . . With the east or air? Did you ever feel as though you could receive or project information to other realms? What did you learn during this period about communication that is still with you today? [*longer pause*] Before you leave this space, express gratitude for the development you experienced here . . . and bless the part of yourself you have brought with you from this space. . . .

You continue to walk the path of the labyrinth . . . soon it begins to make another turn . . . and as it does the path opens into a small clearing

. . . in the center of the clearing is an altar on which sits a bowl filled with hot coals . . . next to it is a feather fan and a container of orange incense powder . . . pour the powder into the censer and use the feather fan to help the incense catch . . . it smells like orange blossoms . . . keep fanning the incense until billows of smoke surround you . . . As you breathe it in, you see that you are now a young adult. . . . Your ability to receive and process information is becoming quite developed . . . you want the information you take in to be rational, or you will reject it. . . . You are imaginative and willing to bend the rules. . . . You do not want to engage in spiritual rituals because you are told to, but only if they make sense to you. . . . Let this time of your life speak to you. . . . What did you think of divination then? . . . Did you have experiences you could not rationally explain? . . . How did you explain intuitive impressions? . . . Did you have any experiences with air or the east? . . . What did you learn during this period that is still with you today? [*longer pause*] Before leaving, express thanks for the development you experienced here and may still be experiencing . . . and bless the part of yourself you have brought with you from this space. . . .

There is only one turn left in the labyrinth, and you walk toward it. . . . Make the last turn and step into a small open clearing . . . in the center of the clearing is an altar on which sits a bowl filled with hot coals . . . next to it is a feather fan and a container of green incense powder . . . pour the powder into the censer and use the feather fan to help the incense catch . . . it smells of mint . . . keep fanning the incense until billows of smoke surround you. . . . As you breathe it in, you see that you are continuing to grow and develop as a person . . . the sharing of information multidimensionally is even more important to you because community is important . . . you want fair treatment for all beings, and a chance for all to share and be heard. . . . You want your experiences with divination to be helpful to others that all may continue to grow. . . . Let the green part of you, whether present, past, or future, speak to you about divination and the value of communication. . . . What spiritual meaning does it have for you? . . . Have you had any experiences with air or the east? . . . What are you currently learning about insight, intelligence, and communication? . . . Before leaving, express thanks for the development you experienced and may still be experiencing in this space. . . .

You are now at the end of the labyrinth . . . waiting for you at the end of the path is the Keeper of Air . . . he stands waiting for you beyond a row of trees that marks the exit from the labyrinth. . . . You approach the ring of trees and listen to what he has to say . . . he wants to speak to you about how you express yourself . . . how you choose to share your thoughts, dreams and desires . . . what you hear and what listens to you, what instructs you, what you do with flashes of insight . . . in what ways you hear and share information across the multidimensional spectrum of the universe. . . . He wants to talk to you about how you connect with others in order to exchange values and information. . . . What does the Keeper of Air say to you? [*long pause*] Ask him questions if you wish. [*long pause*] When your conversation is near an end, the Keeper of Air tells you that to leave the labyrinth you must pass through a row of trees, which are hung with hundreds of wind chimes . . . he tells you that as you walk beneath the trees he will give you a gift . . . it could be an object, a message, a challenge, or opportunity to develop a skill . . . whatever it is, it is something that you need right now in your growth in divination . . . so you walk toward the row of trees, and as you enter it the Keeper of Air raises his arm and with it raises the wind . . . the wind blows through the trees and sets the hundreds of wind chimes to singing . . . you can feel their vibrations all through your body . . . as you pass beneath the chimes, the Keeper of Air tells you what gift he is giving you. . . . What is it? [*longer pause*] Thank him and say whatever more needs to be said between you, if anything. . . .

You turn and leave the labyrinth behind you, and ahead see the carpet waiting to take you home. . . . You step onto the carpet and sit down, and it slowly begins to lift and fly away. . . . You bid farewell to the labyrinth . . . you will return to it again. . . . As you sit on the carpet, you think about your experience . . . What parts stand out in your mind, that made an impression on you? [*longer pause*] How have your ideas and experience of divination changed throughout your life? [*longer pause*] What do you believe now about it as compared to earlier times in your life? [*longer pause*] How do you feel about your encounter with the Keeper of Air? . . . What do you want to do with what he gave you? [*longer pause*]

The carpet is carrying you back toward where you began your journey [*adjust for your setting*] . . . you see the buildings ahead of you, the houses around where you sit, and finally this building. . . . The carpet brings you to the window where you started . . . you step off the carpet and float back in the window, across the room, and to yourself where you are now sitting or lying. . . . Feel yourself come back into your body and take a deep breath . . . move your fingers and toes and stretch a bit . . . take another deep breath . . . and when you are ready, open your eyes.

Be sure you are back. If you are leading a group in this visualization, encourage those who wish to share their experiences, including their conversation with the Keeper of Air and what they received.

Blessing Ritual

Return to the altar you have used in the prior rituals. You will need a third candle to set in the eastern (lower right) quadrant and a stick or cone of incense, wind chime, bell, or feather to represent the element of air. Decorate the eastern quarter of your altar as you like, and again leave room for the candle and other items you choose to represent your experience in the labyrinth. As before, find ways to express the experiences you had in the labyrinth and with divination. Write a poem, draw a picture, or make a figure out of clay. If the Keeper of Air gave you an object as a gift, find a similar object if you can or create a representation of it. If he gave you a quality or ability, create a symbol of it and place this symbol in the eastern quadrant.

When you are ready, take several minutes to relax and cleanse your mind. Breathe deeply and let your thoughts go. Relax all your muscles from your feet upward, breathing slowly and deeply as you do so. Sit and listen quietly for a while. When you feel you are ready you may choose to cast a circle, and call the directions and deities you work with if it is part of your spiritual practice. Light the candle in the eastern quadrant, and if you have not already done so, invite the energies of air, the east, and divination to be present at your ritual. If you wish, also invite the Keeper of Air from the labyrinth.

Then pick up your knotwork cord, which you placed in the southern quadrant in the prior ritual, and acknowledge the you that it represents at this time. Repeat again words which express something like "this is my self, my body, mind, emotions, and spirit. This is who I am here and now as I continue in my journey of self-discovery and spiritual growth." Take a few moments and acknowledge the self you bring to your work with divination, and your relationships with air and the east. Pass the cord through the smoke of the smudge or incense, ring the chime or bell over it, or brush it with the feather. Then place your cord in the eastern quadrant. Next bless yourself with your chosen symbol for air—smudge yourself, fan yourself with the feather, or ring a bell or chime over each of your chakra points. As you do so, say words which honor the intelligent, communicative aspects of yourself, the connection you share with the entire multidimensional universe, the parts of you which discern and choose.

Then bless each of the items you made or found and placed in the eastern quadrant with the smoke, bells, or feather. As you do, describe aloud what the item means to you. Why is it on your altar? What challenge, gift, or ability does it represent and what do you think you are to do with it? How do these things relate to your goal of spiritual growth, and the experiences you have had in your life that have brought you to where you are now?

Express aloud the value of this quadrant's gifts to you, how it helps you sense probabilities, receive and exchange information, and how you wish to continue to grow in divination. Give thanks to the deities you honor, to the vast ground of potentiality, to all the creativity and vitality in the universe, and to all other consciousnesses that support you in your journey and your growth in divination. Bless them and your growing relationships with them.

When you are finished, sit quietly for several minutes and be present to the feelings and thoughts this ritual has raised for you. When you feel ready to end the ritual, thank the east, the element of air, the Keeper of Air (if invited), and dismiss the directions and deities you invoked, if any, according to your tradition.

Blow out the candle in the east but leave it and the items on your altar if possible. Let their presence remind you of your gratitude for the gifts of this quadrant and your work in deepening your spiritual relationships in divination.

Checking in with Your Magickal Plan

Take a moment to review your magickal plan for the year and look at the items you have chosen to work on at the present. Does your plan contain any goals related to divination or are elements of divination contained in them? Identify the extent and nature of the divinatory skills each item on your plan will tend to use, and ask yourself what kind of experiences you want to have with each. If you can detect little to no divination in your plan, why do you think this is so? Is divination something you want to work on now, or something you want to avoid? What are your reasons? Is there anything in your plan that relates to the east and air, to insight, communication skills, mental abilities, education, joy and enthusiasm? Feel free to adjust your plan as you wish to work some of these elements into it. Take some time to journal about divination and its relation to your spiritual development.

7

Conscious Creation

THE FOURTH AND FINAL type of magick we identify is *conscious creation*. Its focus is the manifesting of goals, desires, and beliefs into physical reality. It is likely that most people who hear the word magick are thinking of conscious creation. It is likely they are also thinking of potions, spells, incantations, and bubbling cauldrons. In reality, conscious creation is a lot less dramatic than Hollywood would have you believe. Conscious creation is so ordinary, in fact, that we believe everyone engages in it everyday regardless of religious or cultural background, age, or experience. You could say that for many people it is subconscious creation. Where Paganism differs from some religions is that it names the process and hopes to bring what is often an automatic function to the awareness of the conscious mind, and seeks to help individuals learn to participate in the process in a deliberate way.

Our view of every magickal practice, conscious creation included, is based on the presumption of a living, creative, and communicative universe, which may enfold and unfold itself into existence billions of times a second. Conscious creation is a cooperative process in which individuals strive not only to give their own desires shape and form but are willing to join with other consciousnesses, in both manifest and unmanifest realms, to help give form to the desires of others.

And so the flow and exchange of the universe continues, given concrete shape in this existence by means of this creative process.

Stepping Into the Exchange

The process of conscious creation is reliant upon the cooperation of many consciousnesses that wish to combine forces to produce a result. Without this cooperation and exchange, conscious creation will not happen. From our perspective, then, there is no need for the conscious creator to try and force his or her will on other beings. The degree of force you are willing to use over others is not an indication of your power or accomplishment as a magician. If anything, it takes courage to step up to the plate and announce that you are prepared to be a part of the universal exchange, and then surrender to its process.

The nature of cooperative magick is that it is, well, cooperative. You do not have to participate more than you choose, whether consciously or subconsciously. As always, it is our position that you are in control of your involvement and that you can move from the sidelines to active involvement and back again as you choose. You can also change your mind.

Our view of conscious creation as a magickal practice relies on two underlying presumptions. The first is that the universe is intelligent, creative, able to communicate, and exists at levels deeper than the physical world, levels which operate beyond the constraints of space and time. The concept of the universe as one which enfolds and unfolds allows for communications to occur rapidly through all levels of multidimensionality, both in manifest and unmanifest levels of reality. Potentials and probabilities can be created or dismantled in this enfolded state out to the limits of the vitality and creativity of the universe. The unfolding of the universe into the realm of physical reality allows for the constant influx of energy and information, and for what can appear to be instantaneous changes in exterior conditions.

The second presumption is that the universe is trustworthy. This stems from the belief of inherent blessedness which is somewhat unique to Paganism. Many Pagans embrace the belief that the universe is unflawed and that human beings are unflawed as well. By this we mean unflawed by nature. We recognize that bad things happen and that people make poor choices, but Pagan philosophy does not tend to attribute such events and choices to an inherently corrupt human nature which requires some form of salvation. Pagans generally reject the belief that the physical universe is a prison or punishment for past lives or rebellion against God; it is not a battleground between the forces of good and evil; it is not the domain of Satan until God returns to destroy the universe. Pagans generally agree that human beings are not born with a nature which damns them to eternal punishment. You may wish to see our introductory book for a discussion of human nature from the Pagan perspective.

The blessedness of the universe translates into an essential trustworthiness which exists throughout each part of its multidimensional grandeur. You can enter into relational exchange with this grandeur and be spiritually safe. You can participate in conscious creation and trust that you will not be misused or taken advantage of, or deceived into hell. Every consciousness is blessed and precious and important. Your participation and contribution is as important as that of any other part of consciousness. However, coming to trust in the supportiveness of the universe can be something of a challenge, especially because many of us were raised to believe it is untrustworthy. Building a sense of trust can take time and is best done, we think, in the context of building spiritual relationships. As your spiritual relationships develop, you will probably discover that so also does your sense of safety.

Your opportunities for interaction and exchange with the universe are essentially infinite. But to make it more manageable, you can approach this exchange from within the same spiritual relationships you have developed in your other magickal practices. You can enter into conscious creation with the consciousnesses that form this physical world, such as the earth, trees, animals, ocean, sun, and moon. You can interact with the deeper layers of your own consciousness, that of other people, or groupings such as the collective unconscious, archetypes, and what some refer to as soul families. You can consciously create with the assistance of the Divine—whatever your concept of it—and with beings such as angels, guardians, saints, faeries, and devas. You can interact directly with the multidimensional universe, and with the consciousnesses there that wish to help you in your endeavors. All of these relationships and connections are possible for Pagans. Rather than be overwhelmed by all of your choices, pick a relationship that you are comfortable with and have been working on for a while and go with it. You can always expand to include others later.

The mechanics of conscious creation are fairly simple and include the formation of an intention, the projection of the intention, and the releasing of the intention to do its work. When done in private or public ritual these steps are often observed in sequence separately and formally, but this is not a requirement.

Do not assume that intentions can only be formed to benefit yourself. They can also relate to the needs of others, individually and en masse. They can be directed to the planet and its ecosystems. They can serve as notice to the greater whole that you are available to participate at conscious or subconscious levels in helping bring about the intentions of others. Such an invitation is subject to your choosing to participate in a given instance, an opportunity that can be declined. Since we are proposing that deeper layers of the universe exist outside of space and time, keep in mind that participation may involve events in the past or future, or even in other dimensions of reality. This view opens up intriguing possibilities, such as doing conscious creation to assist your future or past self in manifesting a particular characteristic or outcome, and by extension, to the past and future probabilities of others and the planet.

As far as ethics are concerned, it has been our experience that you will be drawn to do work that matches your current ethical position, or moral embrace. As you know from prior chapters of this book, the extent of a person's moral embrace is generally determined by the worldview of the developmental space he or she has reached. This is all the more reason to continue to push for your continued growth and expansion, and to assist others in theirs. Form your intentions as best you can and trust in the rest. If the universe is not sure of your meaning, ask it to touch base with you as needed to get clarification. If your intention relates to others and you do not know what is needed or is best in a given situation, your intention can ask generally for whatever the recipients most need and leave it at that.

The projecting of your intention can be done as simply as with a thought. It can be supported by ritual actions, such as writing your intention on a paper, burning it, or throwing it into a river. You can visualize it going out as a magickal page, or discuss it in a conversation with the Divine, a patron saint, spirit guide, or the universe.

If you prefer to work with deities and spirit beings, you can present your intention as a petition and leave the matter in their hands. Letting go of your intention means that you free it to travel wherever it needs to go multidimensionally, and trust that it is doing its work and being heard. While you may want to limit the ways in which the universe provides your intention, in the interests of practicality and safety, you probably cannot even begin to imagine all the ways in which it could respond to you. Again, encourage the universe to come check with you before choosing a course that may be unpleasant or undesirable to you. You can certainly recharge your intention as often as you like. For more detailed suggestions on this process, do the exercise below called Manifesting a Desire.

Once you have formed and projected an intention, don't forget to begin your own work. Magick is a team effort. In order to help you succeed, many synchronicities and connections will be pulled together. You need to do what you can to see that they are put to good use. Some Pagans get the mistaken impression that doing magick means they can be passive or even lazy. No doubt their magickal work does not often bring very satisfactory results. Another reason to be actively involved with the process is so that you will more likely find yourself in the right places at the right times in order to do the things and meet the people needed to achieve your intention.

Why would anyone want to do conscious creation? For one thing, it is fulfilling and exciting. For another, humans are part of a creative universe and have a strong urge to be innovative and join in creative endeavors with others. There is a joy and energy that flow from conscious creation which you will discover as you work with it. Artists know this joy and energy intimately in their work, as art itself is an example of direct conscious creation.

Why would the universe care to be bothered with your little intentions? Because the universe is an explosive creative force that cannot find enough avenues in which to express itself. The universe leans in your direction. It yearns for intimacy with you as much or more as you do for intimacy with it.

questions to discuss

1. What does conscious creation mean to you? Do you think it works? Why or why not? Make a note of several of your beliefs about conscious creation and the nature of the universe. How and when did you form these beliefs? Did you learn them from others or are they based on your own personal experience?

2. If Paganism's view of the universe is accurate, what does that mean for you? For your spirituality?

3. What personal and spiritual value does conscious creation have for you, if any? Why?

4. Is art a spiritual or magickal practice for you? In what ways are you artistic? In what ways does your art express your connection to the universe?

 exercise

The Unfolding of Reality

Find a time and a place that is relatively quiet and where you can be undisturbed for about fifteen minutes. You may play music, light candles, and burn incense during the exercise if you wish. Feel free to sit or lie down, as long as you can be comfortable throughout the meditation. When you are ready, close your eyes and breathe slowly and deeply for several minutes. Pay attention to your breathing. Notice the air flow in, and the air flow out. Feel the rhythm of your breath expanding and then subsiding.

After several minutes of quiet awareness of your breathing, gradually shift your focus to your thoughts. As a thought crosses your mind, label it "thinking," and watch it float across the screen of your awareness until it subsides. As another thought makes its appearance, watch it arise, label it "thinking," and watch it subside. Notice that the thought arises and subsides into the ground of your consciousness. See if you can observe the thought in the act of arising and subsiding. Do this for several minutes.

Consider the possibility that what you call an object does not differ greatly from your thoughts, as far as consciousness is concerned. Perhaps objects also arise from some ground and subside back into it. Imagine that an object is a solidified thought. Some scientists, such as David Bohm, propose that the physical universe enfolds and unfolds, or blinks in and out of existence, from its own Ground of Being billions of times a second. Go with that concept for a moment. Allow the thought of the floor or chair on which you are resting to arise in your mind, and feel the reality of this thought beneath you, supporting your weight. See if you can sense its flux in and out of existence. From what does it arise, and into what does it subside?

As the chair or floor subsides, you realize that it has existence beyond this reality. It does not cease its existence because it is no longer unfolded in this reality. There are deeper levels to it than what you experience of it in the physical world. Let it speak to you of what its deeper levels are like, its experience of consciousness. What does it have to say to you?

Continue for several minutes but not to the point of fatigue. When you are ready, bring your awareness back to your breathing and breathe in and out slowly several more times. Gradually return your awareness to yourself and end the exercise. Extinguish any candles or incense you may have lit.

Do not be discouraged if you find this exercise difficult or if you do not have instant success with it. For the vast majority of us it is an engrained habit to see thoughts and matter as discrete objects—which have no reality at deeper levels—and it can be difficult to experience them in other ways. You might repeat this exercise once or twice a week for a while and see if your results change over time.

my journal

If you could create whatever you desire in this reality for yourself, what would it be? Take out your journal and list between ten and twenty things that come to your mind. Why are these things important to you? Which are the most important and which are less? Pick two or three of the most important and list what you are now doing to help bring these desires into reality. What are you willing to do in the future and what are you not willing to do? How much time are you willing to invest in them? Have you consciously communicated your desires to the universe?

If you were to be willing to participate with others in bringing about certain events or conditions in the world, what would they be? List several that come to your mind. What are you willing to do to cooperate in bringing these purposes into reality? What are you not willing to do and why? How much time and effort are you willing to invest? Have you consciously communicated your interest to the universe?

Do you feel you have ever been a part of helping to manifest a larger purpose, one that required the participation of many consciousnesses? If so, what happened? Did any synchronicities or "strange coincidences" occur during the process? What was your reaction to the experience?

exercise

Manifesting a Desire

This exercise is one that you will be involved with for the next few weeks. Begin by taking a look at the goals and desires you listed in the journaling above. Choose one that you would most like to see manifested at this time. It may or may not be a goal that is related to those on your magickal plan for the year. Have pen and paper at hand.

Choose a time when you have thirty or forty-five minutes available, and are in a place that is relatively quiet where you will not be disturbed.

Write your goal at the top of a page. Then take several minutes to think about it. Imagine that your goal has already been accomplished—what is your situation and how do you feel about it? Why is this goal important to you? Do you feel your life lacks something without it? What beliefs, assumptions, and values underlie this feeling of lack? Is your goal the best way to meet this need within yourself? Look at your goal from several angles, and identify the aspects of it that are most important to you.

On the paper begin a column or list called "absolute necessities" and list here everything you think is an essential aspect or quality for your goal to be successful. Include less obvious things, too, such as that no one suffer emotional or physical harm during the manifestation process, which species is involved (we recall a friend who wanted to fall in love with a "guy" and when she adopted a male puppy she adored, she laughingly noted she had neglected to specify that the "guy" be human), whether you are willing to move, lose a job, or make other changes in order to see your goal come to pass. Include the time frame you prefer to work within, and consider how flexible you can be with the timing of results. Be as thorough as you can now and leave plenty of space to add more thoughts later as they come to you.

Either below this list or on another page begin another list called "nice to have but not essential." List here all the aspects of your goal that you find delightful and appealing but that you view as a bonus. Let your imagination run wild and brainstorm freely. The universe is far more creative and surprising than you can imagine, so do not be afraid that you are being unrealistic. Leave space at the bottom to add ideas you think of later. As you make these lists you may discover that some items you thought were necessary can be moved to the list of nonessentials, and qualities you first considered nonessential get moved to your necessity list. This is perfectly okay. You can go through several sheets of paper and revisions if you need to.

We suggest you continue this process for the next week or two and that you read over your lists every day during this period. You do not have to wait two weeks to begin projecting your intention, though you might want to give it several days to be sure you have covered most of the aspects that are important.

Before you begin projecting your desire, there is one more list you need to make, however, which is labeled "things I need to do." On this list identify all the steps you must take, and those which you could take but might be less essential, to bring your desire into reality. Do you need a certain degree or training, do you need to join a particular group or association, are there situations and relationships you need to let go of, do you have issues to be resolved, do you need to go to therapy, or work on beliefs and attitudes? Are there behaviors you need to change, choices you need to make? Will any of your priorities need to shift?

Spend a couple of days reviewing and refining your lists. What these lists do is help you articulate your goal and decide what you are and are not willing to do to bring it about. This inner process is very important and will stand you in good stead as things progress.

Once your lists are in order and you feel clear about your intention, find a time when you have about fifteen minutes available to begin the process of projecting. Feel free to light candles and incense. If you can, have a bell, chimes, or gong to play. If you do not have any of these things, you can always use a kitchen pot. Although we don't believe it is absolutely essential, if you would like to do this projecting within a more formal ritual, feel free to cast a circle and call in quarters, deities, or spirit guides according to your tradition and practice. When you're ready, stand up and ring the bell or chimes, or bang on the pot. Ask the universe for its attention. If you work with deities or spirit beings, invite them to attend and listen to what you have to say. Begin by explaining your intention; do this clearly and out loud. Say why this goal is important to you. Go through each item on your list of necessities and explain why it is essential. Then go through each item on your nice-to-have list and explain why it is there but not considered essential. Tell the universe, or deities, what it is you plan to do to help the manifestation along. Ask for assistance from those consciousnesses that are willing to help you create this piece of reality. Let the universe or deities know you will be expecting magickal pages, synchronicities, "chance" meetings, and so on, and will not dismiss such events as unimportant. Ask the universe or your deities to come and check with you if there is any aspect of your intention they are unclear about. No doubt you have forgotten to list something. Rather than have the universe or your deities guess what you want, ask them to come to you in dreams, meditation, or daydreaming, and check with you. Request them to ask clearly enough that you will realize you are being approached and that you will understand the nature of their question. Assure the universe that you, too, are willing to help in the unfolding of reality for others, and that you stand ready to consider any such requests.

End the projection and extinguish the candles and incense. While you do not need to stand up, strike a pot, and speak out loud for any of this to work, we have found this technique to be very effective. Unlike quiet, sedentary methods of projection, this one engages your body, voice, ears, and kinesthetic energy. Symbolic gestures, such as burning a paper on which you have written your intention, can also be effective but are frequently done only once. It has been our experience that many people need more than one act or gesture in order to feel that their conscious creation is being successful. However, the mode of projection we've presented here is just our suggestion. Feel free to experiment until you find a way that works for you.

Repeat the projecting of your intention every day for several days, as you wish. Make a note of information that comes to you in dreams or daydreaming and talk to the universe about it. If you feel you've been asked a question, by all means answer it. Pay attention to the magickal pages you receive, and the "coincidences" that begin to happen. Are you following through on the items that require action on your part? If this is a longer term goal, you can reduce the number of times you project to perhaps once a week or some other periodic number. Some people choose not to project repeatedly, but do so once or twice and then stop. If you like, take a reminder of this working with you in the car or to work. You can be thinking about your intention and musing on ideas and plans even when you are not actively projecting.

When the date for the goal to be accomplished arrives, evaluate your progress. Was your time frame realistic? Have you accomplished what you needed to do in order to be ready for this reality in your life? Has your intention been met in ways other than you anticipated? Did you discover that you needed to change your intention part of the way through the process?

Journal about your experiences and how you feel about them. Was this harder work than you expected? Think about what you might want to do differently the next time you engage in conscious creation.

Conscious Creation and the Four Elements

We place conscious creation in the upper right of Wilber's four quadrants, which is in the north and home to the element of earth.

The upper right quadrant is Wilber's realm of *Outer It*, the physical world and all we perceive as real. Everything in this quadrant is observable, measurable, and quantifiable, subject to scientific testing and classification. At first glance, this quadrant does not appear to have anything subjective about it, nor does it seem to contain underlying values or purposes. This is the world of matter, which shows itself in the unfolded world as separate and inert objects which seem to exist in a mechanistic realm governed strictly by cause and effect and natural laws. Paganism offers a twist on this view, as we have seen, especially as concerns the levels of reality that underlie and support this physical expression.

In common Pagan practice, the north is the archetype of strength, endurance, silence, darkness, and faith. On the wheel of the year, the north sits in winter (in the Northern Hemisphere), which in more extreme climates brings bitter temperatures and the death of vegetation and animals. The sun is at its weakest point and there are more dark hours in a day than light. On the wheel of the day, north is represented by night. On the wheel of human life, it is the time of repose, evaluation, aging, and death. The north represents the ending of cycles, an ending which makes room for a new cycle to begin. Earth is the element typically associated with the north in Pagan practice because it is also the element of quiet strength, rest, and endurance. Earth is the dark nurturing womb for all life on this planet. It

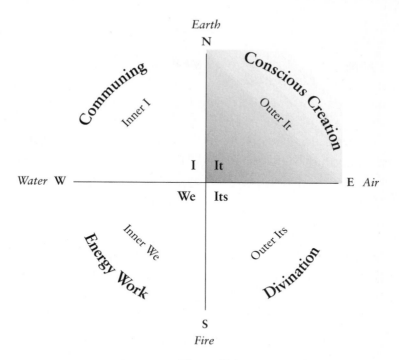

Figure 7.1
The Upper Right Quadrant: Conscious Creation, North, Outer It

serves as foundation and support, and provides all the resources needed by physical life in order to survive.

Developing your experiences with conscious creation can help you move toward the goals of *maximum healthiness* and *maximum expansion* in your spiritual growth by providing the means to put your beliefs, values, and goals into action through physical manifestation. Once a desire or belief achieves physical form, it can be experienced in the exterior world. Pagans test physical reality, and it in turn tests them, challenging them to examine what is of value to them based on the type of world they help create, and what they choose to make real.

Connecting to That Which Endures

This exercise focuses on experiencing that which is lasting, strong, and patient through the element of earth. We suggest that you plan to do this exercise when you can be out of doors, in a location and time of year when you can safely lie on the ground. Check the area you will use carefully for things like poison ivy, stinging nettles, ground bees, and fire ants. Try to find a place that is peaceful and quiet, where you will not be disturbed for twenty minutes or so.

When you are ready to begin, sit on the ground in the place you have chosen and listen to the sounds around you. Relax and let the sounds of the earth, birds, trees, plants, and animals gradually fill your awareness. Sit quietly and calm your mind. If thoughts enter your mind, watch them parade past and keep on going.

Feel the energy of the earth beneath you. Slow your breathing. Try to sense the long, slow vibrations of the earth. How does its energy feel to you? Does it have a sound, do you feel it physically in your body? Does it raise certain emotions in you? Remain open to this energy for several minutes, and pull it up and through you if you wish.

After several minutes, gently turn over until you are lying on the ground face down. Spread your arms out to your sides to a point that is comfortable, and where you have the feeling that you are embracing the earth. Find a comfortable position for your head, close your eyes and relax again. Turn your attention to the pulsing vibrations of the earth. Let these vibrations fill your being until you are resonating in harmony with them. As you do this say, "I open myself to all that is strong and nurturing."

As you lie there, communing with the earth's energy, look within yourself for the parts of you that are strong, solid, and stable. How do you feel about physical existence? What is your attitude toward life? In what ways do you nurture yourself? In what ways do you nurture others? How do you use your resources, and the resources of the earth? Meditate on the patience and quiet strength shown by the earth's mountains, oceans, trees, and soil. Meditate on the faith and courage it takes to trust that life will provide what you need. For all of its quietness, the earth is full of power. Open yourself to how you experience this power, and how you in turn express power in your everyday life.

The earth sustains all of life through her atmosphere, nutrients, and resources. Without her reliable and stable presence, life would perish. The selfless nurturance of the earth is the foundation on which all your days of physical existence are built, even when you are not consciously aware of it. The earth itself, by being what it is and giving of itself, demonstrates the fundamental trustworthiness of the universe. Imagine the sheer volume and abundance of the life forms that the earth supports. Acknowledge its gifts. Just as your arms are outstretched to embrace the earth, so are you embraced by it in return. Open yourself to embrace the joy and beauty of physical existence. It offers untold opportunities to create experiences and explore the meaning of material creations. Acknowledge and appreciate the gift of the physical world.

Gradually bring your attention back to your surroundings. Return to a sitting position and look around you. End the exercise by expressing gratitude for your experience. Feel free to journal about it if you wish, and if you are with a class or group, spend several minutes sharing.

my journal

The most memorable conscious creation experiences I have had are . . .

The impact they had on me was . . .

These experiences were or were not peak experiences because . . .

The aspects of conscious creation I find most challenging are . . .

The aspects I enjoy most are . . .

I would describe my relationship with the north as . . .

Experiences I have had with the north are . . .

My relationship with the element of earth is . . .

Experiences I have had with the element of earth are . . .

Conscious Creation in Developmental Space

We now examine the ways in which conscious creation is experienced by Pagans occupying different developmental spaces. The types of intentions which are chosen, who is permitted to engage in this form of magick, and under what circumstances will take different forms depending on the developmental space the conscious creator occupies. What is considered ethical, in terms of the choices that are made and the methods by which they are carried out, will also vary.

For the **egocentric** Pagan (Purple-Red), conscious creation will likely concern itself with meeting the needs of the individual and of his or her immediate circle. The gods or other recognized beings of power must be consulted to assure that they are not angered. Concern for the greater society, other cultures, or other living creatures on the earth will not be in evidence, since the moral embrace of the egocentric conscious creator extends no further than his or her immediate family. As Red emerges, the conscious creator may have no qualms about trying to create harmful situations for others, or otherwise "smiting an enemy." If they sense that they or their group have suffered an attack or insult, they believe they are ethically justified in protecting themselves and their own.

The acts of forming intentions, empowering and projecting them will likely be surrounded with elaborate rites, music, garb, and processions. Objects may likely be imbued with the power of the ritual and carry within them the intentions of those doing the working. These may take the form of amulets and talismans. The object may be considered to contain so much power, in fact, that it may be left in specific places for the purpose of bringing about the conscious creation on its own. The power of such objects may be considered such that they are even dangerous and must be handled with care by those doing the work, or only by a priestly class. Certain symbols may be adopted to represent the reality these magickal objects are intended to bring about, such as victory in battle, protection from enemies, famine, or drought.

Adult Pagans who get stuck at the egocentric level will likely have many superstitious and irrational beliefs about conscious creation and the power of their rituals and symbols. They may believe that they can perform miraculous deeds, signs, and wonders whenever they choose regardless of circumstance or the will of others. They may interpret ordinary events in which they have participated as providing proof of their miraculous powers despite the fact that no one else present has witnessed what they claim. They may be willing to use their supposed powers to bring about selfish ends without regard to the appropriateness of the work they are doing. If egocentric Pagans are planning rituals or classes which involve conscious creation, they may inject a fair amount of drama into the production and perhaps throw in one or two moments of spiritual crisis. They are likely to believe that everyone wants the same goals which they want, and find it nearly impossible to take the perspective of others. They may see no difficulties in performing punitive conscious creation if they or their group have been attacked or maligned, or even if they simply disapprove of some behavior or attitude. If you are in a teaching or leadership position and encounter any such behaviors, encourage calm action which focuses on the appropriateness of the work and its consequences. Make a point of discussing the perspective of others and encourage those involved to consider other points of view.

Healthy aspects of the egocentric self that conscious creators can bring with them in their development is a confidence in their abilities, an appreciation for symbols and tools, talent in creating beautiful ritual and focusing on goals without distraction, and faith in the successful outcome of their work.

Conscious creation at the **mythic** level (Blue), solidifies the relationship with spiritual beings into a structured mythology which is believed to be literally real. The mythology governs daily reality, and the institutions and structures of the society are created in conformity with it. Any acts of conscious creation—such as prayer and the building of institutional structures—are measured on the yardstick of the mythology and how they serve it. If their usefulness and orthodoxy cannot be demonstrated, then such acts will be prohibited and probably condemned. Most likely the sanctioned acts of conscious creation will be given over exclusively to a priestly or other governing group, so that improper work cannot occur. Conscious creation rituals are very structured and cannot be varied; if someone should attempt to vary them a cry of outrage or heresy will likely erupt.

Mythic individuals cannot tolerate mythologies which differ from their own, and so only their experience and creation of reality is considered good and true. Mythic societies frequently condemn other people's experiences of conscious creation while their own are glorified as being ordained by the gods. Wealth, success in battle, and other accomplishments are produced as proof that the Divine favors them. Other cultures may be demonized and their resources and people turned to the purposes of the mythic society, such as through slavery and conquest. Such behaviors are considered ethical since the moral embrace of the mythic self extends only to its ethnic group, and the mythology is the predominant belief filter. Conscious creation will be viewed as ethical if it helps preserve and advance the group, especially as against all other mythologies. The destruction of competing mythologies is considered a very creative act, as the existence of other belief systems is perceived as a threat.

Pagans who get stuck at the mythic level will tend to be orthodox and believe that a Pagan reality, which rests on their tradition's view of the nature of the universe and the Divine, is the only reality worth having. Only those Pagans who follow the mythic Pagan's own tradition will be viewed as having the truth and capable of doing magick, and therefore conscious creation, correctly. Rituals for conscious creation must be done properly, with the use of specific tools, garb, and words. Mythic Pagans can be very contemptuous of other Pagan traditions, but even more so of non-Pagan religions, especially those they view as having historically sought the demise of Paganism, or who may presently be persecuting it. If you are in a teaching or leadership position when this view expresses itself, try to minimize any negative impact and encourage cooperation and tolerance among all present. Encourage a broader ethical view that looks beyond the preservation of its own belief system.

Healthy aspects of the mythic self that conscious creators can bring with them in their development include respect for custom and practice, an appreciation of order and harmony, loyalty for one's group, dependability, and pride in magickal accomplishment.

Rational (Orange) Pagans look for reasons to explain the myth, while growing into the realization that the myth is a story and not the literal truth. This expansion brings both a freedom and an anxiety, since if they are not doing what the myth tells them to do, then what should they be doing? For the first time they begin to reason through values, practices, and structures, and articulate for themselves what has meaning for them. The main driver of conscious creation ceases to be the myth and becomes what makes sense. The fairness or impact of the realities being created on others outside of one's country or ethnic group are still generally not considered, but all practices which appear superstitious or legalistic are now abandoned.

With the new freedom from the constraints of the old mythology comes a surge of personal autonomy. Since this kind of personal freedom has not been experienced at earlier levels of development, the energy it brings with it can be nearly explosive. Pagans can become exceedingly goal-oriented and insist on their independence. Pagans who get stuck in the rational level can become so fiercely independent that they begin to lose the ability to cooperate with others. Their magickal practices may become self-centered and their conscious creation focused on goals that matter only to them. They may lose their sense of being a part of a greater whole and see no reason to temper their personal needs to take the collective into account. Their conscious creation goals can therefore be short-sighted and sometimes have unpleasant longer term consequences. They may also decide that conscious creation has no spiritual or cooperative dimensions to it, and can be reduced to the sheer force of their will imposed on the world around them. If you are in a teaching or leadership position and encounter this attitude toward magick, present the rational Pagan with reasons why they still need to consider themselves a part of the collective, expand their ethical embrace, and engage in longer term thinking.

Healthy aspects of the rational self that conscious creators can bring forward with them include self-motivation, an interest in how things work, the internalizing and personalizing of ethics, and an attitude that questions and probes the underlying meaning of existence and spiritual practice.

Vision-logic (Green) Pagans become more careful with their conscious creation, and are concerned that the results of their efforts are fair and take into consideration the needs and feelings of others. Since their moral embrace has expanded to include all of humanity, they consider the impact of what they do on all individuals, nations, and ethnic groups. Their ethics are internally driven and they do not seek approval from authority figures for their choices when it comes to the conscious creation work they perform. If it feels right to them, they trust that it is right.

Conscious creation becomes a more intuitive process, and Pagans engaging in it may center their spiritual relating around deep levels of collective interaction, such as the collective unconscious and human archetypal energies.

Pagans who get stuck at this level can become very judgmental of the ethics governing the choices of those at earlier levels of development, particularly the mythic. They cannot understand how anyone would work to manifest a world that does not reflect their Green values, and may be as harsh toward earlier levels on the spiral as those levels are towards them. Conscious creation work can be filtered through an orthodoxy of its own, and individuals made to feel guilty if they do not conform to it. Another way stuck Green can express itself is to be overwhelmed by numerous perspectives. Rather than just the creations of its own mind or those of a mythology, it is faced with the entire range of human experience, choices, and beliefs, and may feel unable to choose a direction in which to move. If taken to an extreme, this relativity of values can lead to hopelessness and cynicism. If you are in a teaching or leadership position when stuck Green appears, gently bring the group or individual back on focus, have them articulate the values that are important to them, and insist that a choice be made in order to move the work of the group or class forward. If judgmentalism makes an appearance, attempt to point out the relativity of the judgmentalism itself, and that many valid points of view can and do exist. A brief discussion of developmental theory may be helpful.

Healthy aspects of vision-logic that conscious creators can benefit from are a concern for the needs and goals of others, a reliance on intuition and feelings, and an appreciation of a truly global vision.

When a Pagan reaches the **psychic** space (Yellow-Turquoise), the inner realms open up. It is as though the Pagan is immediately present to the communications, intentions, and plans of deeper levels of reality. Information is freely available and exchanged. The shape of probabilities and the building of realities soon to be brought into conscious reality can be sensed and sometimes clearly seen in detail. An underlying purpose and intelligence to physical reality may also be perceived. The division between manifest and unmanifest reality, while acknowledged, is readily pierced and both sides are able to be experienced. This leads to a far greater and deeper sense of interconnectedness than has been felt by the individual before. The consciousness of the physical world—rocks, trees, and animals—is the first realm to open up, and spiritual relationships expand to embrace it. Conscious creation is performed with a real sense of communication and participation with these levels of reality and the consciousness of physical things. The moral embrace of psychic conscious creators expands to include all life on the earth. The goals of conscious creation are considered ethical if they do not intentionally harm any life form.

Pagans may get stuck in this level if they become attached to the depth of information and experiences they are having, especially if they fear that moving on developmentally will mean that they lose their newfound sense of connection. In reality, continued growth will lead to an expansion of this sense of connection to include spiritual realms. Pagans who are stuck here may do well to find a good spiritual advisor and be willing to work on releasing their emotional attachment to this level.

At the **subtle** level, Pagans will begin to experience the same type of interconnectedness with spiritual realms as they previously encountered with the consciousness of physical organisms. The world of spirit literally opens up for them and they experience it as naturally and truly as most people experience ordinary reality. This sense of connection brings with it a sense of union with the Divine that results in a hunger to experience more. Pagans at this level may engage in conscious creation simply in the hope of having another moment of ecstatic union. The moral embrace of subtle Pagans expands to include spirit beings, and conscious creation now takes into consideration the purposes and desires of all sources previously recognized, plus those of angels, saints, the Holy Spirit, and spirit guides. Conscious creation will be considered ethical if it does not detrimentally affect humans, earthly creatures and life forms, or the goals of spirit and spirit beings.

At the **causal** and **nondual** levels, Pagans may find themselves very comfortable with the world as it is and their conscious creation may, if they engage in it, occur seamlessly and in harmony with their environment. Their moral embrace expands to include all of manifest and unmanifest reality, and their conscious creation embraces the needs and intentions of the whole.

questions to discuss

1. What view of conscious creation were you raised with? What do you believe about it now?

2. Does Paganism do enough, too much, or too little with conscious creation? What would you do to change this?

3. Have you faced any developmental issues in regard to conscious creation? Are you facing any now?

4. Have you known anyone who has struggled with developmental issues in regard to conscious creation? What happened?

5. Have you had any experience with conscious creation that really stands out in your mind? What happened?

6. How would you explain conscious creation to a non-Pagan?

 visualization

Conscious Creation and the Labyrinth

Get in a comfortable position. If you are sitting, put your feet flat on the floor. If you are lying down, put your arms down beside you and your legs out straight. Close your eyes . . . slow your breathing . . . breathe in . . . breathe out . . . relax your muscles . . . breathe in . . . breathe out . . . feel the tension leave your neck and back . . . breathe in . . . breathe out . . . relax all the little muscles around your eyes . . . relax your spine . . . your legs . . . your feet . . . your hands and arms . . . keep breathing slowly. [*longer pause*]

You feel yourself becoming lighter and lighter . . . you are so light you are able to float right over to the window of this room [*adjust for your setting*] . . . open the window and look outside . . . waiting for you just outside the window is a large carpet that can take you anywhere . . . see yourself floating right out of the window and onto the carpet. . . .

You settle yourself onto the carpet and it begins to fly away . . . over the houses and streets where you live [*adjust to your setting*] . . . the carpet is taking you to the labyrinth for one last visit . . . you can see the trees of the forest now . . . you fly over them and see the clearing where the labyrinth awaits. . . . The carpet enters the clearing and sets you down. . . . You step off of it, knowing it will be waiting for you when you are finished. . . .

You see the entrance of the labyrinth ahead of you and you enter it . . . in this final journey through the labyrinth you will acknowledge your growth in the skills of conscious creation, your awareness of being a participant in the unfolding of reality . . . and you will meet with the Keeper of Earth, who has a gift or bit of advice which you need. . . . You walk into the labyrinth, and soon the path begins to make a turn . . . as it turns it opens into a small clearing . . . in the center of the clearing is an altar on which sits a very large and beautiful white crystal . . . step up to the crystal and look into it. . . . It appears to be gently illuminated from within. . . . As you peer into the crystal, you are transported back to the time when you were an infant . . . your physical reality then was your body and immediate caregivers. . . . Take a moment to get in touch with your basic physical self. [*longer pause*] Before leaving, offer a blessing for this period of your life and the gift of physical existence that has brought you to the present. . . .

You begin to walk again, down the path . . . soon the labyrinth begins to turn . . . as it turns it opens into a small clearing . . . in the center of the clearing is an altar on which sits a very large and beautiful purple crystal . . . step up to the crystal and look into it. . . . It appears to be gently illuminated from within. . . . As you peer into the crystal, you see that you have grown to be a preschooler . . . the world appears to be a mysterious place, and you do not know why it exists or you exist . . . it may seem a bit threatening to you, and so you do as the powerful Others in your life direct you . . . the physical world seems to be alive and full of spirits that talk to you . . . you in turn can communicate with them . . . let this time of your life speak to you about the mystery of reality . . . and the inherent sense of connection children are born with. . . . Before you leave this space, express gratitude for the development you experienced here . . . and bless the parts of yourself you have brought with you from it. . . .

You begin to walk again and the path of the labyrinth stretches out before you . . . soon you approach another turn which opens into a small clearing. . . in the center of the clearing is an altar on which sits a very large and beautiful red crystal . . . step up to the crystal and look into it. . . . It glows softly. . . . As you peer into the crystal, you see yourself as a youth, impulsive and headstrong. . . . You are filled with a love of adventure and you want to experience everything. . . . You want to be powerful and feel as though you have power over your world. . . . The spirit beings that are in charge of how the world runs seem to you to be the most powerful of all, and you do not want to anger them . . . let this period of your life speak to you about what power is. . . . In what ways is your power creative and imaginative? . . . What did you learn during this period about how reality works, how you are or are not in control of your world that is still with you today? [*longer pause*] Before you leave this space, express gratitude for the development you experienced here . . . and bless the part of yourself you have brought with you from this space. . . .

You continue walking . . . soon the labyrinth begins to turn . . . and as it does the path opens into a small clearing . . . in the center of the clearing is an altar on which sits a very large and beautiful blue crystal. . . step up to the crystal and look into it. . . . As you peer into the crystal, you see yourself as an adolescent . . . the world appears orderly to you because people play roles and follow the rules . . . things must be done just so in order to be right and lead to the correct results . . . relationships also matter a great deal. . . . Let this time of your life speak to you about what you believed to be the meaning of this reality [*longer pause*] Did you have any experiences with earth or the north? . . . Did you ever do any conscious creation? . . . Did you begin to experience coincidences? . . . Did you ever have a prayer answered? . . . What did you learn during this period about relationships, nurturing and exchange that is still with you today? [*longer pause*] Before you leave this space, express gratitude for the development you experienced here . . . and bless the part of yourself you have brought with you from this space. . . .

You continue to walk the path of the labyrinth . . . soon the path begins to make another turn . . . and as it does the path opens into a small clearing . . . in the center of the clearing is an altar on which sits a very large and beautiful orange crystal . . . step up to the crystal and look into it. . . . As you peer into the crystal, you see that you are now a young adult. . . . You are creative and independent and ready to try out the world on your own. . . . Understanding how and why things work is important to you. . . . If it doesn't make sense, it doesn't interest you. . . . You are very goal-oriented. . . . Let this time of your life speak to you. . . . What did you think of conscious creation then? . . . Did you have experiences with synchronicities, did you begin to get magickal pages? . . . How did you explain what these things were to yourself? . . . Did you have any experiences with earth or the north? . . . What did you learn during this period about bringing your adult, rational self to your magickal work that is still with you today? [*longer pause*] Before leaving, express thanks for the development you experienced here and may still be experiencing . . . and bless the part of yourself you have brought with you from this space. . . .

There is only one turn left in the labyrinth, and you walk toward it. . . . Make the last turn and step into a small open clearing . . . in the center of the clearing is an altar on which sits a very large and beautiful green crystal . . . step up to the crystal and look into it. . . . As you peer into the crystal, you see that you are continuing to grow and develop as a person . . . a sense of belonging and community is more important to you . . . you care about the earth and the proper use of its resources. . . . You want relationships to be fair, for people's feelings to be appreciated, and everyone to be heard. . . . You want your experiences with magick to be reciprocal and of benefit to others, not just about your own needs. . . . Let the green part of you, whether present, past, or future, speak to you about conscious creation . . . the relational exchange between you and the wider universe which helps to create this world and your experiences. . . . How do you incorporate this exchange in your life? . . . In what ways do you participate in manifesting chosen realities? . . . Have you had any experiences with earth or the north? . . . What are you currently learning about accommodating all the intentions that are being expressed in the universe? . . . Before leaving, express thanks for the development you experienced and may still be experiencing in this space. . . .

You are now at the end of the labyrinth . . . waiting for you at the end of the path is the Keeper of Earth . . . she stands waiting for you just beside a stone arch that marks the exit from the labyrinth . . . she wants to speak to you about anchors, what makes you faithful and brave . . . the things that you love, that you embrace, and choose to nurture in your life. . . . What do you do to regenerate yourself? . . . What supports you, and what in turn do you support with your resources? . . . What world are you creating for yourself and others? . . . She wants to talk to you about how you connect with others in order to give form to desire. . . . What does the Keeper of Earth say to you? [*long pause*] Ask her questions if you wish. [*long pause*] When your conversation is near an end, the Keeper of Earth tells you that to leave the labyrinth you must pass beneath her stone arch . . . she tells you that when you walk beneath it, she will give you a gift . . . it could be an object, a message, a challenge, or opportunity to develop a skill . . . whatever it is, it is something that you need right now in your growth in conscious creation and the nurturance of your inner earth . . . walk beneath the stone arch . . . and as you do the Keeper of Earth tells you what gift she is giving you. . . . What is it? [*longer pause*] Thank her and say whatever more needs to be said between you, if anything. . . .

You turn and leave the labyrinth behind you, and ahead see the carpet waiting to take you home. . . . Before stepping onto the carpet, you take a moment to think about how your ideas and experience of conscious creation have changed throughout your life. [*longer pause*] What do you believe now about probabilities, choice, and conscious creation, as compared to earlier times in your life? [*longer pause*] How do you feel about your encounter with the Keeper of Earth? . . . What do you want to do with what she gave you? [*longer pause*]

As you step onto the carpet, you look back at the labyrinth which you have traveled several times. . . . It has shown you gifts and challenges from all the periods in your life. . . . It has helped you explore your relationship to magick, to power, emotion, choice, and knowledge. . . . It has helped you gain insight into where you have come from and where you are heading in your personal and spiritual development. . . . Through the elements it has provided you with gifts to help you on your path. . . . Acknowledge your experiences here, and offer a moment of gratitude. . . .

The carpet now begins to lift and fly away. . . . It is carrying you back toward where you began your journey [*adjust for your setting*] . . . you see the buildings ahead of you, the houses around where you are living, and finally the place where you began. . . . The carpet brings you to the window where you started . . . you step off the carpet and float back in, across the room, and to yourself where you are now sitting or lying . . . . Feel yourself come back into your body and take a deep breath . . . move your fingers and toes and stretch a bit . . . take another deep breath . . . and when you are ready, open your eyes.

Be sure you are back. If you are leading a group in this visualization, encourage those who wish to share their experiences, including their conversation with the Keeper of Earth and what they received.

Blessing Ritual

Return to the altar you have used in the prior rituals. You will need a fourth candle to set in the northern (upper right) quadrant, and a stone, crystal, or container of salt or soil to represent the element of earth. Decorate the northern quarter of your altar as you like, and again leave room for the candle and other items you choose to represent your experience in the labyrinth. Be creative—draw a picture, write a story, create a clay pot, make a collage—whatever best describes your experiences with conscious creation and in the labyrinth. If the Keeper of Earth gave you an object as a gift, find a similar object if you can or create a representation of it. If she gave you a quality or ability, create a symbol of it and place this symbol in the northern quadrant.

When you are ready, take several minutes to relax and cleanse your mind. Breathe deeply and relax all your muscles. Sit and listen quietly for a while. When you feel you are ready, you may cast a circle, and call the directions and deities if it is part of your spiritual practice. Light the candle in the northern quadrant, and if you have not already done so, invite the energies of earth, the north, and conscious creation to be present at your ritual. If you wish, also invite the Keeper of Earth from the labyrinth.

Then pick up your knotwork cord where you placed it in the eastern quadrant, and acknowledge the you that it represents at this time. Take a few moments and acknowledge the self you bring to your work with conscious creation, and your relationships with earth and the north. Pass the cord beneath the crystal or stone, or sprinkle it with salt or soil. Then place your cord in the northern quadrant. Next bless yourself with your chosen symbol for earth—touch each of your chakra points with the stone or crystal, or sprinkle them with the salt or soil. As you do so, say words which honor the faithful, nurturing aspects of yourself, that point which connects your consciousness and the world of form, and the parts of you which are strong and enduring.

Then bless each of the items you placed in the northern quadrant with the stone, soil, or salt and as you do describe aloud what the item means to you. Why is it on your altar? What challenge, gift, or ability does it represent and what do you think you are to do with it? How do these things relate to your goal of spiritual growth, and the experiences you have had in your life that have brought you to where you are now?

Express aloud the value of this quadrant's gifts to you, how it helps you bring form to intention and use resources wisely, and how you wish to continue to grow in conscious creation. Give thanks to the deities you honor, to the vast ground of potentiality, to all the creativity and vitality in the universe, and to all other consciousnesses that support you in your journey and your growth in conscious creation. Bless them and your growing relationships with them.

When you are finished, sit quietly for several minutes and be present to the feelings and thoughts this ritual has raised for you. When you feel ready to end the ritual, thank the north, the element of earth, the Keeper of Earth (if invited), and dismiss the directions and deities you invoked, if any, according to your tradition. Blow out the candle in the north but leave it and the items on your altar if possible. Let their presence remind you of your gratitude for the gifts of this quadrant and your work in deepening your spiritual relationships in conscious creation.

Checking in with Your Magickal Plan

Take out your magickal plan for the year and look at what you have chosen to work on. Does your plan contain any goals related to conscious creation? Is conscious creation a major theme in your life at the moment, and if so, what is it that you wish to bring into reality? Identify the extent and nature of the conscious creation skills each item on your plan will tend to use. If you can detect little to no conscious creation in your plan, why do you think this is so? Is there anything in your plan that relates to the north and earth, to issues of faith and courage, endurance, acceptance, calmness and nurturance? Feel free to adjust your plan if you wish to work some of these elements into it. In the near future, take some time to journal about conscious creation and its relation to your spiritual development in the coming year.

CONCLUSION

Final Thoughts

Before closing we wish to offer some final thoughts on the formation of an integrated Pagan spirituality. This book has covered a lot of territory quickly and we want you to leave your work here with a sense of the landscape of balanced spiritual development. As we noted at the very beginning, development begins with growth. We all grow at points in our lives, even if we're not aware that we are growing or in what ways we are growing. Growth as an expansion of capacities is a natural process that happens to everyone and everything at multiple levels. Sometimes development unfolds smoothly. Sometimes it is difficult, haphazard, or warps itself to fit the shape of our traumas, fears, and expectations. As adults, growing sometimes takes the form of healing those parts of the self that have been left behind and now need some nurturing attention. While developmental experiences shape you, we also believe that you in turn shape them, especially as you grow into perspectives where you can see the floors of your skyscraper that need support or adjustment, and as you look before you in anticipation of the contours of growth that lie ahead.

We believe that optimal growth, both spiritually and personally, means balancing growth across all of your developmental streams and all aspects of yourself—mind, body, emotions, and spirit. On a practical level this means growing in a balanced way in each of Wilber's four quadrants: private interior experience, shared cultural meanings, exterior social institutions, and the exterior physical world. We go further and relate the four quadrants to Paganism's magickal spiritual practices as we identify them: communing, energy work, divination, and conscious creation. Spiritual development for Pagans in the four quadrants is most likely going to express itself in the context of one or more of these four types of magick. We believe that developing each of them in a balanced manner can lead to a healthy and integrated spirituality. We further believe that helping Pagans grow magickally in such a balanced way should be a primary goal of Pagan teachers and mentors.

Our assigning of the types of magick, the four directions, and the four elements to each of Wilber's quadrants is new and distinctive. We hope that making these unusual correspondences will act as a catalyst for you, offering you new perspectives from which to see your personal development. In order to gain these perspectives, don't be shy about dissecting the material presented in these chapters. Stand all the ideas presented on their heads. Walk around them and view them from every angle. Challenge them, demand their secrets, and their particular significance for you. Be relentless and do not become discouraged. Don't accept that something is true just because someone tells you it is true, including all that we and the scholars cited in this book have said, but demand that reality disclose itself to you directly.

Dare to have relationships with the universe and the Divine you have never considered before. Your point of connection to the multidimensional universe, to the spiritual principles that have ultimate value to you, is absolutely unique. No one else shares your connection to that portion of the whole from which you emerge in each moment, that portion which transforms itself into your experience. Remember, the universe already leans in your direction. The next move is up to you.

The Center Candle

Take the center candle that you have not yet used in the blessing rituals and place it in the center of your altar. Have your knotwork cord at hand. Play some meditative music and light some incense if you wish. Then sit quietly for several minutes and breathe deeply. When you feel calmed and ready, begin by casting a circle and calling the directions according to your tradition. If you have no particular tradition, invite each quadrant, direction, and element to be present for your ritual. As you do, light each of the candles in the quadrants. If you work with deities, call them as well. If you do not, you may wish to call the Keepers of the elements you met in your journeys through the labyrinth.

Then take several minutes and look at all the quadrants before you. Look at the objects you collected or made, the pictures you painted or drew, collages you created, figures you sculpted. Enjoy the memories they evoke, the challenges they raise. This is your journey through the magickal realms laid out before you. What do you see when you look at them, what do you feel? Speak to the quadrants if you wish, tell them what you are thinking and feeling, and the parts of your experiences with them that you will remember.

Look also at the drawings of the spiral or labyrinth you made which you hung or placed near your altar. You have walked the labyrinth several times now. It is more than a mental concept to you, it is a lived experience. What impressions or insights do you have of the labyrinth now that you did not when you began? What insights have you gained concerning the developmental spaces, the colors of the spiral?

Pick up your knotwork cord and hold it in your hand. Breathe deeply and be present with it for a moment. You created this cord to represent yourself. The strands are aspects of yourself which you chose. How do you feel about those aspects now? Notice how they blend together and are bound by the knots, which represent your body, mind, emotions, spirit, and commitment to growth. The knots serve to illustrate in a concrete way the integrating force of your body, mind, emotions, and spirit in your developmental journey.

Now place your cord around the base of the center candle, and acknowledge that you are bringing yourself to the center point, the point of balance and integration. Light the center candle and as you do say the following or similar words: "I affirm and accept all aspects of myself and bring them to the center point of wholeness. I dedicate myself to continued spiritual development and to growth as an integrated being. I commit myself to becoming the happiest and most balanced person I can. I open myself to new relationships with my self, my culture, the physical world, the Divine and the spiritual realms, and all of manifest and unmanifest reality. I embrace my place in the universe, and choose to participate in its creative and magickal exchange. I step courageously into the unknown that lies before me, because I trust myself, the universe, and my concept of the Divine to support me in my journey. So mote it be."

Sit quietly for several moments in the feelings and energies this ritual has raised for you. When you are ready, offer your gratitude for the experiences you have had with the directions and quadrants, and then extinguish all the candles. Thank the deities, Keepers of the directions, and elements you invited according to your tradition. When you feel your work is complete, dismantle the altar.

At the end of the year set aside for working your magickal plan, you may wish to do this ritual or an adaptation of it again, placing a candle in each of the quadrants to represent the elements, and a candle in the center to represent your integrated self. If you design a magickal plan for yourself every year, you can do this ritual annually as a rededication.

NOTES

Introduction

1. Isaac Bonewits, *Defining Paganism: Paleo-, Meso-, and Neo-* 2.2, 1999, located on the internet at http://www.neopagan.net/PaganDefs. html, copyright 1999, c.e., Isaac Bonewits.

2. Wilber, *Integral Psychology*. Boston: Shambhala, 2000, p. 137.

3. Ibid., p. 138.

Chapter 1

1. We gratefully acknowledge the examples Wilber provides of holarchies found in his book, *The Eye of Spirit*, Boston: Shambhala, 1998, p. 41.

2. Koestler, Arthur. *The Ghost in the Machine*. New York: The MacMillan Company, 1967, p. 48.

3. Wilber, *The Eye of Spirit*, p. 39.

4. Koestler, *The Ghost in the Machine*, p. 103.

5. Ibid., p. 68.

6. Eisler, Riane. *The Chalice and the Blade: Our History, Our Future*. San Francisco: Harper & Row, 1979, pgs. 105, 106. We gratefully acknowledge Ken Wilber for drawing our attention to Ms. Eisler's work in this area in his book, *The Eye of Spirit*, p. 33.

7. Wilber, *The Eye of Spirit*, p. 32, 33.

8. Wilber, *Integral Psychology*. Boston: Shambhala, 2000, p. 38.

9. Wilber, Ken. *A Sociable God: Toward a New Understanding of Religion*. Boston: Shambhala, 1984, p. 40.

10. Wilber, Ken. *Sex, Ecology, Spirituality: The Spirit of Evolution.* Boston: Shambhala, 2000, p. 215

11. Ibid., p. 38.

12. Wilber, *A Sociable God*, p. 37.

13. These are our adaptation of the characteristics discussed by Maslow, Abraham in his *Religions, Values, and Peak-Experiences.* New York: The Viking Press, 1970, pgs. 59–68.

14. Ibid., p. 62.

15. Wilber, *Integral Psychology*, p. 15.

16. Ibid., p. 12.

17. Ibid., pgs. 92, 102–108, 197, 198, 215 and page 148 citing Jean Gebser, *The Ever-Present Origin*, Athens: Ohio University Press, 1985.

18. Ibid., p. 96.

19. Marion, Jim. *Putting on the Mind of Christ: The Inner Work of Christian Spirituality.* Charlottesville: Hampton Roads Publishing Co., 2000, p. 38.

20. Wilber, *Integral Psychology*, p. 103.

21. Marion, *Putting on the Mind of Christ*, pgs. 40–44.

22. Wilber, *Integral Psychology*, p. 95.

23. Marion, *Putting on the Mind of Christ*, p. 55.

24. Wilber, *Integral Psychology*, p. 197.

25. Ibid.

26. Ibid., p. 249.

27. Wilber, *Integral Psychology*, pgs. 197, 198.

28. Marion, *Putting on the Mind of Christ*, pg. 109.

29. Wilber, *Integral Psychology*, p. 198.

30. Marion, *Putting on the Mind of Christ*, p. 113.

31. Ibid., p. 117.

32. Wilber, *Integral Psychology* , pgs. 197, 198.

33. Marion, *Putting on the Mind of Christ*, pgs. 185, 193.

34. Wilber, *Integral Psychology*, p. 197.

35. Fox, Matthew. *Breakthrough: Meister Eckhart's Creation Spirituality in New Translation*. Garden City, NY: Image Books, 1980, p. 217.

36. Fowler, James W. *Stages of Faith: The Psychology of Human Development and the Quest for Meaning*. San Francisco: Harper & Row, 1981, p. 17.

37. Ibid., p. 129, citing Ana-Maria Rizzuto's *The Birth of the Living God*. Chicago: University of Chicago Press, l979.

38. Ibid., p. 136.

39. Ibid., pgs. 141, 143, 149.

40. Ibid., pgs. 153, 154.

41. Ibid., pgs. 157, 162.

42. Ibid., p. 178.

43. Ibid., p. 179.

44. Ibid., pgs. 181, 182.

45. Ibid., p. 186.

46. Ibid., p. 201.

47. Ibid., p. 211.

48. Ibid., p. 299.

49. Ibid., p. 296.

50. Ibid., see pages 318 and 319 for statistics from his study.

51. Wilber, *Integral Psychology*, p. 136.

Chapter 2

1. Wilber, Ken. *Sex, Ecology, Spirituality: The Spirit of Evolution*. Boston: Shambhala, 2000, p. 169.

2. Ibid., pgs. 393 and 163.

3. Ibid.

4. Ibid., p. 164.

5. Ibid., citing Chafetz, Janet Saltzman. *Sex and Advantage: A Comparative, Macro-Structural Theory of Sex Stratification*. Totowa, NJ: Rowman & Alanheld, 1984, pgs. 94–97.

6. Chafetz, p. 22.

7. Ibid., pgs. 19, 36, 37, 41, 52.

8. Wilber, *Sex, Ecology, Spirituality*, p. 251.

9. Ibid., p. 127.

10. Ibid., p. 387, citing Taylor, C. *Hegel*. Cambridge: Harvard University Press, 1975. The entire statement goes as follows: "There are seven windows given to animals in the domicile of the head, through which the air is admitted to the tabernacle of the body, to enlighten, to warm and to nourish it. What are these parts of the microcosm? Two nostrils, two eyes, two ears, and a mouth. So in the heavens, as in a macrocosmos, there are two favorable stars, two unpropitious, two luminaries, and Mercury undecided and indifferent. From this and many other similarities in nature, such as the seven metals, etc., which it were tedious to enumerate, we gather that the number of planets is necessarily seven."

11. Ibid., p. 397.

12. Armstrong, Karen. *The Battle for God*. New York: Alfred A. Knopf, 2000, p.61.

13. Ibid., p 63.

14. Ibid., p. 82, citing Jon Butler, *Awash in a Sea of Faith: Christianity and the American People*. Cambridge: Harvard University Press, 1990, pgs 218–226.

15. Ibid., p. 91.

16. Ibid., p. 179.

17. Wilber, *Integral Psychology*, p. 150.

18. Beck, Don Edward and Cowan, Christopher C. *Spiral Dynamics: Mastering Values, Leadership and Change*. Cambridge: Blackwell Publishers, Inc., 1996, p. 32.

19. Ibid., p. 62.

20. Ibid., p. 50.

21. Ibid., p. 300.

22. Ibid., p. 50.

23. Ibid., p. 300.

24. Ibid., p. 50.

25. Ibid., p. 220.

26. Ibid., p. 300.

27. Ibid., p. 230.

28. Ibid., p. 50.

29. Ibid., p. 234.

30. Ibid., p. 300.

31. Ibid., pgs 50, 244.

32. Ibid., p. 301.

33. Ibid., p. 51.

34. Ibid., p. 301.

35. Ibid., p. 274.

36. Ibid., p. 276.

37. Ibid., p. 51.

38. Ibid., p. 301.

39. Ibid.

40. Chafetz, pgs 21–22.

41. Particularly in his citations of Peter Murdock's Ethnographic Atlas.

42. Lenski, Gerhard. *Human Societies*. New York: McGraw Hill, 1970, p. 137, 138, 187, 188.

43. Ibid.

44. Ibid. and Wilber, Ken. *One Taste*. Boston: Shambhala, 1999, pgs. 324, 325.

45. Wilber, Ken. *Sex, Ecology, Spirituality*, p. 172, citing Eisler, "The Gaia Tradition", in Diamond I. and Orenstein, G., *Reweaving the World*, San Francisco: Sierra Club, 1990, p. 32.

46. Ibid., citing Roszak, Theodore. *The Voice of the Earth*. New York: Touchstone, 1992, p. 69. We are indebted to Ken Wilber for drawing our attention to Roszak's writings in this regard.

47. Diamond, Jared. *Guns, Germs, and Steel: The Fates of Human Societies*. New York: W. W. Norton and Company, 1999, pgs. 42, 43, and 47.

48. Chafetz, p. 115.

Chapter 3

1. Roberts, Jane. *The Nature of the Psyche*. New York: Bantam Books, 1979, p. 248.

2. We were introduced to the phrase "conscious creation" or phrases similar to it in George Winslw Plummer's *Consciously Creating Circumstances*, New York: Society of Rosicrucians, Inc., 1992, and in the writings of Jane Roberts.

Chapter 4

1. Wilber, Ken. *Sex, Ecology, Spirituality: The Spirit of Evolution*. Boston: Shambhala, 2000, p. 348. He is using the terms Eros and Agape in a unique manner which most of you will find unfamiliar.

2. Ibid., pgs. 348, 349.

3. Ibid., p. 349.

4. Ibid.

5. Winkler, Gershon. *Magic of the Ordinary: Recovering the Shamanic in Judaism*. Berkeley: North Atlantic Books, 2003, p. 8.

6. This percentage is arrived at by combining the figures for those in Stage 3 and those still in Stage 3 but transitioning to Stage 4. See the bar graphs in chapter 1 in the section on Stages of Faith for specifics.

7. This placement is our own, and is in disagreement with Wilber who puts all levels of the spiral at or below his psychic level.

GLOSSARY

Beliefs. Ideas which are consciously or subconsciously accepted as true.

Blessedness. The belief that physical reality and human beings are not flawed within their natures.

Communing. One of four types of magick which focuses on the building of spiritual relationships.

Conscious Creation. One of four types of magick which focuses on bringing intentions into physical existence.

Cultural Types. Periods of cultural development which are frequently identified as hunter-gatherer, horticultural, agrarian, industrial, and informational. Each of these cultural types is also associated with a type of social organization: the hunter-gatherer with the tribe, horticultural with the village, agrarian with the empire, industrial with the nation-state, and informational with global or planetary systems.

Demythologizing. The process of opening to the realization that myths are stories and do not represent literal truth, and that sacred symbols represent the sacred rather than contain it. This process usually occurs during the rational or vision-logic stages of development.

Divination. One of four types of magick which focuses on the receiving and sharing of information.

Energy Work. One of four types of magick which focuses on the sensing and directing of energies for various purposes.

Four directions. The four compass points of north, south, east and west.

Four elements. The four forms which matter takes in the physical world—solid or "earth," liquid or "water," gaseous or "air," and plasmic or "fire," Each of the elements is traditionally assigned to one of the four directions. Typically air is in the east, fire in the south, water in the west, and earth in the north.

Four quadrants. A model developed by Ken Wilber in which human knowledge and experience is separated into four realms: the *Inner I* (interior subjective experience), *Outer It* (observable physical reality), the *Inner We* (shared cultural meanings such as values and language) and the *Outer Its* (where cultural meanings are given form in laws and institutions). According to Wilber, each of the four quadrants needs to be developed and integrated by an individual or culture in order for it to be balanced and healthy. Additionally, we have placed the four directions and types of magick into Wilber's quadrants, with the *Inner I* and communing in the west, the *Inner We* and energy work in the south, the *Outer Its* and divination in the east, and *Outer It* and conscious creation in the north.

Holons. Term coined by Arthur Koestler, psychologist, to describe the process of growth in terms of "wholes" becoming "parts" of greater wholes, as when the capacity for crawling is subsumed into the greater capacity of walking. The ranking of these skills according to which capacities must come before others he calls a holarchy.

Interconnectedness. The concept that all parts of the universe, whether small, large, "animate," or "inanimate" are connected at deep levels that extend beyond the boundaries of space and time.

Magick. The actions of many consciousnesses voluntarily working together within an aware and interconnected universe to bring about one or more desired results. We identify four types, or applications, of magick: communing, energy work, divination and conscious creation.

Magickal Page. An alert from the universe, often in the form of information or an urge to do something unexpected, which indicates that consciousness has pulled together the people, places, and times necessary to carry out a magickal request.

Moral embrace. A concept articulated by Ken Wilber and based on the work of many developmental psychologists. Moral embrace is the span of ethical consideration, that is, who or what an individual believes is worthy of ethical consideration when making choices. In early development the moral embrace is often limited to one's self, tribe, ethnic group, or country, and later expands to include all humans, all living beings, and the spiritual realms.

Multidimensionality. The proposed existence of multiple levels or layers of reality and consciousness, many of which may lie outside of space and time.

Mythology. The stories created by a culture to explain how and why things are the way they are. A religious mythology tells the stories of the gods, spirits and important people pertaining to a religion.

Paganism or Neo-Paganism. A modern religious movement which encompasses traditions which are generally earth-centered, magickal, or indigenous, stress a connection to and respect for the natural world, recognize both male and female deities, encourage diversity in spiritual beliefs, practices, and lifestyles, do not operate under a centralized hierarchy, have no official or standardized dogma that extends beyond a particular tradition, and stress personal responsibility in matters of belief, ethics, and spiritual practice.

Peak experiences. Term coined by Abraham Maslow, psychologist, which describes those moments when individuals briefly experience a more expansive level of development than the one from which they normally operate.

Principles of Paganism. (1) We are responsible for the beliefs we choose to adopt, (2) We are responsible for our own actions and spiritual development, (3) We are responsible for deciding who or what Deity is for us, and forming a relationship with that Deity, (4) Everything contains the spark of intelligence, (5) Everything is sacred, (6) Each part of the universe can communicate with each other part, and these parts often cooperate for specific ends, and (7) Consciousness survives death.

Spiral Dynamics. Developmental model created by Don Beck and Christopher Cowan based on the work of their mentor, Clare Graves. It identifies worldviews as organizing structures which increase in span, capacity, and freedom as an individual or group travels around the turns of the spiral of development. They identify these levels by colors. The First Tier of levels includes Beige, Purple, Red, Blue, Orange, and Green. The Second Tier is composed of Yellow, Turquoise, and Coral. The meanings of these levels is discussed in chapter 2.

Spiritual relationships. Aspects of being or reality with which Pagans are free to form spiritual relationships. These include the physical world, the self, energetic and archetypal representations of the physical world and the self, other people, all of consciousness, manifest and unmanifest reality, the Divine and spirit beings.

Stages of Faith. Model of faith development created by James Fowler, psychologist, who identifies seven stages of development: the undifferentiated, intuitive-projective, mythic-literal, synthetic-conventional, individuative-reflective, conjunctive, and universalizing.

Wilber's Developmental Spaces. Developmental model created by Ken Wilber in which he identifies five personal levels of development and four transpersonal levels. The personal levels are the archaic, magical (which we refer to as egocentric in this book), mythic, rational, and vision-logic. The transpersonal spaces are the psychic, subtle, causal, and nondual.

BIBLIOGRAPHY

Armstrong, Karen. *The Battle for God*. New York: Alfred A. Knopf, 2000.

Beck, Don Edward and Christopher C. Cowan. *Spiral Dynamics: Mastering Values, Leadership and Change*. Cambridge: Blackwell Publishers, Inc., 1996.

Butler, Jon. *Awash in a Sea of Faith: Christianizing the American People*. Cambridge: Harvard University Press, 1990.

Chafetz, Janet Saltzman. *Sex and Advantage: A Comparative, Macro-Structural Theory of Sex Stratification*. Totowa, NJ: Rowman & Allanheld, 1984.

Diamond, Jared. *Guns, Germs, and Steel: The Fates of Human Societies*. New York: W. W. Norton and Co., 1999.

Eisler, Riane. *The Chalice and the Blade: Our History, Our Future*. San Francisco: Harper & Row, 1979.

———. "The Gaia Tradition," in *Reweaving the World: The Emergence of Ecofeminism*. Diamond, I., and G. Orenstein, eds. San Francisco: Sierra Club, 1990.

Fowler, James W. *Stages of Faith: The Psychology of Human Development and the Quest for Meaning*. San Francisco: Harper & Row, 1981.

Fox, Matthew. *Breakthrough, Meister Eckhart's Creation Spirituality in New Translation*. Garden City, NJ: Image Books, 1980.

Gendlin, Eugene. *Focusing*. Toronto: Bantam Books, 1982.

Grof, Stanislav. *The Holotropic Mind*. San Francisco: HarperSanFrancisco, 1993.

Koestler, Arthur. *The Ghost in the Machine*. New York: The MacMillan Company, 1967.

Lenski, Gerhard. *Human Societies*. New York: McGraw-Hill, 1970.

Marion, Jim. *Putting on the Mind of Christ: The Inner Work of Christian Spirituality.* Charlottesville: Hampton Roads Publishing Co., 2000.

Maslow, Abraham H. *Religions, Values, and Peak-Experiences.* New York: The Viking Press, 1970.

Pennington, Basil. *Centering Prayer.* New York: Image Press, 1982.

Plummer, George Winslow. *Consciously Creating Circumstances.* New York: Society of Rosicrucians, Inc., 1992.

Rizzuto, Ana-Maria. *The Birth of the Living God.* Chicago: University of Chicago Press, 1979.

Roberts, Jane. *The Nature of the Psyche.* New York: Bantam Books, 1979.

Roszak, Theodore. *The Voice of the Earth.* New York: Touchstone, 1992.

Tarnas, Richard. *The Passion of the Western Mind: Understanding the Ideas that Have Shaped Our Worldview.* New York: Harmony Books, 1991.

Taylor, C. *Hegel.* Cambridge: Harvard University Press, 1975.

Wilber, Ken. *The Eye of Spirit.* Boston: Shambhala, 1998.

———. *Integral Psychology,* Boston: Shambhala, 2000.

———. *One Taste.* Boston: Shambhala, 1999.

———. *Sex, Ecology, Spirituality: The Spirit of Evolution.* Boston: Shambhala, 2000.

———. *A Sociable God: Toward a New Understanding of Religion.* Boulder: Shambhala, 1984.

Winkler, Gershon. *Magic of the Ordinary: Recovering the Shamanic in Judaism.* Berkeley: North Atlantic Books, 2003.

INDEX

mythic, 8–9, 11–13, 25, 30–32, 37, 41–44, 51, 53, 62, 68–69, 125, 163–164, 195–196, 223–224, 226
mythic-literal stage, 30
mythology, 13, 35, 43–45, 63, 126, 163–165, 180, 195, 223–226

N

nature mysticism, 14–15, 36, 128
Neoplatonism, 108
New Age movement, 36
Nielsen, Joyce, 65
nondual, 6, 8–9, 17, 25, 36–37, 51, 107, 130, 167, 198, 227
north, 88, 218–219, 221–222, 230–232, 234–235

O

obsessive-compulsive disorder, 12
Orange—spiral, 54–56, 62–64, 69, 94, 96, 126, 134, 165, 171, 196, 202, 224, 231
Outer It, 43, 64, 218–219
Outer Its, 43, 190–191

P

palm reading, 186
path of yogis, 15
peak experience, 7, 14, 27, 30, 58, 83, 90, 119, 128, 162, 193, 221
Pennington, Basil, 107
petitionary prayer, 106
Pledge of Allegiance, 46
plow, 42
postconventional, 31
postmodern, xvi, 31, 37, 62–63, 67, 123
power animals, 84, 118–119, 128

prayer feathers, 29, 152
prayer, 15, 17, 29, 82, 105–108, 111–112, 123–126, 128, 133–134, 136, 139, 152–153, 180, 223, 230
Presbyterian, 31
Principles of Paganism, 80–81
probabilities, 82, 145, 177, 185, 187–191, 205, 208, 210, 226, 232
projection, 13, 32, 210, 217
prophets, 142
psychic, 8–9, 14–16, 25, 30, 36, 51, 57, 63, 69–70, 118, 128–129, 150, 155–156, 166–167, 177, 197–198, 226–227
psychometry, 177
Purple—spiral, 52–53, 59, 69, 93, 96, 98, 123–124, 132, 162–163, 169, 194, 200, 222, 229

R

rational, 8–9, 12–13, 20, 22, 25, 31, 36, 41, 43–47, 51, 62–63, 68–69, 94, 126, 128, 163, 165, 177, 196, 202, 224–225, 231
reaction formation, 13
Red—spiral, 52–54, 59, 62, 69–70, 89, 93, 96, 123–125, 133, 162–163,170, 194, 200, 222, 230
Reformation, 62
relational exchange, 103, 181, 209, 231
Roberts, Jane, 74
roles, 11–13, 16, 20, 42, 44, 46, 55, 67, 74, 80, 94, 125–126, 133, 145, 153, 162–164, 187, 195, 201, 230
Romanticism, 64, 108
rosaries, 107
Roszak, Theodore, 66
runes, 186

64–66, 68–69, 85, 88, 96, 107–108,
112–113, 128–130, 142, 158, 190,
218, 237–238
Winkler, Gershon, 118
World War, 47, 62
worldcentric, xv, 165

Y

Yellow—spiral, 56–57, 69, 96, 98, 128,
154–155, 166, 197, 226
yoga, 108, 130

Z

zone of liberation, 23

Paganism
An Introduction to Earth-Centered Religions

RIVER AND JOYCE HIGGINBOTHAM

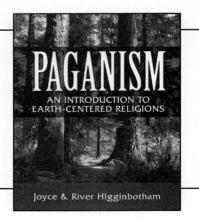

If you want to study Paganism in more detail, this book is the place to start. Based on a course in Paganism that the authors have taught for more than a decade, it is full of exercises, meditations, and discussion questions for group or individual study.

This book presents the basic fundamentals of Paganism. It explores what Pagans are like; how the Pagan sacred year is arranged; what Pagans do in ritual; what magick is; and what Pagans believe about God, worship, human nature, and ethics.

0-7387-0222-6
272 pp., 7½ x 9⅛ $16.95

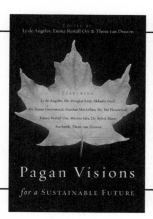

Pagan Visions
for a Sustainable Future

LY DE ANGELES, EMMA RESTALL ORR,
THOM VAN DOOREN

Do Pagan practices lead to an ecological approach to life? What is the role of magic in contemporary Paganism? How can ancient Pagan codes of behavior be applied today?

Representing diverse arenas of Paganism, eleven established activists, authors, and academics passionately debate the critical issues facing modern Pagans. These provocative discussions—exploring feminism, magickal ecology, ancient Egyptian ethics, political activism, globalization, the power of truth, sacred communities, and environmental spirituality—challenge readers to reconsider what it means to be Pagan in the twenty-first century.

0-7387-0824-0
312 pp., 6 x 9 $17.95

Authentic Spirituality
The Direct Path to Consciousness

Richard N. Potter

Our world is plagued with problems related to religions that are based on cultural and historical factors. Many people hunger for a practical and reasonable approach to spirituality that does not insult their intelligence. In other words, they are ready for an authentic spirituality of consciousness.

Lifelong mystic Richard Potter explores consciousness-based spiritual paths and demonstrates how the experience of direct mysticism can help you to open your heart and live a life of clarity, joy, peace, and love. Experiment with practices such as meditation, breathwork, sounding, and retreats.

0-7387-0442-3
312 pp., 6 x 9 $20.95

Postmodern Magic
The Art of Magic in the Information Age

PATRICK DUNN

Fresh ideas for the modern mage lie at the heart of this thought-provoking guide to magic theory. Approaching magical practice from an information paradigm, Patrick Dunn provides a unique and contemporary perspective on an ancient practice.

Imagination, psychology, and authority—the most basic techniques of magic—are introduced first. From there, Dunn teaches all about symbol systems, magical artifacts, sigils, spirits, elementals, languages, and magical journeys, and explains their significance in magical practice. There are also exercises for developing magic skills, along with techniques for creating talismans, glamours, servitors, divination decks, modern defixios, and your own astral temple. Dunn also offers tips on aura detection, divination, occult networking, and conducting your own magic research.

0-7387-0663-9
264 pp., 6 x 9, illus.

$14.95

To order, call 1-877-NEW-WRLD
Prices subject to change without notice

Pagans & Christians
The Personal Spiritual Experience

GUS DIZEREGA, PH.D.

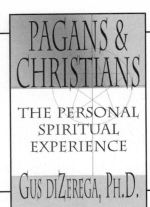

Pagans and Christians have been polarized within the spiritual landscape for two millennia. Recent media reports even talk of efforts by the Christian Right to boycott the U.S. Army for allowing Wiccan soldiers to practice their religion. There is no better time for Western civilization's most prominent religion and humanity's oldest religion to enter into intelligent and respectful dialogue.

Providing something for Pagans and Christians alike, Dr. diZerega presents an important and original contribution for contemporary interfaith understanding. For Pagans, his book deepens the discussion of Paganism's theological and philosophical implications, penetrating its inner truths and examining the reasons for its modern growth. For Christians, it demystifies Paganism, offering respectful answers to the most common criticisms levelled at Pagan beliefs and practices.

1-56718-228-3
264 pp., 6 x 9, illus.

$16.95

Ecoshamanism
Sacred Practices of Unity, Power and Earth Healing

JAMES ENDREDY

In a society riddled with rampant consumerism and unsustainable technology, it's easy for everyone, including shamans, to lose touch with the natural world. James Endredy, who has learned from tribal shamans around the globe, presents a new philosophy of shamanic practice called ecological shamanism, or ecoshamanism. Designed to deliver well-being and spiritual harmony, ecoshamanism is the culmination of the visionary practices, rituals, and ceremonies that honor and support nature.

Exploring the holistic perspective of shamanism, Endredy encourages readers to establish a rewarding connection with sacred, life-giving forces using shamanic tools and practices. The author describes more than fifty authentic ecoshamanistic practices—including ceremonies, rituals, chanting, hunting, pilgrimage, and making instruments—that reinforce one's relationship with the natural world.

0-7387-0742-2
336 pp., 7½ x 9⅛ $19.95

To order, call 1-877-NEW-WRLD
Prices subject to change without notice

Encyclopedia
of Natural Magic

John Michael Greer

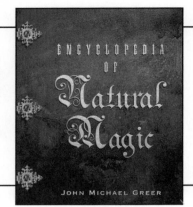

Natural magic is the ancient and powerful art of using material substances—herbs, stones, incenses, oils, and much more—to tap into the hidden magical powers of nature, transforming your surroundings and yourself.

Not just a cookbook of spells, the *Encyclopedia of Natural Magic* provides an introduction to the philosophy underlying this system. It also gives detailed information on 176 different herbs, trees, stones, metals, oils, incenses, and other substances, and offers countless ways to put them to magical use. With this book and a visit to your local herb store, rock shop, or backyard garden, you're ready to enter the world of natural magic!

0-7387-0674-4
312 pp., 7½ x 9⅛, illus. $18.95

High Magic
Theory & Practice

FRATER U∴D∴

Magic may be one of the most difficult, diversified, and fascinating of all the occult sciences. Understanding the theory behind this rich Western tradition is crucial to becoming an accomplished magician. This comprehensive and well-rounded introduction to magical practice provides a solid foundation for furthering one's magic studies.

Instead of issuing spells and rituals like a recipe book, this magic primer explains the basic laws governing magic. The author also discusses what it means to be a "good" magician, emphasizing self-discipline and training one's will, imagination, and trance abilities. Many facets of high magic are covered, including The Lesser Banishing Ritual of the Pentagram, sigil magic, ritual magic, visualization, the Greater Ritual of the Pentagram, planetary magic, tools of the magician, trance work, and much more.

0-7387-0471-7
432 pp., 7½ x 9⅛, charts   **$31.95**

ChristoPaganism
An Inclusive Path

JOYCE HIGGINBOTHAM AND RIVER HIGGINBOTHAM

Witches praying the rosary? Catholics reading Tarot cards?

For some, it's blasphemy. For others, it's a launching pad to enlightenment. But for interfaith experts Joyce and River Higginbotham, it's a new reality begging for intellectual study. More and more, Pagans and Christians are incorporating each other's practices into their own belief systems, forging hybrid spiritual paths that borrow from both earth- and scripture-based religions. Standing in two worlds at once, ChristoPagans are sparking a new conversation about the nature of faith and the evolving spiritual needs of a chaotic world. With scholarly poise, the Higginbothams wade into this provocative religious pairing, deftly navigating its minefield of heresy and personal bias.

Free of political agenda but ripe with open-minded curiosity, *ChristoPaganism* launches a whole new dialogue on the subject of personal belief.

0-7387-1467-4
336 pp., 7½ x 9⅛ $19.95